ACHIEVEMENT and ADDICTION

A Guide to the Treatment of Professionals

ACHIEVEMENT
and
ADDICTION

A Guide to
the Treatment
of Professionals

Edgar P. Nace, M.D.

BRUNNER/MAZEL *Publishers* • NEW YORK

Library of Congress Cataloging-in-Publication Data

Nace, Edgar P.
    Achievement and addiction : a guide to the treatment of
professionals / Edgar P. Nace.
        p.   cm.
    Includes bibliographical references and index.
    ISBN 0-87630-753-5
    1. Professional employees—Substance use. 2. Substance abuse—
Treatment.   I. Title.
    [DNLM: 1. Substance Dependence. 2. Substance Abuse.
3. Professional Impairment.   WM 270 N118a 1995]
RC564.5.P76N33 1995
616.86′008′622—dc20
DNLM/DLC
for Library of Congress   95-2834
                                                    CIP

Published by
BRUNNER/MAZEL, INC.
19 Union Square West
New York, New York 10003

Manufactured in the United States of America

10 9 8 7 6 5 4 3 2 1

To the loving memory of my parents, Kenneth Beyer Nace and Sara Grater Nace; and with love to my parents-in-law, Dr. Sidney A. Charlat and Lucia G. Charlat

Contents

List of Tables and Figures

Foreword

A decade ago, the American Academy of Psychiatrists in Alcoholism and Addictions was launched and Edgar Nace, M.D., its current president, was among its founders. I am honored and pleased to introduce this volume, which is important to those who treat professionals with addictive disorders. It is written by a national authority on addiction treatment, especially the treatment of impaired professionals. Dr. Nace has been director of large alcohol and drug treatment programs at the Institute of Pennsylvania Hospital, Timberlawn Hospital in Dallas, and recently at Charter Hospital in Dallas. In his role as director of addiction treatment services, he has been involved in the direct and indirect care of thousands of addicted patients, including many professionals. They have provided source material for this book. He is an unusual combination of an academician with vast direct clinical experience and a writer with a gift for expounding on his work.

Treating addicted patients is full of paradoxes. Addiction can strike the most talented, highly rewarded, goal-directed persons, and those with a keen sense of responsibility. When professionals are addicted, these valued traits and the very nature of professional life are threatened by a process that "erases achievement, provokes punishment, and potentially compromises skills and abilities." Professionals who have great insight into others may have great denial in themselves. The lies they tell themselves and others often seem shocking considering that before the regressive effects of addiction, many had well-functioning superegos. The same people with the potential to harm themselves, their profession, and the public, also have the talent and ability to achieve the greatest good when sober. Professionals may also have skills in intellectualization, isolation of affect, rationalization of behavior, avoidance, and resistance to acceptance of a problem. On the other hand, the considerable ego strengths that have led to success can be applied to this situation. More often than not, this leads to a positive treatment outcome. Another paradox is that some recovering professionals that find insight and knowledge of the disease opt to help others. Their personal experience with the illness poses opportunities and challenges. When they use their knowledge to help others, they raise their own self-esteem.

Dr. Nace's sophisticated, synthesizing, broad-based biopsychosocial perspective encompasses recent advances in the addiction treatment field and targets them to a population of high achievers. He also synergistically and practically applies a solid understanding of psychodynamic, cognitive, behavioral, 12-steps, family and social models of treatment, and psychoeducational approaches. Dr. Nace reminds us that it is as great a mistake to avoid the unique problems and needs inherent in treating addicted professionals as it is to make errors because of demands to give VIP patients special treatment.

During the past few years, professionals, particularly in the health field, have experienced increased stress, a higher emphasis on productivity, decreased job security, and the need for flexibility. Therapists who see professionals clinically will benefit from the timing of this publication. Studies have found that top-ranking medical school students are as likely to develop problems with alcohol addiction as are lower-ranking students.

Of the eight Americans awarded the Nobel Prize for literature, five were alcoholics. A long list of American writers has been afflicted, with few other major creative talents spared. Addiction has been called an American writer's disease. It is also very much a disease of lawyers, doctors, nurses, and business managers. Liberation of talents is found more often with recovery than from the disinhibiting effects of chemicals sought by creative persons and those seeking solace from toil. Dr. Nace presents examples of this in detailed and evocative case vignettes. When high achievers develop addiction, the consequences in health, marital, legal, and psychiatric problems, including suicide, are of tragic proportions. The ramifications affect not only the individuals involved, but those affected by them.

Achievement and Addiction is clearly and scholarly written. It should be read by physicians interested in addiction medicine. Psychologists, nurses, social workers, alcohol counselors, and employee assistance counselors and managers who seek guidance in the treatment of addicted professionals will also find this text very informative. The book has chapters that discuss the problem from the point of view of medical students, residents, physicians, nurses, pharmacists, attorneys, and executives. It presents a full, literate review of what has been written about each group and clinical vignettes that provide pearls of wisdom in a case history format. These are helpful in practically approaching issues in each profession.

Introductory chapters on features, etiology, diagnosis, evaluation, and treatment provide an effective overview that sets the stage for guidelines. The text stresses the importance of helping the professional recognize the diagnosis and to accept recommendations through proper treatment selection and the recovery process. Concluding chapters focus on issues of transference, countertransference, dealing with professional concerns, setting priorities, dealing with families, dual diagnosis, and incorporating self-help.

Approximately 10,000 major companies have developed employee assistance programs and most professional organizations have recognized the need for the support and treatment of addicted professionals. However, those at higher levels of the corporate or professional ladder are often the last to have their addictive disorder confronted or treated. In these hard-driving persons, work is often the last component of their lives to suffer. In the 1980's, my colleagues and I studied alcoholic lawyers and doctors hospitalized at Cornell. This led to a surprising finding. Although the lawyers were much more difficult to treat and more resistant in the treatment process, they achieved equally favorable treatment outcomes as did physicians. This is probably due to their high ego strength and resourcefulness. Clearly, working with these interesting patients can enhance our knowledge of the manifestation and treatment of addictive disorders.

This book will become the standard text for anyone interested in the challenge and rewards of working with addicted professionals. It will improve the depth of understanding, the timing, and the descriptive, interpretive, and technical skills of both the beginner and the expert. Dr. Nace's keen observations are based on clinical wisdom and wide experiences with this population. He integrates the art of clinical description with a scientific and pragmatic approach that employs psychodynamic ideas in a meaningful way.

RICHARD J. FRANCES, M.D.
Director, Department of Psychiatry
Hackensack Medical Center
Hackensack, New Jersey

Professor of Clinical Psychiatry
University of Medicine and Dentistry
* of New Jersey*
Newark, New Jersey

Acknowledgments

I am grateful to the many men and women who, in the course of their efforts to recover from drug or alcohol dependence, shared their experiences with me. Their demonstration of courage and hope in the dark hours of their lives is remembered. In particular, I thank those who provided their "stories" for this volume. They did so voluntarily and with the understanding that their experience may benefit others.

My thinking on and understanding of addictions has been influenced by many clinicians, researchers, and scholars in the field. I have done my best to adequately reference these sources. I am particularly indebted to Edward J. Khantzian, MD, Ernest Kurtz, PhD, and John Chappel, MD.

My training years at the Institute of Pennsylvania Hospital were enriched by the example of Manuel Pearson, MD, who was known for his dedication to the care of impaired physicians. Decades later, I have the honor to serve as Chair of the Texas Medical Association Physician Health and Rehabilitation Committee. From the latter vantage point, I have been inspired by the efforts and dedication of recovered physicians as they assist colleagues. My role with the Physician Health and Rehabilitation Committee has been bolstered and supported by the skill and hard work of our coordinator, Linda Kuhn, and our education consultant, Rudi Arrendondo, DEd.

Virginia Phillips reviewed this manuscript and provided constructive criticism and consistent support throughout. Bernadette Williams loyally and skillfully assisted in the typing and final preparation.

ACHIEVEMENT
and
ADDICTION

A Guide to
the Treatment
of Professionals

CHAPTER 1

The Professional Paradox

> It is to no purpose, it is even against one's own interest, to turn away from the consideration of the real nature of the affair because the horror of its elements excites repugnance.
>
> —Clausewitz

Over the past three decades, Americans, with the rest of the Western world, have witnessed the spread of drug abuse. Drug abuse has been superimposed on the preexisting scourge of alcoholism and has been accompanied by the development and increasing use of pharmaceutical products with addictive potential (Mellinger, Balter, & Uhlenhuth, 1984). A "modern epidemic" (Nicholi, 1983) is now endemic.

As awareness developed and concern grew over the toll taken by substance abuse, extensive efforts were undertaken to characterize those addicted, as well as those who may be subject to addiction (Brooks, Whiteman, Gordon, & Cohen, 1989; Kandel & Logan, 1984). Profiles of drug abusers emerged: They were poorly motivated and were poor academic performers; they had few religious convictions, were rebellious and depressed, had low self-esteem, and were maladjusted (Nicholi, 1983). Alcoholics had been viewed negatively long before characterizations of modern drug users were drawn (Chappel, Jordan, Treadway, & Miller, 1977; Fisher, Mason, Keeley, & Fisher, 1975). Alcoholics commonly have been viewed as morally weak, unmotivated to change, irresponsible, weak-willed, and passive (Morse, Mitchell, & Martin, 1977).

The usual images, stereotypes, and profiles of substance abusers, whether drawn from empirical studies or from clinical frustration, are confronted when alcoholism and drug dependence present in professionals. In that circumstance, glib assumptions about etiology and character are challenged. The professional patient forces us to reexamine our understanding of and attitudes toward addiction. For, now, we face a

1

patient not unlike ourselves in so many ways: background, training, aspirations, fears, and, in many instances, personality structure. The professional—achievement-oriented and typically devoted to his or her vocation—enables us to appreciate in *bas relief* how the tentacles of addiction choke and potentially destroy character, ambition, accomplishment, reputation, health, family, and future.

It is my hope that this book will help physicians and other professionals recognize the presence of chemical dependence, guide their approach to professionals with substance use disorders, and encourage active involvement in forwarding the process of recovery.

To provide a text on addicted professionals implies that they are different from others with similar problems. Is this true and, if so, to what extent? This text argues that professionals often present "special" problems, which the skilled clinician needs to appreciate.

ATTRIBUTES OF PROFESSIONALS

The term "special" is used in this context conservatively and does not refer to elitism. Special is derived from "species"—a kind or sort. Webster (1980) defines special as "unusual, uncommon; differing from others; designed for a particular purpose."

How then do the men and women who enter professions fit the above definition? For one, members of professions are *well rewarded and compensated* by our society in many ways—by esteem, status, privileges, and better than average earnings. The edge of financial peril is commonly dulled for professionals by job security, demand for services, and a "market" that bears lucrative salaries. Respect for their special knowledge and training and a favorable standing in the social order continue to be endowments of public opinion.

Secondly, a high sense of *self-efficacy* that bolsters their ability to focus and fix on distant goals contributes to the "special" characteristics of professionals. According to Bandura (1986), "perceived self-efficacy underlies the motivated forces which propel goal directed behavior." Perceived self-efficacy is defined as "judgments of [one's] capabilities to organize and execute courses of action required to obtain designated types of performances" (Bandura, 1986, p. 391). The individual aspiring to a profession is unusually goal-directed; certainly well beyond the average.

Associated with self-efficacy and goal-directed behavior is a third attribute: a capability for *endurance*. Long, intense academic preparation and additional years of apprentice-like training are required. For those preparing for a profession, goal-directed behavior, endurance, and a focused, sustained level of motivation cut a swath through youthful years where personal experimentation and immediate gratification are more typical.

A fourth attribute is a keen sense of *responsibility*. Professionals are generally very reliable. They accept the need to be accountable, and they fulfill obligations. In order to be accepted in graduate school, outstanding letters of recommendation are necessary. The academic record reflects intellectual ability, but the letters of recommendation address character. Such letters often describe stability, conscientiousness, and reliability, and frame a portrait of responsibility reassuring to admission committees. Intellectual abilities substantially greater than average would also be expected in professionals because of the competition for admission into professional schools and the rigor of the curriculum.

Finally, I believe that those who choose a professional career have a strong desire to *help their fellow humans*. The origins of this desire may be complex and multidetermined, while the aim, professional success, may sometimes be misguided. The same complexity of motivation may apply to the other attributes referred to above, such as goal-directed behavior, endurance, and responsibility. Nevertheless, my impression is that most men and women in the professions want to do good, want to help clients/patients, work hard, and conscientiously strive to fulfill both societal and self-expectations.

There are, of course, many other factors that direct one toward or deter one from a professional career, and these factors have no relationship to ability or character. The values of one's parents, money, availability of scholarships, exposure to appropriate and effective role models, peer examples, and good health are but a few determinants that can propel one toward a successful career or deny one such opportunity.

The external rewards of pay and recognition for professionals have been briefly mentioned. The rewards of success, esteem, power, and financial gain account, in part, for the goal-directed, achievement-oriented behavior of those who enter the professions. Professional life, however, is enriched by "rewards" less obvious; that is, by rewards that are part of the preparation for and practice of a profession. If the rewards of professional standing were bounded only by purchasing power or public image, the substance of a professional's accomplishments would be little different from those of a lottery winner, rock star, or other form of celebrity. The external compensation is important, but there are rewards, less acquisitive in nature, that stamp professional life. Compared to these, remuneration and status are weak competitors.

INTRINSIC REWARDS OF PROFESSIONAL LIFE

Preparation for a professional career can be likened to a drama. Who can fail to recall the protagonists in one's own drama? Each stage of a career calls forth a cast that provides the tempo, mood, and action for the "scenes" that follow. An intrinsic reward is this *legacy of relationships* through which a professional identity is ultimately formed. These relationships have involved teachers, mentors, and role models, and are characteristically intense and ambivalent. That the feelings about those who taught and directed our professional development would be strong and often conflicted follows from the demands put on students, the rigors of training, and the subsequent sacrifices and deprivations. The years of training extend the dependent status of the trainee, and a prolonged adolescence results.

Out of this difficult journey the student emerges with a mosaic of affect and recollection. Gratitude, humiliation, awe, contempt, and devotion are but some of the emotional elements through which personal and professional identities fuse. No matter what the complexity of emotion may be for any one physician, attorney, or other professional, each has been the beneficiary of a legacy of accomplishment passed on. Those who preceded us, through their scholarship or practice, have transmitted by social process an identity with their profession that is, perhaps, as unique as the biologic transmission of the genetic code.

The professional identity emerges almost imperceptibly as role development proceeds. The third-year medical student is awkward and self-conscious with patient contact. "Do I have a right to ask these questions; to touch his or her body" are unvoiced questions as the student confronts self-doubt as to whether or not he or she is a legitimate member of the medical profession. In contrast, a senior resident has no doubt whatsoever, and expects role confirmation and role support from staff, patients, and families.

A second intrinsic reward is that of *service*. As with one's relationship to mentors, the concept of service deepens the sense of professional identity and belonging. Here, also, relationships are the vehicle by which the legacy of dedication to the welfare of others is transmitted. The concept of service and welfare of others is contained in the following definition of a profession: ". . . a socially sanctioned activity whose primary objective is the well-being of others above the professional's gains" (Racy, 1990).

Involvement in the lives of clients or patients over years and decades, or briefly during crises, exposes the professional man or woman to the vulnerable and the tragic, as well as to the sublime facets of others' lives.

This is a privilege the weight of which each individual suitable for the professions will appreciate. Cynicism, fatigue, and apathy are often ameliorated by a remembrance from a patient, an unexpected thank you, a recommendation. I believe this to be true even in a climate where practice is often defensive and the spectre of litigation omnipresent. Satisfaction in professional work is significantly related to sharing one's wisdom with clients, patients, peers, and students; to the sense of accomplishment from assisting in the resolution of complex problems; and to the stimulation and esteem gained through meeting diverse challenges.

A third intrinsic reward is that of having *chosen one's vocation*. The satisfaction of having reached a goal, of having followed one's calling, is largely an intangible asset, sometimes forgotten as the demands of increasing responsibility and high performance are encountered. Most professionals will find, however, these demands preferable to the tedium, monotony, and anonymity that characterize many less deliberately selected occupations.

PROFESSIONAL SUCCESS VERSUS SUBSTANCE ABUSE

In the context of native ability, personal achievement, and substantial financial and social rewards, how are we to understand the emergence of a process that erases achievement, provokes punishment, and potentially compromises skills and abilities? This is the paradox of professional addiction. Shouldn't professionals, with their education and advantageous position in our society, know better than to get themselves into such difficulty? Indeed, this criticism is familiar to the chemically dependent professional; he or she expects to be subjected to greater stigma for a substance use disorder because of the higher expectations others put upon professionals. Professionals have a highly developed sense of self-efficacy, and individuals who perceive themselves as highly efficacious attribute personal failure to lack of effort, while individuals with a low sense of self-efficacy attribute failure to deficient ability (Bandura, 1986). Thus, professionals are particularly likely to go through a process of self-castigation, believing they should have "known better" or "seen it earlier," and they may assume that their own self-directed efforts will be sufficient to correct a growing dependence on substances. Paradoxically, their achievements, self-expectations, and sense of self-efficacy can delay the acceptance of the need for help. The professional's strength becomes a weakness, at least initially, often because of this inability to ask for help.

Clashing with this belief in the efficacy of self-direction are the complex variables that compose the etiology of substance use disorders. These include a genetic vulnerability to alcoholism or drug dependence; the high degree of stress common to professional life; the availability of drugs, especially in the medical field; and certain personality vulnerabilities, such as self-efficacy, that may propel a person to achievement on the one hand, yet eventually, may undermine the individual's functioning, when taken to extremes.

A military analogy reflects the addictive process: As an advancing line of troops spearheads an attack, military commanders are aware of the potential for a segment of this advancing line to undermine the overall effort. This segment is referred to as a "reverse salient." The reverse salient exposes the vulnerability of the operation and is the point that collapses and reverses the fortunes of the mission. Certainly, the addictive process is the professional's "reverse salient." What accounts for the presence of this vulnerability varies from individual to individual and can be considered a blend of the etiologic variables already mentioned. The chapters that follow explore this paradox and offer clinical guidelines for the diagnosis and treatment of addicted professionals.

Many occupations are considered professions. The professions chosen for this discussion are medicine, law, nursing, pharmacy, and business. The selection of these particular professions is based on the availability of studies on these groups and the author's clinical experience with members of these professions. It is likely that the basic factors leading to addiction are similar across most professions.

This book does not serve as a textbook on addiction. Several excellent general textbooks are available (See Frances & Miller, 1991; Lowinson, Ruiz, & Millman, 1992; Miller, 1991).

This text describes the clinical expression of addiction in a selected sample of the population. The etiologic factors believed to cause an addiction are reviewed, as well as the neurochemical mechanisms of the major drugs of abuse. The processes of intervention, diagnosis, and evaluation, and guidelines for matching the patient to level of treatment are described. Of special importance are the case histories, which are written by a member of each of the professions specifically for this volume. The candid contributions of these professionals enrich and bolster the educational value of this text. I am deeply grateful to them for their willingness to help. I have not altered their presentations except to assure confidentiality.

Specific therapeutic approaches are reviewed in the context of their application to professional patients and not as a review of such therapies themselves. The uses of psychotherapy, medication, and monitoring are discussed. The chapter on 12-step programs emphasizes the importance of Alcoholics Anonymous in the recovery of the professional patient.

Finally, the terms *addiction, substance abuse,* and *chemical dependence* are used interchangeably. For the purposes of this text, I find it useful to think of substance abuse in a generic sense, without emphasizing specific drugs. The next chapter describes why the numerous drugs that produce an addiction can be viewed generically.

CHAPTER 2

The Generic Concept
of Chemical Dependence

The drugs of abuse possess a remarkable variety of properties. Tolerance, withdrawal patterns, effects on neurotransmitters, and sites of action in the brain vary across the broad categories of stimulants, hallucinogens, opiates, and central nervous system depressants. Yet, from this pharmacologic diversity there arises a set of phenomena common to the experience of chemical dependence and independent of the specific drugs involved. These phenomena enable us to clinically conceptualize substance use disorders from a generic point of view. The adjective *generic* is defined as "relating to or descriptive of an entire group or class" (American Heritage, 1987).

The features of drug dependence that transcend the specific drugs used include social effects, poly-drug use, affective functions, and subjective and behavioral phenomena. Further, Beck (1993) maintains that the "same beliefs underlie all addictions."

SOCIAL ASPECTS

Regardless of the type of drugs used, a number of experiences are common at a social level. For example, social interaction is enhanced and interpersonal tensions are relaxed. Thus, an adolescent may relate more easily to an adult employer, and the college student finds confidence when dating. In addition, peer identity may be established by drug use. "Head" or "freak" may be identifying labels for drug cognoscenti; young affluent urbanites may flock around fashionable new drugs, such as they did with cocaine in the early and mid-1980s. An awkward student, who transfers to a new high school, may find quick acceptance and a sense of group identity if he or she is identified as a drug user. A need to rebel may find expression in relationships with drug-using peers. Friendships

8

may revolve around the interest in and use of particular drugs. For example, a married couple developed their relationship around the use of amphetamines. Subsequently, they named their daughter "Crystal."

Another social factor may be the development of a "career" from involvement in drugs. A young college graduate flew marijuana and cocaine into the United States from South America, financially rivaling his father's success in business. A senior at a major university enjoyed a life style beyond the means of his middle-class parents; dealing cocaine quickly yielded him ample sums of money. Eventually, his own habit indebted him to a more experienced dealer, which necessitated parental involvement to pay off his debt in order to avoid physical harm.

Any variety of drug use patterns may facilitate social experiences that have positive reinforcement for the user. Improved social interaction, identity, relationships, and "career" represent a sampling of possible social effects.

POLY-DRUG USE

To find a drug-abusing patient whose use is confined to a single substance is unusual. This is especially true for those under 40 years of age. Typically, the history reveals either an interchangeability of drugs or a simultaneous pattern of abuse of various drugs. For example, a 35-year-old physician presented with opiate dependence, which varied among hydrocodone, codeine, and propoxyphene. Years earlier, he had used marijuana daily and had abused alcohol during student days. At time of treatment, his alcohol use was infrequent, and he no longer used marijuana.

Another patient presented with cocaine dependence, but further inquiry revealed that, in the few months prior to referral by his employer, he had begun intravenous heroin use. If he could not afford cocaine or heroin, however, he would substitute marijuana and alcohol.

In a third case, ethchlorvynol dependence and an associated withdrawal seizure led to treatment for a 62-year-old woman. For over two decades, she had used benzodiazepines or other types of anxiolytics, hypnotics, or sedatives. These were prescribed by physicians, but ultimately overuse led to dependence. In this case, the poly-drug abuse was contained within the class of anxiolytics, hypnotics, and sedatives, but varied with the changing preferences of the prescribing physicians and the patient.

Survey data document that multiple drug use is the prevailing pattern among drug abusers. A study of Vietnam veterans who had used narcotics during the war revealed that poly-drug use characterized their usage patterns during the first two years post-service. Although narcotic use declined significantly after return from Vietnam, the use of alcohol, marijuana, amphetamines, and barbiturates significantly increased (O'Brien, Nace, Mintz, Myers, & Ream, 1980). A veteran who abused alcohol was likely to abuse marijuana, amphetamines, and narcotics, as well. Concurrent multiple drug use was the prevailing pattern (Nace, O'Brien, Mintz, Ream, & Myers, 1977).

In a random survey of households, patterns of drug use, including cigarettes, were assessed. The patterns of concurrent and cumulative drug use are described by Voss and Clayton (1987):

> It is important to recognize that persons who move to the stage in which they smoke marijuana do not use it as a substitute for alcoholic beverages and cigarettes. On the contrary, they commonly increase their levels of consumption of cigarettes and beverage alcohol. In fact, a relatively widespread pattern among young persons involves the use of marijuana and alcohol simultaneously or in combination to produce an interactive effect. Of the individuals who had used marijuana in the year preceding the interviews, approximately one-half of them indicated that they had, on one or more occasions, used marijuana and alcoholic beverages on the same occasion. Similarly, people who move to the stage in which they use illicit drugs other than marijuana do not terminate their use of marijuana; rather, the other drugs are used in addition to, and at times in conjunction with their use of marijuana. A sizeable majority of the individuals who use marijuana or other illicit drugs also smoke and drink—they are multiple drug users.

A variety of poly-drug abuse patterns, gathered from clinical practice, have been listed by Wilford (1981):

- persons who are dependent on one drug and use other drugs only when they are readily available
- persons who are dependent on one drug and use other drugs only when the preferred substance is not available
- persons who prefer one drug but use a second drug to diminish the side effects of the primary substance
- persons who abuse any drug and also consume large amounts of alcohol
- persons who abuse different drugs at different times of the day, perhaps using stimulants in the morning, tranquilizers during the day, and hypnotics at night
- persons who have no drug preference but take any drug that is available
- persons who use one drug to enhance or prolong the effect of another drug

AFFECTIVE FUNCTIONS

The third experience common to drug abuse is a change in affect. Put simply, drugs change the way a person feels. Relief, escape, euphoria, relaxation, energy, sedation, and peace may be commonly described. This alteration in feelings is a primary reinforcement for drug use.

- A physician was administered Demerol following minor surgery. He felt "wonderful." A decade of opiate dependence followed.
- A graduate student rapidly became a daily user of marijuana after first using it late in his doctorate program. After three years of regular use, marijuana began to produce anxiety, irritability, and mild "paranoia." Sedatives were administered to counter this effect. Why not just discontinue the marijuana? The immediate euphoria, the "mellow" initial effect, remained sufficiently compelling to motivate both acceptance of the negative consequences (anxiety) and procurement of additional drugs to counter the dysphoria.

The relationship between drug use and affect is complicated. When we consider the disorders of substance abuse or dependence, we find that the relationship between a drug's effect and emotions transcends the experience of recreational drug use, a term that refers to the casual, less frequent level of involvement with drugs analogous to the social use of alcohol. The man or woman who smokes marijuana occasionally, or uses cocaine infrequently, experiences, of course, a change in feeling during the period of the drug's effect. The experience is similar to the "time out" of the cocktail hour. Fatigue may be relieved temporarily, inhibitions lessened, care blunted. However, the social use of drugs and alcohol and the associated changes in mood do not embrace the depth of the relationship between drugs of abuse and changes in affect when the condition of drug dependence has been established.

When drug dependence is present, the individual's affective status is intertwined with the drug's effect—the issue is now closer to a matter of survival rather than a change in sensation. Two broad functions are served by the drug in individuals who have become drug dependent. These functions are *defense* and *repair*.

The function of defense is provided by the ability of a drug to counter threatening feelings or feelings that are intolerable to the individual. According to Wurmser (1974), " . . . the importance of the drug effect in the inner life of these patients can perhaps be best explained as an artificial or surrogate defense against overwhelming affects." Examples of the defensive function of drugs are provided by Khantzian (1985): The cocaine dependent individual may be self-medicating against chronic depression or residual attention deficit disorder; the opiate dependent patient finds relief in the anti-aggression and anti-rage actions of opiates.

The function of repair refers to the enhancement of well-being and functioning the drug provides. A reduction in distress occurs, which the individual has not been able to find through his or her own mental efforts. Wieder and Kaplan (1969) consider drug use to serve a "corrective" or "prosthetic" function. Along the same lines, Khantzian (1985) describes the role of cocaine as replacing boredom and emptiness with feelings of self-sufficiency.

It is apparent that the subjective effect of drugs, particularly the change in affect, ranges from the relatively simple, brief period of euphoria, through escape from or "self-medication" for physical or emotional pain, to intrapsychic functions analogous to mental defenses and ego enhancement (repair). These effects occur across the broad spectrum of intoxicating substances, and any one person may utilize a variety of drugs for essentially the same result.

ADDICTIVE PHENOMENA

The condition of being drug or alcohol dependent brings forth a set of phenomena that transcends the pharmacologic properties of any specific drug (Nace, 1987). Collectively, these phenomena comprise the syndrome of chemical dependence, in the same way physical findings are used for criteria in syndromes such as hypertension or congestive heart failure.

The first phenomenon·common to the drugs of abuse is *psychological dependence*. A World Health Organization panel stated: "All of these drugs have one effect in common: they are capable of creating, in certain individuals, a particular state of mind that is termed 'psychic dependence.' Indeed, this mental state is the most powerful of all the factors involved in chronic intoxication . . . " (Eddy, Halback, Isbell, & Seevers, 1965).

Psychological dependence is best understood in terms of changes in one's thinking, changes caused by the drug experience. Commonly, the changes are misunderstood to reflect the values of the drug dependent patient. When this misunderstanding occurs, the drug dependent person is easily seen as "weak-willed," morally irresponsible, or in other terms of disapproval.

These cognitive changes, which are derived from the effect of drugs, are:

- Psychological primacy: This aspect of psychoactive substance dependence refers to an ever increasing importance or salience of the drug and its effect on one's life. As the dependence progresses, the person's preoccupation with obtaining and using the drug mounts. One of the American Psychiatric Association's criteria for the diagnosis of substance dependence reflects this phenomenon: "Important social, occupational, or recreational activities are given up or reduced because of substance use. The person may withdraw from family activities and hobbies in order to spend more time with substance-abusing friends, or to use the substance in private" (American Psychiatric Association, 1987).

The preoccupation with the drug is not a reflection of the patient's value system, but rather reflects the dominance of the chemical on cognitive and behavioral processes. By the same token, this preoccupation is not, at least initially, derived from an effort to forestall or avoid the discomfort of withdrawal syndromes. Later, the effort to curb such discomfort adds to the salience of drug-seeking behaviors. It is, however, the psychic need that carries the day, and from which the perplexing, seemingly self-defeating behaviors of the dependent person are derived.

- Self-doubt: A second aspect of the psychic need or dependence established by psychoactive substances is that of a profound erosion in self-confidence. A conviction of inadequacy in the face of daily work or family demands impels one to seek the "boost" from the drug, an effect that further reinforces self-doubt.
- Sense of loss: The prospect of living without drugs conjures feelings of emptiness, boredom, and depression. A "grief reaction" can be expected when abstinence is anticipated.
- Inability to abstain: As the patient becomes aware of his or her dependence on drugs, there are grave concerns that the ability to quit is lost. The fear of failure to abstain may be one of the factors that block the patient's willingness to seek treatment.

Other addictive phenomena that will be present in varying intensity include:

- Craving: the subjective experience of desiring, needing, or longing for the euphoria or sedative properties of a drug.
- Personality regression: the erosive effect of intoxicating substances on personality functioning and the resultant return of immature defense mechanisms and behaviors.
- Denial: the commonly observed tendency to minimize, rationalize, or totally disavow the effects of drugs or the consequences of use.
- Conflicted behavior: the actions and events resulting from drug use (e.g., accidents, loss of income), which result in guilt, shame, and loss of self-esteem.

The addictive phenomena described above, together with the affective functions of drug use, poly-drug use, and the social aspects of the drug experience transcend any intoxicating drug or class of drugs. Together, these phenomena enable us to consider the substance use disorders in a generic sense.

CLINICAL IMPLICATIONS

From the generic concept of substance use disorders certain clinical implications can be derived. The first is the necessity for abstinence from all intoxicating substances. Recovery from alcoholism requires abstinence from marijuana, cocaine, and other drugs. Similarly, the cocaine dependent patient will edge closer to relapse if his or her drinking continues. The use of any one drug, even if not previously abused, affects judgment in regard to one's use of previously abused drugs. Further, even if the initial drug that produced dependence is avoided, the use of other drugs is accompanied by an increased probability of dependence.

A second implication concerns the prescribing patterns of physicians. The use of anxiolytic, sedative, and hypnotic drugs must be considered carefully in the patient with a prior history of drug dependence. The same applies to opiates, as any "opportunity" to reexperience the affective changes associated with intoxicating substances may rekindle a return to a pattern of abuse. For example, a young man had abstained from marijuana and cocaine use for eight months, when a skiing accident led to use of oxycodone. The reexperiencing of a drug effect led to opiate dependence and eventually a return to treatment.

Third, the generic concept deemphasizes physical criteria of dependence. Tolerance and withdrawal symptoms assume less importance in the description and diagnosis of substance use disorders. The American Psychiatric Association's revised diagnostic criteria (1987) reflect this lessened emphasis on physiological criteria.

Fourth, our treatment approaches are simplified by an understanding of the generic aspects of drug dependence. It is not necessary to establish separate rehabilitation programs for each class of drugs. The experience of being chemically dependent is common to all the different types of addicting drugs, and this experience needs to be the primary focus of treatment.

In summary, the treatment of substance use disorders includes recognition of aspects of these disorders that are not specific to a particular drug but, rather, are common across diverse pharmacologic groups. Such aspects of the drug experience validate a generic concept of chemical dependence and include social aspects, poly-drug use, affective functions, and addictive phenomena.

CHAPTER 3

Etiologic Variables of Addiction

NEUROCHEMICAL MECHANISMS

From the late 1960s to the present, a series of scientific discoveries have heralded a new era of interest in the biological aspects of addiction. First, the concept of an opiate receptor as the mechanism whereby opiate drugs exert their effects was proposed (Martin, 1987). A receptor is a protein complex in the cell membrane to which selected molecules attach and thereby initiate their pharmacologic effects. The receptor and its ligand (any molecule that binds to a given receptor) have a very specific fit and operate, like a key (ligand) in a lock (receptor). Opiate receptors were soon demonstrated in the central nervous system (CNS) (Pert & Snyder, 1973); if the "lock" was present in the human brain, then nature likely provided "keys," as well. A series of naturally occurring opiate-like compounds were discovered in vertebrates (Goldstein, 1978; Pasternak, 1988). These were called endorphins, a generic term for any internal morphine-like peptide. Endorphins and enkephalins (small morphine-like peptides) and their interaction with opiate receptors constitute a major neurotransmitter system in the CNS and involve regulation of mood, pleasure, and perception of pain.

These findings spurred theories attempting to link addictive conditions, such as alcoholism, to a deficiency in endogenous opiate-like substances (Blum & Trachtenberg, 1988) or to the formation of tetrahydroisoquinolines (THIQs) from metabolites of alcohol. The THIQs could act as surrogate opiate ligands and temporarily compensate for a presumed genetic deficiency in endorphins. A deficiency in endorphins has not been demonstrated, but the formation of THIQs in mammalian species has been (Cashaw, Geraghty, McLaughlin, & Davis, 1987; Davis & Walsh, 1970), and a THIQ compound has been reported to increase alcohol drinking in animal models (Myers & Melchior, 1977). However

15

intriguing the THIQ theory may be, it recently has fallen out of favor because THIQs are not found in mammalian brains by most investigators, THIQs bind weakly to opiate receptors, and the quantity of THIQ formed from condensation reactions may not be high enough to affect the opiate receptors (Wallace, 1988).

Neurochemical Actions of Opioids

More germane to our understanding of the biology of addictive states is the developing understanding of how opioids work. Within the midbrain, the ventral tegmental area (VTA) and the nucleus accumbens (NA) contain neurons highly sensitive to the administration of opioids. The lateral hypothalamus also is stimulated by opioids, and the nerve tracts from the lateral hypothalamus to the VTA to the NA with subsequent projections to the cortex constitutes a "reward" center mediating the effect of opioids. Animals will work to self-administer opioids into the VTA and NA, indicating cells rich in opiate receptors. Interestingly, the reward centers for opioids are not the same neuronal pathways that mediate withdrawal symptoms. Cessation of opioid administration into the VTA and NA does not lead to opiate withdrawal symptoms. If opioids are injected into cerebral ventricles (thereby affecting other neuronal areas), withdrawal symptoms are observed when administration of the opioid is stopped (Koob & Bloom, 1988).

There are several types of opiate receptors, but within the CNS, the major types are the mu and kappa receptors. The opiate mu-receptor is activated in the VTA, and thereby stimulates dopamine-containing neurons within the above described "reward" circuit. Another nucleus within the brain, the locus ceruleus (LC), located in the pons, is activated by mu opiate receptors. The LC is the largest collection of noradrenergic neurons in the CNS. It develops tolerance to opiates, and its cells fire excessively when opiates are withdrawn. The increased LC activity resulting from discontinuance of opiates is the basis for much of the opiate withdrawal syndrome. As a result, clonidine, an alpha-2 agonist, is useful in treating the opiate withdrawal syndrome, as alpha-2 agonists inhibit by binding presynaptically to the noradrenergic LC neurons (Gold, Pottash, Sweeney, & Kleber, 1980).

Neurochemical Actions of Cocaine and Amphetamines

The neuropathways that reinforce cocaine and amphetamine use are similar to those involving opioid reinforcement. Dopamine-containing neurons of the VTA project to the NA and other limbic areas, as well as to the frontal cortex. Amphetamines release both dopamine and norepinephrine from cellular sites, whereas the effect of cocaine is due primarily to its blockade of dopamine reuptake. This effect prolongs the action of dopamine (Koob & Bloom, 1988).

Cocaine affects the serotonin system, as well as the dopamine and norepinephrine systems. It is postulated that stimulant-induced euphoria involves an interaction between serotonin and dopamine systems. Research with animal models indicates that agents with only serotonin or only dopaminergic activation are less effective in producing self-administration than are agents that have a combination of serotonin and dopamine effects (Gawin, 1991).

Prolonged use of cocaine depletes neurons of dopamine, norepinephrine, and serotonin, the result of which is the "crash"—the anhedonia, fatigue, and depression—that follows a cocaine binge. Postsynaptically, there is down-regulation of dopamine receptor sites, an effect that may stimulate craving. These neurophysiological changes are the basis for treating cocaine addicts with tricyclic antidepressants, such as desipramine or imipramine (Gawin & Kleber, 1984). The tricyclics down-regulate presynaptic receptor sites, thereby allowing more dopamine to reach the postsynaptic neuron. In addition, bromocriptine has been used in the treatment of cocaine dependence, as it binds to D2 dopamine receptors and serves as a dopamine agonist (Dackis & Gold, 1985).

Neurochemical Actions of Marijuana

Marijuana is highly lipophilic, and initial efforts at understanding its psychotomimetic effects focused on its ability to "stick" to membranes. A "membrane perturbation" hypothesis has been proposed to account for cannabinoid action due to the observed increased fluidity within the phospholipid vesicles of cellular membranes. The calcium channels in cellular membranes are impacted by cannabinoids. Less calcium enters the intracellular space, and this depresses the release of neurotransmitters (Martin, Bloom, Howlett, & Welch, 1988).

More recently, this very general effect of cannabinoids has been supplemented by a specific effect, the discovery of a marijuana receptor and its gene (Marx, 1990). Cannibinoids inhibit formation of cyclic AMP through suppression of adenylate cyclase activity. These effects are not blocked by naloxone nor are they synergistic with morphine, indicating that the marijuana receptor is distinct from opioid receptors (Martin, Bloom, Howlett, & Welch, 1988). The marijuana receptors are found in areas of the brain that correspond to known behavioral effects. For example, the cerebral cortex, hippocampus, and cerebellum are rich in marijuana receptors, which accounts for the drug's impact on cognition, memory, and the coordination of movements. Conversely, marijuana receptors are few in the brain stem, corresponding to marijuana's minimal effect on cardiac and respiratory function (Marx, 1990).

Neurochemical Actions of Hallucinogens

Hallucinogens only rarely produce hallucinations. Typically, they intensify sensory experience and produce illusions and pseudohallucinations (a misperception that the subject recognizes to be a misperception) (Cohen, 1984). Their mechanisms of action are less well-known than the mechanisms for opiates, stimulants, or alcohol.

LSD (lysergic acid diethylamide), a derivative of the rye fungus ergot, is similar in structure to the neurotransmitter serotonin and is believed to inhibit serotonin's activity at the serotonin receptor. LSD has been demonstrated to inhibit cell firing in median raphe nuclei and cerebral cortical cells, both of which are areas of the brain rich in serotonin. Psilocybin (derived from mushrooms) and mescaline and peyote (derived from species of cacti) affect the serotonin system, as well. The raphe nuclei act as sensory input filters; when inhibited by hallucinogens, the amount of information available to higher brain centers is considerably increased, accounting for the visual and the sensory experiences (Blum, 1988).

Neurochemical Actions of Ethanol

Ethanol has numerous neurochemical effects in the brain. Which ones are clinically significant in terms of explaining intoxication, tolerance, and withdrawal syndromes remains to be determined. Similarly, determining the sites of action that may be fruitful for pharmacologic intervention awaits future research.

One of the known actions of ethanol is the disruption of the phospholipid molecular chains in the nerve cell membrane. The result is an increased "fluidity" of the membrane. This disturbance in the structure of the membrane impacts the functional protein systems (enzymes, receptors, and ionophores), which are attached to the membrane (Tabakoff & Hoffman, 1988). For example, adenylate cyclase and monoamine oxidase activity are lower in alcoholics than in controls. Adenylate cyclase is important in the formation of cyclic adenosine monophosphate (CAMP), which, in turn, influences metabolism within the cytoplasm. Of particular interest is the finding that adenylate cyclase remains inhibited in alcoholics 12 to 48 months following abstinence (Tabakoff, Hoffman, Lee, Saito, Willard, & DeLeon-Jones, 1988).

Neurotransmitter systems are affected by alcohol. The glutamate system and the glutamate receptor, N-methyl-D-aspartate (NMDA), may mediate acute effects of alcohol. Alcohol inhibits the activity of glutamate, possibly by blocking NMDA-stimulated calcium uptake. The NMDA receptor is believed to be a factor in consolidation of long-term memory and, when abnormally activated, contributes to hypoxic damage and seizure activity. Alcohol's action at the NMDA site may partially account for alcohol-related problems, such as memory dysfunction, seizures, and brain damage (Chandler, Sumners, & Crews, 1991).

The effect of ethanol on norepinephrine and dopamine neurotransmitter systems is better known. Low doses of ethanol activate norepinephrine systems via the reticular activating system in the brain stem. This effect activates behavior and arousal by increasing the flow of sensory input to the cortex. Interestingly, tolerance to this arousal/activating norepinephrine-mediated effect does not develop and, therefore, the expectation of further reinforcement is established. As the concentration of ethanol in the brain increases, the dopamine pathways in the mesolimbic system assume importance as a reward center. This system, which involves the ventral tegmental area and projections to the nucleus accumbens, is the same neuronal system activated by opiates and cocaine. Alcohol at this concentration, with its impact on dopamine, becomes a primary reinforcer (i.e., a reward unto itself rather than an enhancement of experience by increased arousal). Tolerance develops within the dopamine system necessitating higher concentrations of alcohol to capture the "reward" (Tabakoff & Hoffman, 1988).

Studies of serotonin have stimulated interest in the role of this neurotransmitter in drinking behavior and alcoholism. Low brain serotonin levels have been associated with increased spontaneous alcohol consumption in rodents, and serotonin uptake inhibitors have been associated with decreased alcohol consumption (Gill & Amit, 1989). The effect of increasing serotonin is to decrease alcohol consumption, an effect opposite that of an increase in norepinephrine and dopamine. It should be appreciated that, thus far, demonstrated decreases in alcohol consumption in humans secondary to serotonin uptake inhibitors is slight and temporary.

The major inhibitory system of the brain has been demonstrated to be affected by alcohol. The gamma-aminobutyric acid (GABA) receptor/chloride channel complex is the site for GABA (the brain's major inhibiting neurotransmitter) and is also the recognition site for barbiturates and benzodiazepines. The binding of these latter compounds to their recognition sites on the receptor causes an ion channel to open temporarily, in order to emit chloride ions into the cell (Suzdak, Glowa, Crawley, Skolnick, & Paul, 1988). The chloride ion influx is enhanced by the presence of alcohol and may represent one of the mechanisms for alcohol's anxiolytic effects (Linnoila, 1989).

SUMMARY

Continuing advances in neurobiology enable the clinician to appreciate the basic and profound impact that alcohol and other addicting drugs have on brain functioning. The primitive, subcortical areas of the brain are profoundly impacted (e.g., the VTA to nucleus accumbens tract). The reinforcing power of overly stimulated neurotransmitter systems drives drug-seeking behavior beyond the boundaries of rational consideration. It is often helpful for patients to understand that drug usage tampers with major, basic, life-sustaining brain centers and pathways. As the chemically dependent patient gains appreciation for the neurobiologic forces that affect behavior, motivational forces nourished by such information may emerge to counter the addictive process.

GENETICS

The study of genetics has raised hopes for a straightforward understanding of alcoholism and drug addiction. Lewis Thomas (1979) writes of disease as having "a single switch at the center of things." Proponents of a genetic etiology of alcoholism range from advocating a "switch" model (Goodwin, 1983), to a more complex model of multiple genes interacting with the environment (Schuckit, 1985a), to an acknowledgment of the critical importance of sociocultural influences (Cloninger, Bohman, & Sigvardsson, 1981).

It is well known that children and first-degree relatives of alcoholics are more likely to develop alcoholism than the general population (Schuckit, Goodwin, & Winokur, 1972). Evidence supporting a genetic contribution to alcoholism is found in twin studies, adoption studies, family studies, and in studies searching for biological markers (Devor & Cloninger, 1989). Critical reviews of the literature can be found in Murray, Clifford, and Gurling (1983) and in Lester (1988).

When viewed broadly, the majority of twin studies find a concordance rate of 60% or higher in identical twins and 30% or less in fraternal twins (Schuckit, 1985a). The twin studies, however, are more complex than the above summary would suggest, and a shared genotype is not the only variable impacting identical twins. For example, frequent social contact or cohabitation is related to similar drinking patterns. Identical twins have more social contact with each other in adulthood than do fraternal twins, and the higher concordance rates for drinking patterns in identical twins are influenced by this variable (Kaprio, Koskenvuo, Langinvainio, Romanov, Sarma, & Rose, 1987). Marital status also influences whether identical twins have similar (concordant) drinking patterns. Married twins have been found to be much less similar in their drinking patterns than are twins who have not married (Heath, Jardine, & Martin, 1989). Twin studies continue to be inconclusive; a large study based on United States veterans' records found a concordance for alcoholism in 26.3% of monozygotic twins and 11.9% of dizygotic twins (Murray et al., 1983).

Adoption studies investigate the rates of alcoholism in individuals who have an alcoholic biological parent, but who were adopted into nonalcoholic homes. A study conducted in Denmark (Goodwin, Schulsinger, Hermansen, Guze, & Winokur, 1973) stimulated strong interest in the genetic theory of alcoholism. Eighteen of 55 adopted sons of alcoholic parentage were found to be alcoholic, compared to 5 of 78 adoptees without a biological alcoholic parent. Thus, sons of alcoholics were nearly four times more likely to develop alcoholism than sons of nonalcoholics.

A larger and more complex adoption study was conducted in Sweden. If the biological father was alcoholic, the adopted sons were found to be alcoholic in their adult years in 22.4% of cases, compared to 14.7% of adoptees without an alcoholic father. If the biological mothers were alcoholic, adopted daughters had a three-fold increase in alcoholism (10.3 versus 2.8%), compared to controls (Cloninger, Bohman, Sigvardsson, & von Knorring, 1985). Other major adoption and family studies are reviewed by Devor and Cloninger (1989) and methodologically critiqued by Lester (1988) and Murray et al. (1983).

An important contribution to the genetic theory would be the discovery of a marker that predicts susceptibility to alcoholism (or other substance use disorders). A marker could be biochemical, electrophysiological, or behavioral. The marker may be merely correlated with the expression of alcoholism or it may bear a direct relationship to the formation of alcoholism.

The search for biochemical markers has been extensive and includes studies on human leukocyte antigens (HLA). Certain of these antigens have been found more frequently in alcoholics than in controls, particularly alcoholics with liver disease. In numerous studies, platelet monoamine oxidase (MAO) and adenylate cyclase activity have been found to be reduced in alcoholics (Devor & Cloninger, 1989). The naturally occurring brain peptide, beta endorphin, has been found in several studies to be lower in the cerebrospinal fluid of alcoholics. Nonalcoholic relatives with a family history of alcoholism have lower resting epinephrine levels and a lessened response to stress-induced epinephrine release (Topel, 1988).

Replication of findings is essential if true differences between those at high risk for alcoholism and those at lower risk are to be discerned.

The report of a particular variety of the dopamine D2 receptor being associated with a virulent form of alcoholism was of potential importance (Blum, Noble, Sheridan, Montgomery, Ritchie et al., 1990). However, subsequent studies have failed to link this finding specifically to alcoholism (Bolos, Dean, Lucas-Derse, Ramsburg, Brown, & Goldman, 1990; Gelernter, Goldman, & Risch, 1993; Holden, 1991).

Biochemical markers are also being investigated in an effort to distinguish subgroups of alcoholics. For example, alcoholics with onset of heavy drinking before age 20 were found to have lower concentrations of somatostatin and diazepam-binding inhibitor in the cerebrospinal fluid than older age onset groups. Behaviorally, the younger age onset group are more antisocial and have more associated mental disorders (Roy, DeJong, Lamparski, Adinoff, George et al., 1991).

Electrophysiological studies have found differences in samples known to be at high risk for alcoholism, for example, the sons of alcoholics. Alpha rhythm may be decreased in sons of alcoholics, but is subject to enhancement when alcohol is consumed. The alpha rhythm reflects a capacity for relaxation, and if this capacity is diminished (less alpha activity) under normal conditions, but increased considerably with alcohol ingestion, a physiologically different "high" may be presumed for those known to be at risk for alcoholism (Pollock, Volavka, Goodwin, Medrick, Gabrielli et al., 1983).

Brain-stem event-related potentials are computer-averaged brain waves that are evoked when an unusual stimulus is presented to the subject. For example, presenting a tone of a different frequency compared to a preceding tone evokes a brain wave called the P300 wave. Preadolescent sons of alcoholics were found to have a lower amplitude P300 wave than a control group of boys (Begleiter, Porjesz, Bihari, & Kisson, 1984), indicating that the sons of alcoholics may have difficulty in focusing their attention. As with most efforts at identifying markers, some studies provide replication, for example, lower P300 waves in sons of alcoholics (Whipple, Parker, & Noble, 1988), while others find no differences (Polick & Bloom, 1988).

The impact of alcohol on performance and subjective affects has been the focus of studies on behavioral markers. Subjects with a family history of alcoholism differed from controls without a family history of alcoholism, in that the former reported significantly less feelings of intoxication after a dose of alcohol. The family history positive group also demonstrated less body sway (ataxia) after ingestion of alcohol and showed less deterioration in performance on psychological tests than did the control subjects who were at lower risk for alcoholism (family history negative) (Schuckit, 1985a, 1985b).

If confirmed, the differences, whether biochemical or behavioral, hold promise for education and early intervention efforts. Future studies will determine whether individuals with "markers" for alcoholism do, in fact, become alcohol dependent.

TEMPERAMENT

An important area of research has centered on the question of whether individuals at high risk for alcoholism have a disturbed neurological organization which is reflected in temperament. Temperament refers to the emotional sensitivity and responsiveness of the central nervous system and makes up the biological and constitutional template from which personality develops.

There is evidence that neurobehavioral disturbances comprise a vulnerability to alcoholism and that these disturbances are "the final link in the chain of genetically determined biological procession" (Tarter, Alterman, & Edwards, 1988). Following is a summary of neurobehavioral findings that antedate the onset of alcoholism and are suspected to be associated etiologically with alcoholism:

1. Many alcoholics were hyperactive as children.
2. Children of alcoholics exhibit faster waveform activity on the electroencephalogram (EEG).
3. Patients with essential tremor have a higher incidence of alcoholism.
4. Static ataxia is greater in nonalcoholic relatives of alcoholics than in control groups.
5. Left-handers are more prone to alcoholism.
6. Adolescent sons of alcoholic fathers show more neuropsychological impairment and lower academic achievement than sons of nonalcoholic fathers.
7. Nearly one in three alcoholics meet criteria for attention deficit disorder.
8. On tests of abstracting and problem solving, first-degree relatives of alcoholics performed worse than controls.
9. Pre-alcoholics are often impulsive, aggressive, and emotionally labile.
10. Antisocial tendencies frequently predate the onset of alcoholism (Tarter et al., 1988, pp. 76–77).

Initial observations (Tarter, McBride, Buonpane, & Schneider, 1977) linked childhood history of hyperactivity and/or minimal brain damage with the risk of future alcoholism. Subsequent studies led to a revision of these findings. The risk for alcoholism was found to be related not to hyperactivity but to the presence of conduct disorder (Tarter, Hegedus, & Gavaler, 1985), and a history of childhood hyperactivity in adult alcoholics was related to the presence of a personality disorder (Alterman, Tarter, Baughman, Borber, & Fabian, 1985).

A current model for the role of temperament is Cloninger's (1987) discussion of genetic variation in the sensitivity of neurotransmitter systems. Differing sensitivities lead to specific personality traits, from which are derived a Type 1 and Type 2 classification of alcoholics (Table 3.1). Cloninger's model integrates neurophysiological data with observed differences in the behavioral patterns of early and late onset alcoholics. The three major neurotransmitter systems (dopamine, norepinephrine, and serotonin) are considered to facilitate three dimensions of personality: respectively, novelty seeking, reward dependence, and harm avoidance. These latter traits are considered to be determined genetically and are independent of each other.

The dopamine system is a behavioral activation system primarily involving neuronal circuitry in the midbrain between the ventral tegmental area and the nucleus accumbens.

Stimulation of this system—for example, by alcohol—leads to novelty-seeking behavior, exploratory activity, and exhilaration. The norepinephrine system, involved in behavioral maintenance, anatomically includes the locus coeruleus in the pons with pathways projecting to the hypothalamus, limbic structures, and throughout the cerebral cortex. This system modulates reward seeking behaviors and responses to rewards, such as social approval. The personality trait of reward depen-

TABLE 3.1
Distinguishing Characteristics of Two Types of Alcoholism*

	Type of Alcoholism	
Characteristic Features	*Type 1*	*Type 2*
Alcohol-related problems		
Usual age of onset (years)	after 25	before 25
Spontaneous alcohol-seeking		
(inability to abstain)	infrequent	frequent
Fighting and arrests when drinking	infrequent	frequent
Psychological dependence (loss of control)	frequent	infrequent
Guilt and fear about alcohol dependence	frequent	infrequent
Personality traits		
Novelty seeking	low	high
Harm avoidance	high	low
Reward dependence	high	low

*Data in table collected from Cloninger, 1987.

dence depends on the sensitivity (genetically determined) of the norepinephrine pathways. The serotonin system mediates harm avoidance behaviors. The major pathways project from the raphe nuclei in the brain stem to the limbic system and prefrontal cortex. In addition, cholinergic projections from the midbrain reticular formation to the frontal cortex modulate harm avoidance behaviors. This system facilitates learning to inhibit behaviors to avoid punishment and frustration (Cloninger, 1987).

These genetically based neurotransmitter systems are assumed to account for the traits and behaviors observed in alcoholism. Two broad classifications of alcoholics are derived from this model: Type 1 alcoholism is found in those over age 25 who have loss of control over alcohol use once drinking is initiated. Alcoholics of the Type 1 classification are characterized by passive-dependent and anxious features. They typically are sensitive to social cues, are sentimental, emotionally dependent, and eager to help others. These features characterize the reward dependent personality trait. Type 1 alcoholics also exhibit the features of the harm avoidance trait, such as apprehension, caution, pessimism, shyness, and fatigue.

Type 2 alcoholism is found in early-onset alcoholics (under age 25), who are almost always male. This type is characterized by high novelty seeking behaviors, such as distractability, impulsiveness, and excitability. Type 2 individuals are low on the traits of reward dependence and harm avoidance. Therefore, they tend to be emotionally cold and detached, and/or carefree, uninhibited, and confident.

The features of the Type 1 and 2 classification are summarized in Table 3.1. It is important to note that alcoholics may show features of both types and that the Type 2 alcoholic may represent an antisocial personality disorder rather than alcoholism per se (Schuckit, Irwin, & Mahler, 1990).

SOCIAL AND CULTURAL FACTORS

History and culture shape whether—and to what extent—drug epidemics appear. Westermeyer (1988, 1991) has documented the complexity of these processes. Before Columbus sailed to America, Europeans used drugs primarily through oral ingestion. With the colonization of the New World, smoking and nasal insufflation were introduced. Eventually, tobacco smoking was introduced into Asia from the New World, and opium eating, which had not previously resulted in social problems, was replaced by the new technology of opium smoking—adapted from the introduction of tobacco smoking. Drug abuse became widespread and, with it, potential corruption.

In the late 17th and early 18th century, England underwent an epidemic of gin drinking. Gin was produced from cane sugar, grown by slave labor in North America. English ships used barrels of gin as ballast as they returned to England. The importation of this cheap alcoholic beverage coincided with the social cruelty of the Industrial Revolution and the breakdown of rural values. Traditions that governed the use of more familiar products, such as ale, did not exist for gin, and widespread gin drinking emerged (Westermeyer, 1991).

Thus, cultural and social changes since the post-Columbus era led to greater availability of a wide array of intoxicating substances. Among these changes are increased international commerce resulting from more efficient, rapid means of transportation; rising income levels, especially in the Western World, which have resulted in greater interest in recreational drug use and, in turn, increased production and distribution of drugs; technological advances, such as the hypodermic syringe, which rapidly became adapted to illicit drug use, as in the morphine epidemic following the American Civil War; improved techniques for extracting and purifying the active ingredients from plants (e.g., free-base cocaine and the increased content of tetrahydrocannabinol in the cultivated marijuana plant); and laboratory synthesis of new compounds (e.g., the opioid fentanyl, amphetamine compounds, and "designer drugs," such as "ecstasy"MDMA or methylenedioxymethamphetamine), which may be more potent, purer, or cheaper than botanical products (Westermeyer, 1988).

One sociocultural variable, availability, can be considered primary for the development of substance abuse. In a given culture, numerous variables influence drug and alcohol use. Among these variables are attitudes toward use of a given substance, the procedures and rules for use, the social processes served by use, and the expected effects, marketing strategies, values, and revenue derived from sale of substances (Ewing & Rouse, 1978). A reason for considering availability as the primary factor is the obvious, commonsense conclusion that if the drug were not present it could not be used.

The role of availability has been studied extensively, at least for alcohol. A society can regulate alcohol availability by placing restrictions on distribution, such as age limitations, days of sale, hours of operation, and extent and type of advertising. Pricing, taxation, and the density of outlets also affect availability (Janes & Gruenewald, 1991; Single, 1988).

Legal liability of alcohol beverage servers in another variable, which shows promise in preventing inappropriate serving practices and, thus, reducing alcohol-related problems. States that have emphasized server liability have been documented to have different serving practices from states that have not emphasized server liability. In the former states, the owners and managers of establishments serving alcohol show higher concern over serving practices and have been exposed to greater publicity about potential liability (Holder, James, Mosher, Saltz, Spurr, & Wagenaar, 1993).

Availability affects not only the social drinker, whose consumption may be light, moderate, or heavy, but also the extent of alcohol-related problems. The price of alcoholic beverages affects per capita consumption and correlates inversely with cirrhosis rates. Pricing, therefore, is a social mechanism for regulating availability (Popham, Schmidt, & de Lint, 1978). Changes in consumption can have far-reaching consequences. A French study (Pequegnot, Cholert, Eydonx, & Courcoul, in Single, 1988) found that the consumption of 60 to 80 grams of alcohol (4 to 5 "standard drinks") per day carried twice the risk of death from cirrhosis than a consumption level of 40 to 60 grams of alcohol per day.

The impact of price on availability has been demonstrated recently in the United States. The cocaine epidemic in the late 1980s and early 1990s in the United States was fueled by the increased availability of inexpensive, highly purified "crack" cocaine. Prior to the mid- to late 1980s, cocaine was expensive and associated with a "glamorous," affluent lifestyle. The image of the drug changed as "crack" flooded the market and swept through deprived urban areas, boosting crime rates. Unlike alcohol, which can be taxed, thereby making it more expensive and relatively less available, cocaine availability is less easily modified through interdiction of imports or by lower production in drug producing countries.

Availability, of course, interacts with a society's shared beliefs and patterns of behavior. "The rules of the game" (Heath, 1988) determine substance use patterns, such as who may use (age, sex), when to use, and where to use. Some cultural groups highly value sobriety (e.g., Jews) as a means of demarcation from less temperate groups, while other groups sanction drunkenness as a selective period of disinhibition valued for its "time out" from normal social sanctions (Heath, 1988).

The power of sociocultural factors, such as attitudes toward drinking mediated by ethnicity or cultural background, has been demonstrated by Vaillant and Milofsky (1982). Their longitudinal study of several hundred males followed over 33 years found that, along with having alcoholic fathers, ethnicity accounted for most of the variance in the development of alcoholism. This juxtaposition of a biological variable (genetics) with the sociocultural variable of ethnically determined attitudes and behaviors serves as a reminder of the complex forces that shape substance use and substance use disorders.

STRESS

Finally, the role of stress as an etiologic variable will be considered in the chapters on the professions. Stress is intrinsic to the preparation for and practice of a profession and is best considered within specific professional contexts.

CHAPTER 4

Initial Steps: Intervention and Diagnosis/Evaluation

This chapter reviews two processes that logically precede treatment decisions. The first process described is that of "intervention." There is no perfect way to undertake an intervention, and this process may vary from informally offered expressions of concern and help to a formal (and usually more successful) intervention technique (Crosby & Bissell, 1989). The essential elements of an intervention as formulated by the Texas Medical Association Physicians Health and Rehabilitation Committee are described.

The second process reviewed is diagnosis and evaluation. This process requires data from numerous sources, including the information that may have prompted an intervention. Emphasis is placed on obtaining properly qualified physicians to proffer the appropriate diagnoses.

INTERVENTION

Intervention is a process that increases the likelihood that an impaired individual will accept the need for help. An intervention "confronts" the individual with evidence of his or her impairment. The evidence is presented by loved ones or concerned others in a systematic manner and with care and concern. This process is likely to evoke strong emotion in both the individual who is the object of the intervention and the other participants. For this reason, it is best to have an objective professional to "coach" those participating in the intervention and to maintain control.

Fact Finding

The professional, who agrees to assist a family, corporation, or group of friends in planning an intervention, will need to determine first whether there is evidence of disability from alcohol or drugs, of cognitive decline, or of other psychiatric disorders. This can be accomplished by reviewing the professional and personal activities of the prospective patient through interviews with family members, friends, associates, or other health care professionals.

Such an evaluation of allegations and the obtaining of additional information will help determine: (1) whether or not the individual is impaired, (2) the degree of impairment, (3) the appropriateness of intervention, (4) who should be asked to assist in the intervention, and (5) who may sabotage an intervention. Once sufficient information is obtained and the above are determined, the second phase of the process begins.

The Intervention Team

The intervention team should consist of two or more persons who are connected personally or professionally to the prospective patient. Those individuals chosen to work with the professional intervener should have directly observed the behavior of the impaired person. The team members should have some understanding of substance abuse and dependence and should accept the definition of these conditions as illnesses and be free of judgmental attitudes. It is crucial that the team members maintain a nonjudgmental stance. All persons participating in the intervention process need to be genuinely concerned about the health and well-being of the prospective patient. Once the team is assembled, the next phase of the intervention process can begin.

Pre-Intervention Team Preparation

Seven preparatory steps are outlined for this phase of the intervention process:

1. The team members are educated on addiction as a disease. Particular emphasis is placed on the defense mechanisms that can be expected to be encountered during the actual intervention. For example, denial, rationalization, minimalization, projection, blaming, anger, and defocusing can be expected to be manifested by the impaired professional, and it is important that the team members not be intimidated or thrown off the track by this possible defensive display.
2. Each team member is asked to list specific incidents or conditions related to the impairment of the professional.
3. Specific treatment options are determined so that the impaired professional can be promptly referred for evaluation or treatment.

It is important that the prospective patient be given meaningful choices as to where he or she will seek an evaluation or treatment.

4. The professional conducting the intervention designates himself or herself as a chairperson and is in charge of the flow of the intervention and is responsible for maintaining control.
5. A rehearsal of the intervention is carried out with the team members. This helps alleviate tension, provides mutual support and understanding, keeps team members focused on their task and the possible outcomes of this task, and empowers the team members to establish the conditions for change.
6. Each team member reads his or her written list of concerns and observations.
7. The team decides the order in which team members will read their list during the intervention.

With this preparation completed, the intervention can be conducted.

The Intervention

The intervention may be held in the office of the professional intervener, in the home of the prospective patient, or in any setting deemed suitable by the team. Once that decision is made and the prospective patient and team members are assembled, the professional intervener makes a simple and empathic introductory statement addressing the reasons for the meeting. This chairperson then clearly points out to the impaired professional that his or her role is to be a listener and the direction of the group is to maintain that stance. Each member of the team presents his or her observations in a caring manner, with the hope and expectation that the impaired professional will seek help. The impaired professional is given the opportunity to respond at the end of the intervention, with the understanding that the goal of this intervention is immediate referral for evaluation and treatment.

The team should have a back-up plan, if the prospective patient refuses to cooperate with any recommendations. For example, an employer may refuse to have the employee return to work until an evaluation is completed. Hospital-staff privileges may be suspended until cooperation is obtained, and family members may withdraw support until constructive, definitive action is taken by the impaired professional. It is necessary to point out certain risks related to an intervention. The shock may provoke anger, relief, or suicidal impulses. The professional intervener and the team members must have some understanding of the mental state of the individual prior to the intervention and must be prepared to respond constructively.

In some cases, confrontation should proceed gradually (Schuster,

1993). If the individual being intervened upon poses a threat to himself or others, implementation of an involuntary mental health or chemical dependency commitment procedure should be anticipated. If the results of the intervention are inconclusive, that is, the impaired professional refuses to cooperate or delays implementation of the intervention team's recommendations, a future meeting should be arranged as soon as possible, in order to sustain the pressure for constructive action.

I will briefly describe two interventions, of differing styles, which were very effective. The first involved an attorney who was suspected of cocaine addiction. As evidence was gathered by his law partners, the professional intervener—in this case, a licensed chemical dependency counselor—formed the team, went through the pre-intervention preparation, and conducted the intervention at the offices of the law firm. Clear-cut consequences regarding the attorney's status with the law firm were provided, and the attorney readily agreed to enter an inpatient treatment program by that afternoon. He was accompanied by one of his partners to his home, where he explained the nature of his problem to his wife and the fact that he was leaving for treatment that afternoon. Special support was provided to the wife, who was unaware that drugs were involved but knew that something was wrong. The wife was not included in the intervention because the law partners did not know her and were concerned that she would not support an intervention process or treatment recommendations. Fortunately, this did not prove to be the case. The attorney cooperated fully with treatment recommendations after overcoming initial resistance and went on to enjoy a long-term successful outcome.

A second successful intervention involved a physician who had avoided and/or deflected the urgings of his medical partners that he "do something about his drinking." Through the guidance of a county medical society's impaired physicians committee, a professional intervener was obtained, and an intervention was held in the physician's home. The physician's wife and son were part of the intervention team, and the physician recalls walking into his home study, seeing the assembled guests (family, a few friends, and colleagues) and knowing instantly what it was about. He accepted treatment recommendations and was admitted that evening.

At times, interventions may be flawed by being either too "passive" or "heroic." Either extreme is a mistake. An example of a passive intervention was provided to me by a residency training director. A resident, older than most residents, was reported to the training director as behaving bizarrely and having had the odor of alcohol on his breath several times. These reports were provided by different members of the nursing staff. The training director felt ill at ease, because he admired and respected this older resident and felt particularly supportive toward him. He casually encountered the resident in the hospital hallway a few days later, called him aside, and asked him if there were any problems. He mentioned that several complaints had been brought to his attention. The resident quickly and confidently assured the training director that "there was no problem" and that there would be no repetition of any behavior that might provoke such concern. About two months later, the same resident was found unconscious in a men's room in the hospital with a needle in his arm. He suffered no serious medical sequelae but clearly had been in danger of tragic consequences from an escalating substance abuse problem. The latter incident, of course, prompted immediate treatment.

In contrast to the passive, casual form of treatment, which is practically guaranteed to be unsuccessful, is the "heroic" confrontation. The heroic confrontation is often too vigorous, may be conducted without sufficient evidence, and allows the impaired professional little or no choice in selection of treatment options. A middle-aged gynecologist was reported to have had the odor of alcohol on his breath. The department chairman was notified, and he attempted to conduct an investigation to see if further action was necessary. This same physician was known to have been depressed and possibly alcoholic several years earlier but, as far as anyone knew, had apparently shown considerable improvement until the recent report.

An intervention was arranged, utilizing two physicians from an impaired physicians committee. The physician interveners did not investigate to obtain further information. They assumed that the gynecologist was an alcoholic, gave him no choice but to catch a plane that afternoon to a distant treatment center, and threatened him with being reported to the National Practitioners Data Bank if he did not cooperate. The gynecologist was stunned and intimidated. He left that day for treatment. After he got on the plane, the physicians met with the gynecologist's wife and explained what had happened. She was devastated and quite frightened about their future. She denied that he had a problem. One of the physicians explained that his marriage had not survived his own personal treatment.

The gynecologist spent several days undergoing an evaluation at the treatment center and requested discharge. He returned home insisting that a second opinion be obtained. This was subsequently carried out and involved interviews with the gynecologist, his wife, and physician colleagues. It was determined that the gynecologist had a past history of severe depression with alcohol abuse. He was treated successfully by a psychiatrist. He acknowledged current depression, but denied alcohol abuse. He was on a complicated medical regimen for a chronic unrelated medical condition. There was no current or recent history of substance abuse. He agreed to resume treatment for depression with his psychiatrist. Both he and his wife were very angry over the way they had been treated. They obtained an attorney and considered bringing suit. This apparently was deflected as he regained his staff privileges and clarification of his status was provided.

This section has described the technical process of an intervention. Many interventions are done less formally, that is, respected colleagues and concerned friends can often share their concerns with an impaired colleague, and an acceptance of the need for treatment or evaluation may result. Should this straightforward, sensitive, and courteous effort fail, the more formal process described in this chapter would be indicated. It is a matter of judgment as to whether to proceed with the less formal or opt for a formal intervention as described above. In either case, intervention is not necessarily completed with one meeting; it may be necessary again once treatment has been initiated if the denial system reemerges to the extent that the individual refuses to adhere to treatment recommendations.

DIAGNOSIS AND EVALUATION

The identification of an impaired professional begins by observing indicators of impairment as described in the chapters specific to each professional group. The presence of numerous signs, symptoms, and aberrant behaviors point toward a diagnosis of a substance use disorder, but do not in themselves determine such a diagnosis, just as ankle edema or an attack of dyspnea does not necessarily determine the presence of congestive heart failure. These "red flags" alert one to the need for further evaluation.

It is essential that an accurate diagnosis be obtained, though this elementary point is often breached in practice. Vastly different responses to the question of whether an individual is impaired may be encountered: Either indications of a substance use disorder are dismissed casually without any effort at comprehensive evaluation, or vigorous intervention and rapid placement in intensive treatment take place in the absence of an accurate diagnosis or a consideration of the individual's specific needs.

A proper evaluation will consist of the following:

1. Referral to a physician experienced in the treatment of substance use disorders, such as a psychiatrist with American Board of Psychiatry and Neurology Added Qualifications in Addiction Psychiatry. Alternatively, a physician recognized as an addiction specialist may be used.

The American Society of Addiction Medicine provides a certifying examination for physicians, which indicates experience and knowledge in addictions. It is important that the evaluating physician be in a position to make the assessment with objectivity.

In some instances, physicians who are asked to evaluate other professionals assume an addiction is present even without supporting evidence. Such physicians may be acting out of their own experience with recovery from a substance abuse problem and may lack the experience needed for an objective evaluation. On the other hand, evaluation by a physician unfamiliar with the manifestations and dynamics of addiction may lead to a missed diagnosis.

A crucial issue is one of attitude. If an evaluating physician believes that alcoholism and drug addiction are found only in ill-kempt, careless individuals, then the well-dressed, well-spoken professional will not fit the stereotype and may be dismissed as not having a problem. Or an evaluating clinician may overidentify with a referred professional and find ways to convince himself/herself that the colleague "does not deserve" a substance abuse diagnosis.

2. Accumulation of data from collateral sources, such as a spouse, family members, partners, colleagues, friends, or other relevant and appropriate sources. Obtaining such data is done best through face-to-face interviews whenever feasible, but it may be obtained by telephone if the first option is not possible.

3. Interview(s) with the professional in question. This often requires more than one session. A careful assessment of psychiatric comorbidity is an important aspect of this interview. Guidelines for taking a substance abuse history are presented in Appendix A.

4. A physical examination and laboratory studies (Table 4.1).

TABLE 4.1
Laboratory Tests Useful for Diagnostic Evaluation

1. Urine screen for drugs of abuse: opiates, cocaine, marijuana, amphetamines, benzodiazepines, phencylidine, and barbiturates; LSD, fentanyl, and so-called designer drugs are not detected by routine laboratory procedures.
2. Complete blood count (CBC)
3. Blood chemistry profile (SMAC-23) to include gamma glutamyl transpeptidase (GGTP)
4. Hepatitis antigen and antibody tests
5. HIV test for exposure to AIDS virus (with patient's permission)
6. Carbohydrate deficient transferrin test determines chronic heavy alcohol intake. For example, use of 60 g of ethanol for one week will produce an evaluation of carbohydrate deficient transferrin (Behrens, Worner, Braly, Shaffner, & Lieber, 1988; Stibler & Hultcrantz, 1987). This test is not widely available but holds promise if further developed.

The above data sets usually enable one to make an accurate diagnosis: substance use disorder and/or other psychiatric disorder, or no diagnosis. Table 4.2 lists DSM-IV (APA, 1994) criteria for substance abuse and dependence. Despite extensive evaluation, however, the existence or extent of a substance use disorder may remain uncertain. In such an instance a period of observation and reevaluation is indicated. The evaluating physician may remain in contact with the professional and monitor the clinical course through periodic appointments and contact with significant others.

Useful Diagnostic Instruments

A variety of questionnaires and interview schedules have been developed to assist in the diagnosis of substance use disorders (Jacobson, 1989). Well-known self-administered questionnaires include the Michigan Alcoholism Screening Test (MAST), a 25-item list of common signs and symptoms of alcoholism (Selzer, 1971). A score of five or more has been the traditional definition of alcoholism, but a more conservative use would be 10 or more as indicative of alcohol dependence. The Self-Administered Alcoholism Screening Test (SAAST) is a 35-item checklist with a score of 10 or more indicative of alcoholism (Davis, de la Fuente, Morse, Landa, & O'Brien, 1989). For drugs, the Drug Abuse Screening Test (DAST) is a 28-item list with a cutoff score for dependence of 10 (Gavin, Ross, & Skinner, 1989). Self-administered tests are, of course, easily falsified. Nevertheless, they often serve the purpose of enhancing self-recognition by presenting the far-ranging signs and symptoms.

A widely administered diagnostic interview schedule is the Addiction Severity Index (ASI). A trained interviewer assesses 180 items across six domains: drug/alcohol use, legal status, physical health, employment/support, family/social relations, and psychological/psychiatric status. An assessment of severity in each of these domains is made through a combination of both patient and interviewer ratings (McLellan, Luborsky, Woody, & O'Brien, 1980). A comprehensive review of available instruments is provided by Jacobson (1989).

Although essential for research purposes, standardized instruments should not be used clinically in place of careful, open-ended interviews, during which the patient experiences the interviewer's attention and interest (Senay, 1992).

Diagnostic Pitfalls

In conducting an evaluation certain considerations bear emphasizing in order to avoid under- or overdiagnosing:

TABLE 4.2
DSM-IV Diagnostic Criteria for Substance-Related Disorders*

Criteria for Substance Abuse

A. A maladaptive pattern of substance use leading to clinically significant impairment or distress, as manifested by one (or more) or the following, occurring within a 12-month period:

(1) recurrent substance use resulting in a failure to fulfill major role obligations at work, school, or home (e.g., repeated absences or poor work performance related to substance use; substance-related absences, suspensions, or expulsions from school; neglect of children or household)

(2) recurrent substance use in situations in which it is physically hazardous (e.g., driving an automobile or operating a machine when impaired by substance use)

(3) recurrent substance-related legal problems (e.g., arrests for substance-related disorderly conduct)

(4) continued substance use despite having persistent or recurrent social or interpersonal problems caused or exacerbated by the effects of the substance (e.g., arguments with spouse about consequences of intoxication, physical fights)

B. The symptoms have never met the criteria for Substance Dependence for this class of substance.

Criteria for Substance Dependence

A maladaptive pattern of substance use, leading to clinically significant impairment or distress, as manifested by three (or more) of the following, occurring at any time in the same 12-month period:

(1) tolerance, as defined by either of the following:

(a) a need for markedly increased amounts of the substance to achieve intoxication or desired effect

(b) markedly diminished effect with continued use of the same amount of the substance

(2) withdrawal, as manifested by either of the following:

(a) the characteristic withdrawal syndrome for the substance (refer to criteria A or B of the criteria sets for withdrawal from the specific substances)

(b) the same (or a closely related) substance is taken to relieve or avoid withdrawal symptoms

(3) the substance is often taken in larger amounts or over a longer period than was intended

(4) there is a persistent desire or unsuccessful efforts to cut down or control substance use

(5) a great deal of time is spent in activities necessary to obtain the substance (e.g., visiting multiple doctors or driving long distances), use the substance (e.g., chain-smoking), or recover from its effects

(6) important social, occupational, or recreational activities are given up or reduced because of substance use

(7) the substance use is continued despite knowledge of having a persistent or recurrent physical or psychological problem that is likely to have been caused or exacerbated by the substance (e.g., current cocaine use despite recognition of cocaine-induced depression, or continued drinking despite recognition that an ulcer was made worse by alcohol consumption)

The need for collateral information. Of all psychiatric disorders, the substance use disorder demands the most far-reaching search for information. Shame, denial, and fear of consequences merge to minimize one's awareness and one's account of the experience with alcohol or drugs. Fear of loss of professional standing with decline in status, position, or income is nearly ubiquitous. Less obvious, but just as real for the individual, is the fear of not being able to cope or endure without chemical assistance. And an unspoken dread of failure may cloud the slowly emerging recognition that abstinence will be necessary (Nace, 1987).

Collateral sources of information are necessary because dependence on a substance often distorts the clinical inquiry. Preferably, such sources of information will be available to the evaluator before meeting with the prospective patient. No one source is entirely sufficient. In some cases, medical data confirm a diagnosis, whereas the spouse may be naive and unsuspecting. In other cases, a family member or colleague is key to understanding the prospective patient's clinical status.

The following case illustrates the problem of underdiagnosis because sufficient collateral sources were not available:

> An intern was referred for evaluation. He was new to the city, single, and emotionally and geographically remote from his family of origin. His performance had been less than marginal, but the event that precipitated a request for an evaluation involved his behavior, while off duty, in the hospital emergency room. He arrived at the emergency room with a friend who needed medical attention for a severe asthma attack. He was demanding, loud, and offensive to the nurses in attendance to the point that he was reported to the training director.
>
> Evaluation revealed depression related to the loss of a relationship shortly before the start of his internship. He appeared haggard with the possible odor of alcohol on his breath during one clinical rotation. This young physician had, in fact, discontinued alcohol use at least a month prior to the time of evaluation on the basis, he said, that he feared it would worsen his depression. There were no corroborating medical data, and no family or close friends were available. The interviewer was moved by the intern's loss of a fiancée, his struggles adapting to a strange city, and the stress of internship. He concluded that the intern was severely depressed but not alcohol or drug dependent.
>
> Months later, this assessment was proven wrong, and, on reevaluation, the intern openly presented a pattern of pathological alcohol use extending back into medical school, which had also contributed to the breakup of his engagement. Collateral sources, although geographically distant, and an extension of the evaluation over time may have yielded a clearer diagnosis and more prompt treatment recommendations.

Aberrant behavior is not necessarily substance abuse. An individual who acts out or is obnoxious or offensive is not necessarily a drug or alcohol abuser. Consideration of a substance use disorder may be warranted, but the diagnosis is not assured. A case history illustrates this point.

> A prominent radiologist was being sued for sexual harrassment by two former employees. The members of his group practice were alarmed and arranged an intervention. The interveners, several physicians from the medical society's impaired physicians committee, assumed alcoholism to be responsible for this physician's recent suits and his well-known expansiveness and, at times, abrasive interpersonal style.
>
> An inpatient evaluation was arranged, which included a medical and psychiatric evaluation, including neuropsychological and personality testing. This prolonged assessment in a setting where the physician was free of the distraction of professional and family concerns allowed significant emotional material to come to the fore. Although he was very successful, the physician had poor stress management skills, but he was quick to strengthen such skills through participation in the inpatient program. Interviews with his wife, colleagues, and a former therapist determined that alcohol abuse or dependence was not present. A return to his former therapist was arranged.

Ask about each and all possible substances of abuse. Appendix A outlines guidelines for taking a substance abuse history. In this process, the interviewer needs to recall for the prospective patient the names of all substances that may have been used. Some patients vigorously avow their abhorrence of illegal drugs. Their sense of indignation, however, may not extend to prescription drugs or to alcohol. In other instances, they cannot acknowledge the use of specific drugs, for example, Demerol, morphine, or Dilaudid. The patient, in spite of (or perhaps in denial of) the goals of the interviewer, does not reveal fentanyl use until a specific inquiry is made. The interviewer must proceed with specific examples in the interest of pushing back the barriers of denial and in furthering the patient's health through accurate diagnosis.

Overidentification with the professional. The evaluating physician may project his or her own fears about the consequences of a diagnosis of a substance abuse problem and, thereby, avoid drawing a proper conclusion, either finding no diagnosis or another diagnosis. Imagining how one would feel if sent away for treatment and then, upon return, explaining the absence to staff or patients could lead an evaluating professional into "protecting" the patient from "embarrassment." The counterbalance to overidentification is the recognition of the losses, em-

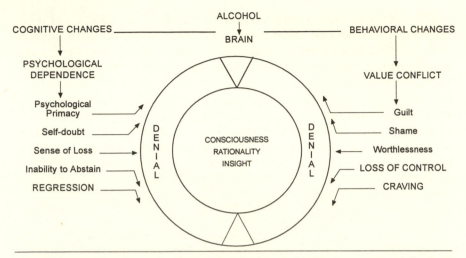

Figure 4.1. Denial Blocks the Conscious Mind from the Consequences of Alcoholism (Reprinted with permission from *Texas Medicine*, 79, p. 38, December 1983.)

barrassment, and shame for the professional rooted in the chemical dependence and the consequences if not treated. Treatment and successful recovery lead to a restoration of self-esteem and a preservation of professional activity.

This is not to say that the moments of confrontation and realization of impairment are not acutely painful for both. His or her shame and disappointment are almost always very acute and require reassurance that facing the problem squarely will be an investment in the future—not a liability. When the evaluating physician has witnessed the destructive consequences of alcohol or drug abuse on the personal lives and careers of professional men and women, but has also seen the restoration and growth from treatment, the natural tendency to identify with the patient and the attempt to prevent the early humiliation associated with diagnosis can be counterbalanced.

Appreciation of the power of denial. It is essential that the evaluating professional fully appreciate the patient's natural tendency to deny or minimize treatment needs and not allow this process to cloud his judgment as well. Denial arises, on the one hand, from the need to protect the addiction, that is, the fear that one could not cope or survive without drugs or alcohol. On the other hand, denial is an attempt to preserve self-esteem in the face of increasing powerlessness over alcohol or drugs. Denial, since it is a primitive defense, can be expected to emerge as the traumas of chemical dependence lead to personality regression (Bean, 1975). Figure 4.1 illustrates the experiences that account for denial (Nace, 1987).

For example, alcohol and drug abuse lead to behavioral changes, which conflict with one's values or expectations, therefore, guilt, shame, and feelings of worthlessness develop. These painful emotions are shielded from awareness by the process of denial. By the same token, the powerlessness and loss of control over chemical use is threatening— not only to one's well-being but to the ability to continue use of the substance. Recognition of these threats is blocked by the denial mechanism. Similarly, psychological dependence is manifested by the priority or primacy of the drug in the person's life, feelings of doubt as to ability to function without the drug, sense of loss and grief if the substance is not available, and a fear that one cannot actually discontinue use. Again, denial "rescues" one from facing the fear of discontinuing alcohol or drug use and from facing the regressive consequences of continued use.

As the clinician gains sensitivity to the shame, fear, and dependence that underlie the defense of denial, he or she can be more effective in addressing denial. Similarly, one learns to develop curiosity about the patient's denial and the purposes it serves in lieu of responses such as frustration, anger, or confusion.

CHAPTER 5

Medical Students and Residents

Consideration of physician impairment raises many questions. Medical school and residency programs are settings where depression, anxiety, and substance abuse often occur. Are such pathological states present before the training years or are they phase-specific to medical school and residency? Do these experiences predict future impairment? To what extent do students bring to the medical setting a vulnerability for impairment that is independent of reactions to the stress and pressure of training?

The possible sequences of symptom development include the years prior to medical school; the training years (medical school and residency); and the postgraduate years (practice). The most unusual sequence would be clinically significant symptoms prior to training, during training, and into practice. Psychopathology extended in time to that extent could often interfere with admission to medical school, with training, or with practice. The most common sequence is the absence of clinical syndromes prior, during, or after training (that is, no impairment); whereas the most studied situation is impairment in the graduate physician. This chapter reviews the growing concern for impairment as it presents during medical school or residency training.

MEDICAL STUDENTS

Medical school is widely recognized as being academically rigorous, physically demanding, and emotionally draining. Highly competitive men and women enter medical school on a crest of prior academic achievement. They confront, usually for the first time, a body of knowledge and a system of education that precludes the satisfaction garnered by a prior sense of mastery. There is too much to learn, insufficient time in which to learn it, and uncertainty about which knowledge will remain relevant.

The successful student of any graduate curriculum is often compulsive in nature. Compulsive attributes, such as thoroughness, conscientiousness, and attention to detail, are taxed by the demands of the medical school curriculum. Doubt, guilt, and an exaggerated sense of responsibility may emerge (Gabbard, 1985). A shift in identity also occurs. The student certainly does not feel like a doctor, yet may be expected by family and friends to provide medical information and, in some ill-defined sense, act like a doctor. Time spent with friends or family decreases, and former interests are typically usurped by academic and clinical demands (Nadelson, Notman, & Prevem, 1982). The losses of previous identity structures, such as roles (e.g., athlete, literature major, fraternity member) and relationships are replaced hesitantly over several years with an identity as a member of the medical profession.

In addition to the losses engendered by the cloistered environment of the medical school, the struggle with finding an emerging identity and the stress of encountering a workload that can be only partially mastered, the student encounters a series of phase specific stressors.

For example, in the first two years, exposure to pathology and mechanisms of disease raise hypochondriacal fears. The third year involves patient contact, and issues of intimacy and boundaries are faced, while the fourth year heralds anticipation of and doubts about managing greater responsibility (Sachs, Frosch, Kesselman, & Parker, 1980).

A study of 230 medical students found that 36% reported being very depressed or anxious most of the time. Significantly more women students (42%) reported anxiety and depression than male students (33%) (Hendrie, Clair, Brittain, & Fadul, 1990).

A quantitative study, measuring intensity of perceived problems, revealed that medical students experience problems more intensely than students in other health-related areas (e.g., dental, nursing, or pharmacy students). Significant differences occurred in complaints about learning environment. Competition, professional ambivalence, and not feeling valued by their families were greater problems for medical students. In addition, medical students reported a greater intensity of problems with feelings of loneliness, helplessness, apathy, self-confidence, self-dissatisfaction, and inhibition. Interpersonal relationships were influenced significantly, with students not having friends, feeling distant from others, feeling ill at ease with others, and feeling shyness. Medical students also reported greater problems in dating and with sleep disturbances. Married medical students in this study reported fewer problems than single students (Bjorksten, Sutherland, Miller, & Stewart, 1983). An increase in negative emotional status (depression, worry, feelings of inferiority and loneliness) from the beginning of the first year of medical school to four months later has been documented (Alagna & Morokoff, 1986; Clark, Dougherty, Zeldow, Eckenfels, & Silverman, 1986).

First-year medical students at Duke University reported a worsening of their health status on all ten parameters assessed. Male students reported statistically significant changes in physical health, general health, depression, and pain. For female students, only a significant increase in depression was found (Parkerson, Broadhead, & Tse, 1990).

Medical students certainly are not the only graduate students who experience stress. Compared with law students, medical students have been found to be significantly less depressed, anxious, and angry, and less obsessive-compulsive (Heinz, Faher, & Leiden, 1984; Kellner, Wiggins, & Pathak, 1986). Yet high rates of depression and anxiety are reported by medical students (Clark & Zeldow, 1988; Michels & Johnson, 1990). Anxiety has been documented in first- and second-year medical students, utilizing the anxiety scale of the Symptom Checklist-90 (SCL-90) (Derogatis & Melisanatos, 1983). Thirty-four percent of students reported symptoms of anxiety, which is above the median reported by psychiatric outpatients. The experiences most anxiety-provoking for students during preclinical years are fear of not being able to master the knowledge, competition, feelings of anonymity, perceiving medical school as a threat more than a challenge, and a sense of loss of control over one's use of time (Vitaliano, Russo, Carr, & Heerwagen, 1984).

A similar study (Zoccolillo, Murphy, & Wetzel, 1986) of first- and second-year medical students evaluated the presence of depression, using the Beck Depression Inventory (BDI) (Beck, Ward, Mendelson, Mock, & Erbaugh, 1961). The incidence of major depression in this study was 12%, with a lifetime prevalence of 15%. This finding is nearly three times greater than the rate of major depression in the general population.

A study of Harvard and Tufts medical students as they began their first year found no differences between male and female students or between minority and nonminority students in number or types of recent life changes or in number or intensity of perceived stressors. The five areas of greatest concern for these students were found to be in decreasing order, schoolwork, intimate relationships, money worries, family, and living conditions (Notman, Salt, & Nadelson, 1984). Another study of first-year medical students found, initially, no differences in psychological adjustment between men and women. But later in the year women were experiencing more depression, more somatic symptoms, and more dissatisfaction than males (Lloyd & Gartrell, 1981).

That medical students will avail themselves of psychiatric consultation has been documented by Dickstein, who treated over two hundred medical students in an eight-year period. Thirty-four percent of the female students were seen in brief therapy. Adjustment disorder, depression, anxiety, and marital problems were the most common syndromes (Dickstein, Stephenson, & Hinz, 1990).

The ultimate concern in medical student adjustment and mental health is the problem of suicide. A survey of U.S. medical schools (Pepitone-Arreola-Rockwell, Rockwell, & Core, 1981) found the male student suicide rate to be 15.6 per 100,000, which is comparable to that of males in the general population. Female student suicide rates were the same as those for male students, but were over three times the rate for the general female population. Seventy-six percent of the suicides were committed by sophomores and juniors, and 50% occurred in the months of November, December, and January. The same survey found that the percentage of students in the different medical schools who sought psychiatric help ranged from 0% to 43%.

In a longitudinal study of over 1,300 Johns Hopkins medical students (Thomas, 1971), it was found that 14 former students had committed suicide. The average interval between graduation and suicide was 8.9 years, with those committing suicide ranging in age from 22 to 48 years. Eleven males and three females committed suicide. Those who committed suicide reported significantly greater "habits of nervous tension" during the medical school years. Six symptoms were most effective in discriminating future suicides: difficulty sleeping, urinary frequency, loss of appetite, urge to be alone, irritability, and lack of urge to confide. The same students, however, did not report feelings of depression.

In addition to symptoms of depression and anxiety, substance abuse has been of paramount concern in the medical student population. For the past 25 years, students have entered medical school following years of exposure to drugs and alcohol on high school and college campuses. By the time they reach age 26, graduates of our nation's colleges have used illicit drugs and alcohol in high percentages: Nearly 100% have drunk alcohol; over 75% have used marijuana; about 33% have used cocaine; over 10% have used LSD or other psychedelics; and nearly 1% have used heroin (Johnston, O'Malley, & Bachman, 1989).

By 1970, marijuana use was extensive among medical students. In a survey of four medical schools in different parts of the country, it was revealed that 50% of students had used marijuana at least once, and 30% of the students were current users. Of the nearly 10% of students who had used marijuana 100 times, 93% were current users (Lipp, Benson, & Taintor, 1971). At the University of Pennsylvania, students in all four years were surveyed in 1970 and 1972. Fifty-three percent of students in 1970 and 70% of students in 1972 had tried marijuana, but in 1972, 57% of users had stopped or decreased use compared to 37% in 1970. In both years, 7% reported use in the past week, and these recent users had used marijuana over 50 times in their lives. This study provided evidence for a wave of marijuana use in the late 1960s and 1970s, which impacted medical students, but showed a decline over the course of several years (Mechanick, Mintz, Gallagher, Lapid, Rubin, & Good, 1973).

Another study from the mid-1970s found all medical students had drunk alcoholic beverages and that alcohol use remained steady over the four years. Ten percent were drinking in a manner that was "problematic." Over 50% of the students had used marijuana and over 20% had used amphetamines. Six percent of students had experienced withdrawal symptoms, and 4% reported having had substance abuse treatment. Longer hours of study and church attendance were associated with less alcohol and drug usage (Thomas, Luber, & Smith, 1977).

Not surprisingly, medical students may reflect usage patterns of the larger society and show a decline in use as a drug fad wanes (Mechanick et al., 1973). On the other hand, there are data confirming a dimension of drug involvement that precedes medical school and continues across the medical school years. For example, the class of 1986 at a midwestern medical school was studied over the first two years (Clark, Gibbons, Daugherty, & Silverman, 1987). The heaviest drug users in the first two years of medical school were extensive users prior to medical school. The number of drugs used, the frequency of drug use, and high levels of drug use were associated with higher levels of alcohol use. If new drugs were added to the students' usage pattern, prior drugs of use were not dropped. Rather, an accumulation of used drugs developed similar to patterns noted in young Vietnam veterans (Nace et al., 1977). A senior medical school class in Texas demonstrated similar patterns, as students who used any alcohol in their lifetime used, on the average, an additional 2.6 drugs. If marijuana had ever been used, an additional 3.7 drugs were used, and if hallucinogens had ever been used, 5.9 additional drugs had been used. Use of any drugs was more frequent for this class in the years prior to medical school than during the medical school years. Mean age of first alcohol use was 15 years, while mean age of first benzodiazepine use was 24 years. Eleven percent of the senior students had been symptomatic from drug use within the past year, and 12% were using one or more substances daily. Use of illicit substances or symptoms secondary to drug or alcohol use was associated with depressed mood (Maddux, Hoppe, & Costello, 1986). By contrast, heavy drinking did not differentiate depressed from nondepressed students in another sample (Clark, Eckenfels, Daugherty, & Fawcett, 1987), but a similar percentage of students, as in the Texas class, were considered substance abusers. Nearly one half of the alcohol abusers (10.6% of the class) also met criteria for drug abuse compared to 7% of the remaining class. Symptomatic drinking was found in 20% of medical students when surveyed at the end of the first year of medical school at the University of Minnesota. Recent drug use was low (less than 2%

of students), except for marijuana, where 15% reported use in the week prior to the survey (Westermeyer, 1988).

A longitudinal study of drinking patterns over the first two and a half years of medical school found that 7% of students had experienced work or school problems secondary to alcohol use. There were no significant gender differences in drinking behavior in this sample, and the incidence of problems was less than that found in college samples (Richman & Flaherty, 1990). The variability in substance-related problems from school to school is highlighted by a survey of freshman and sophomore classes at the University of South Carolina School of Medicine, where less than one percent of the students drank daily or used other drugs regularly (Michels & Johnson, 1990).

As indicated earlier, societal drug use trends may penetrate medical school classes. This fact is illustrated in a survey of 263 second- and third-year students surveyed in 1987. Use of tobacco and marijuana decreased substantially when medical school started, but cocaine was used by 17% of the students prior to medical school and by 17% during medical school. Frequent use of cocaine (i.e., greater than 10 times during medical school) was associated with what might be called a dimension of drug involvement as those students demonstrated excessive alcohol intake, tobacco dependence, and frequent use of marijuana (Schwartz, Lewis, Hoffman, & Kyriazi, 1990).

Two large and methodologically sophisticated studies are available. The first (McAuliffe, Rohman, Santangelo, Feldman, Magnuson et al., 1986) involved a 1984 survey of 504 medical students in New England. Seventy-nine percent (483) completed an anonymous questionnaire. The survey did not include questions about alcohol use. Seventy-seven percent of students had used nonprescribed drugs, 16% were using once per month or more, and 5% believed that they were or had been drug dependent. In all of the categories, the students' use was significantly greater than that of graduate physicians who were simultaneously surveyed. Significantly more students used drugs during their clinical years (50%) than their preclinical years (38%). Religious medical students were significantly less likely to use drugs. Over the five-year period 1979 to 1984, recreational drug use remained constant in these medical schools, except for the use of cocaine, which doubled during this period. The authors conclude: "Perhaps for the first time, appreciable although small proportions of persons entering medicine have histories of extensive drug use and dependence" (p. 809).

A more recent major study surveyed 2,046 senior medical students (67% response rate) in 23 schools. Ninety percent of students began use of substances prior to medical school. Only the use of tranquilizers began more often during medical school than prior to medical school. Only

1.6% of the students believed they currently needed help for substance abuse. Higher percentages reported a history of dependence: for example, tobacco dependence, 8.1%; alcohol, 3.4%; marijuana, 3.2%; and cocaine and amphetamines, about 0.5% each. Compared to national norms, the medical students had used less tobacco, marijuana, and cocaine in the past 30 days than their age peers, who were college and high school graduates. The medical students' use of alcohol in the past 30 days was, however, greater than that of their age peers (Baldwin, Hughes, Conard, Storr, & Sheehan, 1991).

In summary, the literature on medical students documents substantial symptom (e.g., anxiety and depression) development, which seems to peak during the sophomore year. Women students usually, but not invariably, experience more symptoms than male students. Psychological characteristics of students may prove to be more important than gender in the etiology of symptom formation, as "maturity" and traits of masculinity (whether in males or females) were associated with better adjustment, but "Type A" traits or high needs for both power and intimacy were associated with less successful adjustment (Boyle & Coombs, 1971; Hill, Krantz, Contrada, Hedges, & Ratliff-Crain, 1987; Vitaliano, Maiuro, Russo, Mitchell, Carr, & Van Citters, 1988; Zeldow, Clark, & Daugherty, 1985; Zeldow, Daugherty, & McAdams, 1988).

Substance abuse is prevalent in the medical student population, though there is evidence that drug abuse drops off somewhat during medical school, and medical students are using less of most drugs than their age peers who completed high school or college. Nevertheless, a dimension of drug involvement predating and continuing during medical school has been documented. Also of concern is the use of alcohol by medical students, which does exceed usage patterns of their nonmedical age peers, and the introduction of new usage patterns, for example, tranquilizers. A history of substance dependence could be expected in at least 5% of medical students, yet perceived need for help remains low.

RESIDENT PHYSICIANS

Entering medical school initiates a major transition for the student. Similarly, graduation from medical school and the assumption of house-officer status in a residency program entails another significant transition in a medical career. One is no longer a student, but now has an M.D. after his or her name. The former student now expects more of himself or herself, and, indeed, clinical responsibilities take a quantum leap. The excuse of "I'm only a medical student" is no longer available. Clinical decisions, although supervised, are initiated by the resident. Work hours are notoriously long and fatigue is expected. Once again, relationships may be strained by long days and nights in the hospital.

Learning is now less formalized and occurs both continuously and haphazardly. The pressure to know and to be "up on" appropriate clinical management is keenly felt by the resident, who grasps for further knowledge through the supervisory process with attending physicians and by intense glimpses at the latest journals. Competition with fellow residents is often keen. Future fellowships or staff positions are at stake. Some residency programs operate under a pyramid system, whereby fewer residents are retained in the advanced years of training. Coincident with these years, the young physician may be entering into marriage or parenthood.

Depression is the most common symptom in the residency years. Nearly 30% of residents will experience depression, particularly in the PGY-1 year and during rotations with long working hours (Clark, Salazar-Grueses, Grabler, & Fawcett, 1984; Valks & Clayton, 1975). Female residents may be somewhat more susceptible (Hendrie, Clair, Brittan, & Fadul, 1990; Smith, Denny, & Witzke, 1986). Alleviation of symptoms occurs as one advances in the residency years and has more elective time (Reuben, 1985; Schwartz, Black, Goldstein, Jozefowicz, & Emmings, 1987).

The variables that account for most stress have been documented (Colford & McPhee, 1989; Laundau, Hall, Wartman, & Macks, 1988) and include high number of hours at the hospital, years of training, lack of athletic activity, sleep deprivation, lack of family and social contact, inability to do errands, debt, time spent doing housework, high number of spouse's working hours, and fewer awake hours at home. Stress was reduced in relationships when there was athletic activity and time to visit family or friends. The importance of social support and contact was demonstrated in a sample of family practice residents. Those with low social support reported more somatic symptoms, symptoms of anxiety, and feeling themselves to be under greater stress (Mazie, 1985).

Psychiatry residents have been the focus of several studies. A comprehensive study of psychiatry residencies in the United States (Russell, Pasnau, & Taintor, 1975) found that 2% of psychiatry residents terminated training because of emotional illness. Women, minority, and foreign medical graduates were not overrepresented in the dropout group. A review of about 200 residents over a 25-year period from one psychiatric center found that 13% were emotionally disturbed with psychiatric, neurotic, substance use, or personality disorders (Garetz, Raths, & Morse, 1976). A similar 13% prevalence of nonpsychotic emotional illness was found in psychiatry residents at two Canadian programs (Garfinkel & Waring, 1981).

Remarkably similar figures for emotional impairment have been reported in two larger Canadian studies of interns and residents, with 12% to 14% having seven psychiatric symptoms (Hsu & Marshall, 1987; Hurwitz, Beiser, Nichol, Patrick, Kozak, 1987).

In addition to the problem of depression and other manifestations of emotional distress, the issue of substance abuse arises during residency years. Often, studies of house staff officers have not investigated alcohol and drug abuse (e.g., Garfinkel & Waring, 1981; Hendrie et al., 1990; Hsu & Marshall, 1987; Landau et al., 1988; Reuben, 1985; Russell, Pasnau, & Taintor, 1975; Schwartz, Black, Goldstein, Jozefowicz, & Emmings, 1987). An early study (Valko & Clayton, 1975) found no evidence of drug abuse or alcoholism in either depressed or non-depressed interns. Other studies found rates of substance abuse varying from 7% of interns with a history of alcohol abuse to 9% with a history of illicit drug use (Clark, Salazar-Grueso, Grabler, & Fawcett, 1984); 3% meeting criteria for alcohol abuse (Hurwitz, Beiser, Nichol, Patrick, & Kozak, 1987); 4% with substance abuse (type unspecified) (Davis, 1989); and of the 1% of internal medicine residents who took a leave of absence for emotional reasons, only 2% of these were admitted to a facility for treatment of chemical dependence (Smith, Denny, & Witzke, 1986).

Studies that have focused on substance use have found extensive use among resident physicians. A survey of anesthesia training programs for the years 1970 to 1980 found that nearly 2% of residents were drug dependent (Ward, Ward, & Saidman, 1983), whereas a 30-year survey (N = 183) from one anesthesia training program reported that nearly 16% of respondents considered themselves to be substance abusers during their training years. Eighty-five percent of the anesthesiologists contacted felt they had inadequate knowledge of drug abuse or treatment while in residency, and 70% felt that drug control procedures were "fair or poor" in the hospitals where they trained (Lutsky, Abram, Jacobson, Hopwood, & Kampine, 1991). In a New England survey done in 1981–1982, 2% of respondents reported themselves as drug dependent, and an additional 6% were likely to be dependent (McAuliffe, Weschler, Rohman, Soboloff, Fishman et al., 1984). From the same study, Table 5.1 shows the percentage of resident physicians using drugs for either recreational or self-medication purposes.

McAuliffe et al. (1984) point out the alarming fact that only one in one hundred young physicians reported use of opiates in the 1960s, but 1 in 20 were reporting experience with opiates by the early 1980s. Five years later, a survey of residents at an academic center in Texas found lifetime usage rates similar to that of the McAuliffe study (Maddux, Timmerman, & Costello, 1987). However, in the Texas study, use of tranquilizers seemed to be more extensive as 45% reported lifetime use and 11% use in the previous 30 days.

TABLE 5.1
Nonmedical Drug Use by Resident Physicians (lifetime percentage)*

	Recreational	*Self-treatment*
Marijuana	67	1
Amphetamines	13	4
Tranquilizers	6	17
Hallucinogens	16	0
Sedatives	7	8
Cocaine	21	1
Heroin & other opiates	5	27

*Data in table collected from McAuliffe et al., 1984.

The most sophisticated methodological approach to the question of resident physician substance abuse was a stratified random sample of 3,000 third-year residents, obtained from American Medical Association files (Hughes, Conard, Baldwin, Storr, & Sheehan, 1991). Sixty percent of the surveyed residents responded to mailed questionnaires. Self-reports of drug dependence were very low: 0.2% reported being dependent on amphetamines, and 2.3% reported dependence on tobacco. In the month preceding the survey, the following percentage of residents used these substances: alcohol (87%), cigarettes (10%), marijuana (7%), benzodiazepines (4%), cocaine (1.4%), and amphetamines, LSD, other psychedelics, barbiturates, heroin, and other opiates, all less than 1%. Use of substances was generally greater for male residents than female residents, but differences reached statistical significance only in males' greater use of tobacco in the past year and males' greater lifetime use of marijuana.

Of particular interest was this study's comparison of resident physicians with their age peers, who were high school or college graduates. Male and female residents, overall, used fewer drugs than their age peers. Exceptions were higher rates of alcohol use by male and female residents. Male residents also used more benzodiazepines and opiates than their age peers, but not to a statistically significant degree. Female residents use of benzodiazepines was significantly greater than their age peers. Typically, the residency years were not the years of introduction to substance use (80% of residents began use of most substances before medical school). Benzodiazepines and opiates other than heroin were the two classes of drugs that showed substantial initial use during residency. One third of residents who ever used a benzodiazepine first used them in residency, and the comparable percentage for non-heroin opiate use was approximately 25%. Prescription drug use was largely for "self-treatment" not "recreational" use and was self-prescribed in the majority of cases.

A similar study was conducted on 1,800 resident physicians in Ontario (Myers & Weiss, 1987). Dependence and abuse were not reported, but as with Hughes et al. (1991), the use of drugs and alcohol by these young physicians did not exceed that of their age peers. An exception was the use of sleeping pills by physicians under age 30, which occurred at a rate five and a half times greater than their nonmedical age peers. These data are in line with the findings of Maddux et al. (1987) and Hughes et al. (1991) wherein young physicians show a trend toward greater use of prescription drugs than do their age peers. Female physicians in the Ontario study used significantly more sedatives and tranquilizers than the male physicians.

The data available on substance use by medical students indicate the impact of societal drug use trends on student usage. By the time of the residency years, illegal drugs are being used less by these young physicians than by their age peers, who are either high school or college graduates. Yet, a transition seems to occur that offsets the favorable decline in illegal drug use: an increase in use of prescription drugs (see Figure 5.1).

That residents commonly prescribe for nonpatients, such as family members, friends, and fellow residents, has been documented (Clark, Kay, & Clark, 1988). Although the consequences of this are not known, the potentially tragic consequences of self-administration of prescription drugs has been well established. A study of 113 anesthesiology residency training programs (from 1975 through 1989) revealed that 180 of a pool of 8,810 residents were drug dependent. Of these residents with a *known* drug addiction, 26 died, yielding a 15% mortality rate for chemically dependent anesthesiology residents. Fentanyl was the most commonly abused drug, followed by other opiates, then diazepam and alcohol (Menk, Baumgarten, Kingsley, Culling, & Middaugh, 1990).

A striking finding of that study was that 70% of the residents with a history of self-injection were able to complete their training successfully. Sixteen percent of the residents with a history of self-injection died after reentering training compared to less than 5% of the other chemically dependent residents (Menk et al., 1990).

To summarize, resident physicians are using fewer illegal drugs than their age peers, but a tendency toward increasing use of self-prescribed prescription drugs is alarming. The PGY-1 year is the year in which most emotional distress occurs. Symptomatology decreases as a function of advanced years in the residency and as free time increases and call schedules and difficult rotations decrease. Women residents are more subject to symptoms of depression and anxiety, although marital status offers some attenuation of the latter symptoms.

A willingness to address substance abuse, emotional dysfunction, and stress as they occur in the context of residency training programs has been slow to develop. For example, in the 1970s, only 55% of anesthesia residents with a known drug problem were referred for professional rehabilitation (Ward et al., 1983), and, in an editorial on preventing impairment in residents, it was noted that only one third of program training directors acknowledged that work load might be a factor affecting the residents' health and functioning (Blackwell, 1986).

Colford and McPhee (1989) recommend that hospitals provide adequate salaries, increase benefits, and provide services such as child care and financial counseling. They emphasize the need for "protected time" off, better sleeping conditions, fewer nights on call, and increased availability of faculty. Training in stress reduction, support groups for residents, and regular social events would be expected to boost morale.

The Resident Physician Section of the American Medical Association has recommended that time on duty be limited to 80 hours per week, and that every third night be the maximum on-call schedule. An extensive survey of otolaryngology residents, utilizing a daily time log, determined that they averaged 79.4 hours of work per week. This resident physician group further documented that fatigue compromised patient care, as well as their educational experience. The residents working the longest hours also were concerned about developing negative attitudes toward patients (Strunk, Bailey, Scott, Cummings, Lucente, et al., 1991).

It is to be hoped that studies such as the one by Strunk et al. (1991) will stimulate reforms in the duration and environment of work for physicians in training, and that such reforms will diminish both physician morbidity and potential tragic outcomes for patients (Asch & Parker, 1988).

MEDICAL SCHOOL YEARS **RESIDENCY TRAINING YEARS**

Illicit drug use: Prescription drug use:

reflecting societal ——TRANSITION TO ——→ self-medication and

drug use trends instrumental drug use

Figure 5.1. Transition in Substance Use During Medical School and Residency

CHAPTER 6

Physicians

A review of studies on medical students and resident physicians documents the prevalence of alcohol and drug abuse, as well as symptoms of psychiatric impairment. Clinically, we know that many physicians develop drug and alcohol problems during their practice years without an earlier pattern of abuse or dependence. However, we lack longitudinal studies that could tell us whether graduate physicians who become impaired are more likely to have been alcohol or drug abusers in their undergraduate and training years. Symptoms suggestive of impairment in these early years could reasonably be expected to increase the probability of later problems, as at least one study has demonstrated (Thomas, 1971, 1976).

Our concern, now, is to focus on the practicing physician who experiences impairment from alcohol or drug abuse. First, a definition of the impaired physician:

> one who is unable to practice medicine with reasonable skill and safety to patients because of physical or mental illness, including deterioration through the aging process or loss of motor skill, or excessive use or abuse of drugs, including alcohol. (AMA Council on Mental Health, 1973)

While this definition acknowledges that impairment is not limited to substance use disorders, substance abuse accounts for the majority of cases of impaired physicians. This fact has been widely documented; for example, reports from Colorado indicate that 58% to 79% of physician impairment cases involve alcohol and/or drugs (Casper, Dilts, Soter, Lepoff, & Shore, 1988; Shore, 1982). In North Carolina, 85% of impaired physicians were alcohol or drug dependent (Vanderberry, 1990), and, in California, 93% of impaired physicians were drug and/or alcohol abusers or had a mental illness combined with substance abuse (Gulatieri, Consentino, & Becker, 1983).

54

PREVALENCE OF SUBSTANCE ABUSE

The number of physicians with a substance abuse problem has not been determined with certainty. Among the general adult population (18 years and older) of the United States, the lifetime prevalence rate for alcohol abuse and dependence is about 13%, with a one-month prevalence rate of nearly 3%. For drug abuse and dependence, the lifetime rate is nearly 6%, and the six-month rate is about 1.3% (Regier, Boyd, Burke, Rae, Myers, et al., 1988). The rate of alcoholism and drug addiction in physicians has been subject to sensationalism. A source often quoted in the literature reported physician addiction to be 30 to 100 times greater than the general population (Modlin & Montes, 1964). The source of this misinformation was identified to be the Federal Criminal Office of West Germany during the mid-1950s (Brewster, 1986) and is based on data irrelevant to the United States in the 1990s.

In a 20-year longitudinal study, drug abuse between physicians and a control group did differ, in that physicians were using greater amounts of sleeping pills. Problems with alcohol occurred in 16% of both groups by age 46 (Vaillant, Brighton, & McArthur, 1970). In a random sample of Ontario physicians, 1.2% reported having been treated for drug or alcohol problems (Brewster, 1986), which is similar to the 1.5% who reported treatment in an American sample (Niven, Hurt, Morse, & Swenson, 1984). In a survey of over 1,000 young physicians in New England, 2% reported that they were or had been drug dependent (McAuliffe et al., 1984).

More recently, data from a national sample of over 5,400 physicians (Hughes, Brandenburg, Baldwin, Storr, Williams, et al., 1992) showed a self-reported history of alcohol abuse or dependence of 4.2%. Drug abuse or dependence only was reported by 1.9% and a combination of alcohol and drugs by 1.8%. Overall, a substance abuse problem was reported by nearly 8% of physicians. These physicians were less likely to have used illicit drugs or cigarettes in the past year than their nonphysician age and gender peers, but were more likely to have used alcohol, minor opiates, and benzodiazepines. The above studies most likely underestimate the prevalence of physician addiction. It has been assumed that alcoholism occurs at the same rate as in nonphysicians (Canavan, 1983a) and that the rate of drug dependence is higher in physicians than in matched controls. Data to validate these claims are scarce (Brewster, 1986), but at least one study has documented that physicians used drugs more than a control group of pharmacists (McAuliffe et al., 1986).

Specialties

There is no specialty that "protects" a physician from developing a substance use disorder, yet some specialties have higher rates of addiction than others. The availability of highly addicting drugs or the isolation of the practice setting are associated with higher rates of addiction. Selection of a specialty by a physician on the basis of drug availability—for example, choosing anesthesiology because of the higher utilization of opiate drugs in that clinical setting—is uncommon.

Data on the specialties of addicted doctors comes from clinical programs that have treated large numbers of physicians, from state impaired physician committees, or from state medical boards. At the alcoholism treatment center of Lutheren General Hospital in Illinois, 0.5% of patients were physicians. Anesthesiology and obstetrics/gynecology were the two specialties that were noticeably overrepresented (Goby, Bradley, & Bespalec, 1979) compared to the percentage of United States physicians in those specialties. The addiction program at the C.F. Menninger Memorial Hospital reported that nearly 10% of patients were physicians. The specialties of internal medicine, surgery, and obstetrics/gynecology were overrepresented in the clinical setting (Johnson & Connelly, 1981). The Alcoholism and Drug Dependence Unit at the Mayo Clinic reported that 5% of their patients were physicians, with family or general practice being overrepresented (Morse, Martin, Swenson, & Niven, 1984). In a sample from a private psychiatric hospital, surgeons and obstetrician-gynecologists were overrepresented in admissions to a substance abuse program, but pediatricians and psychiatrists were overrepresented in admissions to a psychiatric unit (Nace, Davis, & Hunter, 1995).

A study of physicians on probation (in 1980) by the Board of Medical Examiners of Oregon found no specialty to be statistically overrepresented, although family practitioners (32%) and surgeons (29%) comprised the majority of the sample (Shore, 1982). Data are reported by the California Medical Association's Impaired Physician Program: general practice/family medicine (20.3%); anesthesiology (13.8%); internal medicine (13%); and obstetrics/gynecology (10.1%) (Gulatieri, Consentino, & Becker, 1983). From a sample of 1,000 physicians, the Medical Association of Georgia found that, compared to the proportion in the physician population in the United States, anesthesiologists and family practice/general practitioners were significantly overrepresented (Talbott, Gallegos, Wilson, & Porter, 1987). The North Carolina Physicians Health and Effectiveness Program identified 118 impaired physicians during its first 13 months of operation. Four specialties were overrepresented compared to the number of physicians in North Carolina in those specialties: anesthesiology, emergency medicine, psychiatry, and urology (Vanderberry, 1990). In a study of women physicians in Alcoholics Anonymous, only psychiatry was clearly overrepresented (Bissell & Skorina, 1987).

Overall, anesthesiology stands out as a specialty at higher risk for developing drug dependence. The presence of potent opiates and sedatives that are short-acting and not easily identified in urine tests (for example, fentanyl citrate) is compatible with the etiologic role of "availability" in the development of substance use disorders. The areas of general and family practice seem to be the second most overrepresented specialties. Often, these practices are marked by professional isolation and little relief from client demands.

Two case vignettes illustrate these risk factors.

> During his residency years and in the early years of practice, Dr. H., an anesthesiologist, used amphetamines for "instrumental" purposes. That is, he was able to work longer hours, avoid fatigue, and prevent weight problems. The drug use was mild to moderate but had not reached a level where overt impairment developed. Nevertheless, the utility of self-medicating had been established. Years later, in the context of marital discord, the self-administration of fentanyl occurred. This potent, short-acting drug was readily available in the operating suite, particularly when stringent criteria for accounting for the amount of controlled substance used was absent. When the procedures in the operating room allowed for the use of fentanyl in the absence of strict accountability, a "window of opportunity" was presented and abuse followed. Eventually, the physician was observed injecting himself with fentanyl, and disciplinary actions by the hospital led to loss of privileges.

The second case, that of an internist, illustrates the impact of personal and professional isolation combined with the demands of a solo practice.

> Dr. K. was older than most physicians who completed residency. She established a solo practice in a rural area, which rapidly became very busy. The demands of her new practice stressed a long and significant relationship with her male companion. The loss of this relationship led to depression and somatic symptoms. Informal advice and casual prescribing from physician friends (in lieu of a thorough evaluation of her clinical needs) provided no relief. Inexplicably, she made the decision to self-inject Demerol to relieve headaches. Over the course of the next several months, use of Demerol increased and, by six months, she had been reported (presumably by a member of her office staff) to the local impaired physicians committee. There had been no prior history of alcohol or drug abuse. Dr. K. promptly complied with treatment recom-

mendations and had a successful outcome. She later avoided solo practice by joining a multispecialty group.

IDENTIFICATION

Physicians are ethically bound to take action in the case of an impaired colleague. In 1982, the American Medical Association prepared the following position: "It is the ethical responsibility of any physician who knows of an apparent problem in a colleague to take affirmative action— to seek treatment or rehabilitation for his fellow physician" (as quoted by Canavan, 1983b).

For such action to be realized, the ability to identify an impaired physician is necessary. Clues to impairment may be identical to those found in the general population (e.g., arrests for driving while intoxicated) or may be specific to a medical practitioner (e.g., writing inappropriate orders). Talbott and Benson (1980) have described six areas in which symptoms of impairment become manifest.

Family. The spouse and other family members are usually the first to witness and experience the impact of a substance use disorder in their physician family member. One of three patterns of behavior is observed: withdrawal from the family in the evenings and on weekends by sedating with alcohol, opiates, or tranquilizers; absence from the home to frequent clubs and bars where alcohol and cocaine are typically used; arguments and/or physical abuse toward the spouse or children at home, usually associated with alcohol intoxication.

General symptoms and signs of family dysfunction are:

- family violence (arguments or physical abuse)
- antisocial or other abnormal symptoms (e.g., school problems in the children)
- depression or anxiety syndromes in the spouse
- sexual problems
- separation or divorce

Not unique to physicians, but often seen in exaggerated form, is the process of "family denial." The "secret" of the physician's problem is strongly guarded. The family's reputation in the community, their financial status, and the wife's social identity are perceived to be threatened by the imagined, inevitable damage of exposure. Codependent behaviors (Cermak, 1986) are often well-established, as the spouse allows his or her life to revolve around the increasingly overlapping circles of the physician's career and state of impairment. The fear and shame common to these physicians' families renders them less able to confront the problem, access helpful resources, or initiate a treatment process. It is necessary, therefore, that medical personnel be capable of identifying impairment and know how to obtain help.

Office. The office setting is the next most common setting for indications of impairment. The physician may simply be seen by office staff— for example, receptionist, clerical workers—to be ingesting pills or even injecting drugs. More subtly, the physician may be increasingly absent from the office, may fail to keep appointments, or may spend excessive time alone in the office or the bathroom. Drug samples may disappear quickly, and controlled substances may be ordered in large quantities from pharmaceutical houses. The physician may have the odor of alcohol on his or her breath, appear dishevelled, or be bright, alert, and energetic at one point in the day (after using a stimulant, for example), but shortly thereafter be irritable and fatigued. Patients may complain of inattentiveness, rudeness, or detect an alcohol odor.

The common signs that may be apparent in the office setting include:

- poor appearance
- erratic scheduling
- withdrawn, irritated, or hostile behavior to staff or patients
- excessive ordering of drugs
- observed usage of substances or telltale odor of alcohol

As with the family, the office staff is dependent on the physician and may have difficulty accepting that there is a problem or confronting it.

A female psychiatrist was known by her children to have an alcohol problem. A daughter worked in the office as receptionist and bookkeeper. Patients began to confide and/or complain to the physician's daughter about obvious signs of intoxication in her physician mother. The daughter quickly went on the defensive and reassured patients that nothing was wrong and if they were unhappy with the care received she would refer them elsewhere.

In the above vignette, the daughter, as both a family member and an employee, colluded with the denial system to enable the mother's alcoholism to progress. More typically, the staff covers up, makes excuses, and generally avoids the issue. Staff may be financially dependent on the physician and fear losing their jobs if they become confrontational. Similarly, the physician, often a male authority figure, may intimidate the lower paid staff, who are usually female. Resignations may be common. If employees in such offices are laid off or fired, they may, out of anger, report the physician.

An internist was struggling with an increasingly large solo practice. Personal and professional isolation led to depression and somatic symptoms. An occasional self-administered injection of Demerol for migraine headaches grew into a regular problem of abuse. When conflict with one of the office staff led to the employee's resignation, she promptly reported the internist to the county medical society.

Hospital. Hospital staff have an opportunity to identify substance abuse problems: for example, through calls to the doctor's home for orders or requests to come to the emergency room to see a patient, the physician may be found to be unavailable or actually unable to respond. Nursing staff who place the calls may note slurred speech, incoherent responses, or inappropriate belligerence. At times, the physician may go back to the hospital after the usual work hours with an odor of alcohol detectable. This does not, in itself, mean the physician is an alcoholic, but it is behavior that requires confrontation. For example, an obstetrician was celebrating his birthday with his family at a local restaurant, where drinks were served. He was paged for an emergency and had to return to the hospital. The nursing staff smelled alcohol on his breath and wrote an incident report. He cooperated with an evaluation as recommended by the head of the medical staff. No pattern of alcohol or drug abuse was found, and he was sensitized to the concerns that had been raised.

In contrast, a young house staff officer brought a friend to the emergency room following a minor injury. The house officer was not on duty at the time. He was belligerent and demanding in the emergency room. His behavior provoked an incident report, which, when evaluated in the context of his performance reports, clearly suggested impairment. Through an extended evaluation it was determined that he was alcohol dependent, and specific treatment was arranged.

The following behavior may signal impairment (Herrington, 1979; Talbott & Benson, 1980):

- erratic behavior characterized by swings in mood leading to conflict with hospital personnel and/or patients
- failure to see patients in a timely manner or doing patient rounds on at odd hours (for example, 2:00 A.M., when very few staff would be around to notice aberrant behavior)
- unavailability or inappropriate responses to phone calls
- deteriorated handwriting
- failure to keep records
- overprescribing or inappropriate prescriptions
- forgotten orders—for example, orders given during a blackout and forgotten the next day

- inappropriate sexual comments or behavior
- ingesting or injecting drugs in the hospital

A nurse noticed an emergency room physician taking pharmaceutical cocaine from the narcotics box. Another time, pills were taken from the prescription bottle of a patient in the emergency room; and on occasion, the physician was seen swallowing several pills at a time during his tours of duty. These behaviors were reported to the hospital administration but not acted upon until a complaint of malpractice was received.

Physical and mental changes. This category includes developing medical or psychiatric symptoms, as well as changes in behavior that are out of character for the physician:

- bruises or lacerations from accidents or fights
- deterioration in dress, grooming, or personal hygiene
- increased number of physical complaints or illness
- medical complications of alcoholism or drug dependence
- excessive medical work-ups or hospitalizations
- signs of depression, anxiety, indecision, or impulsivity
- personal crisis

A physician in his mid-thirties had a physical exam for life insurance. Elevated blood pressure was found. Laboratory work revealed increased liver enzymes, which were recognized as a consequence of heavy drinking. He was advised to have repeat tests done and one year later returned for the same. An attempt to cut down on alcohol use for one month prior to the tests was undertaken without much success. Abnormalities were again found. Through a series of crises, this physician patient eventually accepted the need for alcoholism treatment.

Social. The impairment from alcohol or drugs may present outside family or professional settings. An arrest for driving while intoxicated (DWI) is a common example.

A middle-aged surgeon had concealed his pattern of increasing alcohol use by drinking only in his home after work hours. He was divorced, and occasionally dated, which often involved drinking. One night, while returning from a social outing, he was pulled over by the local police and arrested and jailed for DWI. This physician effectively utilized this legal crisis and his sense of embarrassment to obtain the necessary treatment.

Another common means of identification is through pharmacists. Pharmacists can spot physicians who are overprescribing in the name of family members or for themselves.

> A woman physician was reported to the state medical board when several local pharmacists recognized excessive prescriptions for opiate compounds for herself and family members. An investigation revealed opiate dependence, and she was mandated to treatment.

The symptoms of impairment commonly occurring in the social arena include:

- driving while intoxicated or public intoxication arrests
- embarrassing behavior at social events
- withdrawal from church or other community organizations
- aggressive behavior in restaurants or bars
- pharmacists' refusal to fill prescriptions
- excessive malpractice suits

Employment History

The establishment of the National Medical Practitioners Data Bank in 1990 enabled certain employment problems to be identified by a hospital or medical staff. Malpractice suits and suspension from a medical staff in excess of 30 days must be reported to this data base. Hospitals are required to search this data base prior to appointing or reappointing medical staff.

Clues from the employment history about a physician's having a problem with substance abuse include:

- frequent job changes, usually including geographic changes
- working in a position that is beneath former positions or beneath the practitioner's qualifications
- unexplained periods of unemployment
- delays in obtaining a preemployment physical exam or in providing urine specimen for a drug analysis

Opportunities to identify signs of impairment in a physician—and thereby initiate an evaluation of treatment needs—present in a variety of settings. The physician will present in many of the same ways as nonphysicians (such as with family or legal problems), but is most likely to be confronted by the medical system through patient complaints, nursing reports, pharmacists' actions, medical staff or hospital administration intervention, or partner's concern.

FACTORS CONTRIBUTING TO PHYSICIAN IMPAIRMENT

Why a given physician becomes drug or alcohol dependent cannot be known with certainty. Several factors are well recognized as contributing: availability of drugs, stress of practice, personality factors, and genetics. In the literature, one can find advocates for each as the predominant contributing variable. Similarly, discussion with informed colleagues will reveal strong opinions as to the "primary" cause. Perhaps we desire to find simple, straightforward explanations. Yet, to do justice to physician impairment and professional impairment in general, we must tolerate complexity and inconsistency. On a case-by-case basis, any given factor may seem to stand out, but most often an amalgam of the above factors are present. The combination of factors is kaleidoscopic, with different hues and patterns appearing from a common denominator of background variables.

Availability

As noted, drug use among medical students reflects usage patterns prevalent in society. The influence of *availability* emerges during the residency years as drug use shifts from "street" or illegal drugs to a pattern of prescription drug use, as self-prescribing enters the picture.

Availability is more likely to exert influence on choice of drug rather than to use or not. Those predisposed to drug use will be most influenced by availability. The resident physician with a history of drug abuse throughout college and medical school is more likely to avail himself or herself of the pharmaceutical agents that are plentiful through prescriptions or free samples. Similarly, the physician in recovery for a substance use disorder will find reexposure to drugs a potential hazard. This is particularly the case if the chemical dependence of the physician bears a one-to-one relationship with what is extensively available in the hospital or office setting.

An anesthesiologist had become addicted to fentanyl and had lost his hospital position, but had followed a successful recovery program for 15 months. He recognized his vulnerability for relapse with each exposure to the operating suite, where fentanyl was available. Outside the hospital setting, he was free of drug craving and had no difficulty refraining from alcohol. In other words, the drug abuse was situation specific and was stimulated by reexposure to the stimulus configuration of the operating suite. To manage this predicament he was open about his history of opiate abuse with hospital personnel such as nursing staff and physicians.

Careful procedures to account for the amount of medication used, disposing of unused opiates in front of nursing or pharmacy staff, and random urine tests provided structure and safeguards against relapse. Combined with these technical procedures, the doctor was involved in 12-step programs.

This system worked until the physician began part-time work in a new hospital. It was immediately apparent that procedures to regulate and account for controlled substances used during anesthesia were not in place. Fentanyl was, therefore, relatively more available. An operating room nurse saw him inject himself. He was dismissed from the hospital staff, reported to the state medical board, and lost his license.

Availability provided a "window of opportunity" when it coincided with the decreased attention this physician was paying to his recovery needs. He was not attending 12-step meetings as regularly as in the past, was not in close contact with his sponsor, and had decided not to use (as had been recommended) the opiate blocking drug, naltrexone. Decreased vigilance combined with increased availability led to an unfortunate outcome.

A dentist, after several years of hydrocodone dependence, entered treatment. She instructed her staff to remove hydrocodone products from the office and not to accept samples from pharmaceutical representatives. Several months after returning to practice, she visited the office after hours in order to obtain some stationery. While looking in the supply cabinet, she was surprised to find a package of hydrocodone tablets, which she later learned had been hidden there by the staff in case of an office emergency. Briefly, she experienced a craving for hydrocodone, but quickly left the office and called a staff member who went to the office and removed the product. This helped the dentist appreciate her vulnerability for relapse. She was aided also in this unexpected confrontation by being on naltrexone and by participating in 12-step and psychotherapy programs.

The significance of availability cannot be denied. Our nation's drug epidemic is aided and abetted by a continuous supply of illicit drugs (Bailey, 1989). The relationship between alcohol problems and alcohol availability is also extensively documented (Single, 1988). Use of alcohol is more likely in professionals because of the relationship between increased income and frequency of drinking (Godfrey & Maynard, 1988). On the other hand, the uniqueness of the health professional's position vis-à-vis drug availability is attenuated by the immense availability of illicit drugs in society at large—even prescription drugs may reach the streets. To the health professional, the factor of availability remains dangerous for its impact at the workplace and for the potential the physician has to choose specific pharmaceutical products.

The Role of Stress

That physicians are exposed to considerable stress is widely recognized. In a national survey, physicians' stress scores were above the mean for all occupations in the areas of "work overload" and "too much responsibility for people" (Stout-Wiegand & Trent, 1981). Stress has been considered a more powerful factor in the etiology of physician substance abuse than availability of drugs (Stout-Wiegand & Trent, 1981). Physicians, compared to dentists, abuse drugs at a significantly greater rate, although both professions have access to addicting drugs. Physicians report greater occupational stress than dentists, and severity of occupational stress correlates significantly with drug use (Stout-Wiegand & Trent, 1981). Attorneys report feeling under "high pressure" more frequently than physicians (Wyshak, Lamb, Lawrence, & Curran, 1980), yet physicians, compared to lawyers, respond to professional stressors with more anxiety and depression (Krakowski, 1984).

To consider the role of stress in the development of substance abuse in physicians requires that the relationship between stress and addiction, in general, be considered. The literature on this subject is voluminous, and excellent reviews are available (Chrousos & Gold, 1992; Gottheil, Druley, Pashko, & Weinstein, 1987; Pohorecky, 1991). A useful definition of stress is: "a particular relationship between the person and the environment that is appraised by the person as taxing or exceeding his or her resources and endangering his or her well-being" (Lazarus & Folkman, 1984, p. 19). The stress response is both behavioral and psychological and may become pathological.

Three major degrees of stressors have been described: (a) the usual, ordinary strains of daily life, which are minor in nature; (b) acute, severe stressors, which are generally unexpected and include sudden onset of a serious illness, a major accident, death of a family member, or a natural catastrophe, such as a tornado; and (c) chronic, enduring strains intrinsic to interpersonal relationships, social conditions, or occupation. Chronic stressors are not easily modified or changed and contribute to the stress of medicine (Asby Wills & Shiffman, 1985). The physician is susceptible to the first two categories of stress as well, but enduring occupational demands are usually implicated in the etiology of a substance use disorder.

The relationship between stress and substance abuse has been studied most extensively in regard to alcohol use, and several models have emerged. The dominant theory explaining the link between alcohol use and stress is the Tension Reduction Hypothesis (TRH) (Conger, 1956): Alcohol is used because it reduces tension (stress). Although the TRH is supported in studies of adolescent drinking and studies on rural drinkers, its relevancy to drinking in young adults, women, and married couples has been questioned (Pohorecky, 1991). An Expectancy Model (Marlatt, 1987) attributes the use of alcohol to its arousing and stimulating effects. The Power Conflict Model emphasizes that an increased sense of personal power (McClelland, Davis, Kalin, & Wanner, 1972) is a potent reinforcing effect of alcohol, and the Self-Awareness Model (Hull, 1981) recognizes that alcohol decreases self-awareness; therefore, the individual's sensitivity to criticism and negative self-evaluation are diminished.

Alcohol and other drugs would seem to interact with stress in a variety of ways. Self-enhancement and coping effects interplay with anesthetic or emotional buffering effects. Expectations of the drug, gender, setting, and age mediate the stress-drug relationship.

Stressors in Medical Practice

Stressors vary with the time period studied and with the setting. For example, graduates of a medical school between the years 1938 and 1945 listed time pressure and lack of leisure time as major stressors, but graduates between 1955 and 1965 added fear of malpractice, practicing defensive medicine, peer review, and fear of violence from patients or their families (Mawardi, 1979). Compared to clinical faculty, academic faculty report significantly more stress over decisions about career direction, making enough money, having enough time to spend with family and friends, being pulled in many directions by work, and running behind on a work schedule. Clinical faculty experience significantly greater stress over worry about the oversupply of physicians and about finding meaningful intellectual and educational growth at work (Linn, Yager, Cope, & Leake, 1985).

Commonly described sources of stress for physicians are: not having enough personal time, being on call, heavy workload, caring for dying patients or patients who do not respond to treatment, dealing with noncompliant patients, excessive paperwork, and interpersonal conflicts with nurses and consultants (Krakowski, 1982; Mawardi, 1979). Fatigue, phone calls at night, fears of not keeping up with new knowledge, and making clinical decisions in the face of uncertain results are additional common stressors.

McCue (1982) recognized that the intrinsic stressors of medicine sharpened and enhanced performance in some physicians, but led to dysfunctional or inappropriate behaviors in others. The intrinsic stressors described by McCue (1982) are:

- *Suffering*. Young physicians expected medicine to be rewarding, but find that sick people are unhappy, uncomfortable, demanding, and may not be able to express gratitude. In addition, the physician often has to inflict pain through various procedures or deny pain relief under certain circumstances.
- *Fear*. Fear is universal when one seeks medical care. Physicians may not be well-trained to be reassuring and to alleviate fear. A patient's fear may be contagious and is often fatiguing.
- *Sexuality*. The physician is privileged to explore the physical and emotional aspects of a patient's life in a manner that is taboo in other social settings. Embarrassment and discomfort are the norm for both patient and physician.
- *Death*. Death is seen as a failure of medical care; families may become angry and the physician may experience sadness, but typically will guard against sharing his or her feelings.
- *Problem patients*. Patients who do not comply or are "malingerers" or have psychiatric problems often anger physicians and are time-consuming and frustrating.
- *Uncertainty*. Serious clinical decisions often need to be made in the face of conflicting findings or incomplete data. Other sources of uncertainty include the conflict between being cost-effective versus being thorough and changes in the doctor–patient relationship (more technical, less personal, and often not as enduring as in the past).

In a recent assessment of physicians' stress, a strong relationship was found between stress and work satisfaction. Forty-three percent of physicians who reported low satisfaction with the practice of medicine felt that their work was "very stressful." In contrast, only 15% of physicians with high work satisfaction reported their work to be "very stressful" (see Table 6.1) (Lewis, Barnhart, Howard, Carson, & Nace, 1993a).

In the Lewis et al. (1993b) study, a random sample of physicians in a major metropolitan area reported that the most stressful aspects of their work were factors extrinsic to medicine, such as government regulations, insurance companies, malpractice, and defensive practice style. Relatively few physicians rated clinical aspects of medicine as very or extremely stressful. Overall, 23% of physicians rated work as low on stress, 53% as moderately stressful, and 24% as highly stressful.

TABLE 6.1
Physicians' Level of Work Stress and Work Satisfaction*

Level of Work Satisfaction	Not Stressful	Moderately Stressful	Very Stressful
	NO. (%)	NO. (%)	NO. (%)
High	157 (31)	267 (53)	76 (15)
Low	9 (4)	121 (53)	99 (43)
$x^2 = 103.5(2), p > .0005$			

*Reprinted with permission from *The Journal of Texas Medicine. Lewis et al. 1993a*

Are Physicians under More Stress than Other Professions?

The impact of stress on physical health is highly variable. Job "strain" has been demonstrated to produce serious physical effects, including structural changes in the heart and hypertension (Schnall, Piper, Schwartz, Karasek, Schlussel, et al., 1990). Yet, diseases that were once considered to be "psychosomatic" may, upon closer study, be unassociated with psychiatric factors (North, Clouse, Spitznagel, & Alpers, 1990). In fact, physicians, when compared with United States white males from the general population have fewer expected deaths for all causes (Ullman, Phillips, Beeson, Dewey, Brin, et al., 1991).

In a comparison of random samples of physicians and lawyers, hypertension was diagnosed in 21% of the lawyers compared to 12% of physicians. Prostate disease and degenerative arthritis were more common in the physicians. Lawyers drank more heavily, with 9% reporting problems from alcohol compared to 3% of physicians. The lawyers reported experiencing higher pressure in practice than physicians, whereas the physicians worked longer hours, took more vacation time, and were more satisfied with practice (Wyshak et al., 1980). Responses to stressors are commonly behavioral and psychological, including substance abuse (Krakowski, 1984).

A comparison of lawyers and doctors by Krakowski (1984) found alcohol abuse more frequent in lawyers than in physicians (20% versus 8%); drug dependence was similar (about 5% for each group); but physical illness was more frequent in the attorneys (20% versus 8%). Reports of anxiety and sleeplessness in response to personal or professional stressors occurred at the same rate in both doctors and lawyers. However, 33% of doctors compared to 10% of lawyers reported a history of depression over personal stress, and 15% of the doctors versus only 2% of attorneys reported depression related to professional stressors. Physicians reported more stress than attorneys over client complaints, noncompliance, disputed charges, intervention from supervisors, and loss of a client to another doctor. Physicians' increased sensitivity to depression or criticism was attributed in part to their (80%) having marked compulsive personality traits compared to 28% of attorneys (Krakowski, 1984). A recent extensive comparison of professional groups finds that physicians are comparable to but do not exceed, for example, dentists in the experience of stress (Lewis, Barnhart, Howard, Carson, & Nace, 1993a).

Personality

Chapter 3 indicates that temperament and personality traits may have a role in the etiology of addictive disorders. That temperament and personality traits contribute to physician impairment must be seriously considered. Exposure to drugs and stress are common to all physicians, albeit in varying degrees. Personality, which is shaped by genetically based temperament traits in interaction with environmental influences, could be expected to vary considerably from physician to physician.

Stress, either personal or professional, interacting with personality "vulnerability" is a common paradigm for explaining physician impairment. The definition of stress provided by Lazarus and Folkman (1984) is useful in appraising this interaction: "Psychological stress is a . . . relationship between the person and the environment that is appraised by the person as taxing or exceeding his or her resources and endangering . . . well-being" (p. 19). In the case of physicians, what resources are being taxed or exceeded? Intelligence is not the problem. Medical schools select students on the basis of demonstrated abilities. Physicians are known to be well above average in intelligence and have excellent problem-solving skills (Smith, 1989).

On the other hand, the emotional resources of physicians may vary considerably. For addicted physicians, an emotionally barren childhood (Vaillant, Sobowale, & McArthur, 1972) has been postulated. A study of addicted physicians found only 3% held their fathers in esteem and only 13% felt warmly toward their mothers. As children, these physicians were sickly and compliant (Modlin & Montes, 1964). Krakowski (1982) considers the choice of medicine to be a counterphobic response to an unconscious fear of death. The physicians in his study were considered to be unequal in strength to their peers in childhood and fearful of competition. Their mothers provided support and encouragement, but their fathers were aloof and distant. Of 50 physicians treated for an addiction in a private psychiatric hospital, 72% perceived parental deprivation in childhood (Johnson & Connelly, 1981). In a prospective study, Vaillant et al. (1972) found that physicians who developed problems in adulthood had lower scores on childhood rating scales. The physicians with substance abuse, psychiatric, or marital problems were more likely to have shown excessive dependency, passivity, pessimism, and self-doubt in childhood.

Personality variables influence medical school performance and future practice. The addition of personality variables, such as impulsivity, ego strengths, and sociability, to cognitive variables significantly enhanced the prediction of basic science scores and National Board of Medical Examiners examination scores (Roessler, Lester, Butler, Rankin, & Collins, 1978). Physicians who found practice "vexatious" were found to have scored higher on tests measuring self-derogation, dependency, and a need to appear socially desirable during their medical school years (Boisaubin, Laux, Lester, Rankin, Roessler, et al., 1983).

In treatment settings, addicted physicians have been described as deficient in such ego functions as regulation of feelings, self-care skills, and maintenance of self-esteem. Khantzian (1985) suggests that for some physicians their sensitivity to and capacity to care for patients represents a partially successful transformation of their conflicts in the area of feeling cared for. Physicians prone to an addiction are often unable to recognize, tolerate, or regulate their emotions and fail to value themselves. A deficiency in self-esteem is only partially repaired by professional success. Chronic dysphoria may find relief through self-medication, a process that paves the way for further drug or alcohol problems. Just as Krakowski (1982) views the practice of medicine as an effort to overcome the fear of death, Khantzian (1985a) sees within addicted physicians efforts at self-repair through caring for patients; when this fails, the restorative properties of alcohol or other drugs may be substituted.

The impact of personality variables has not been limited to consideration of addicted physicians. The compulsiveness commonly observed in normal physicians has been described as leading to feelings of doubt, guilt, and a sense of exaggerated responsibility. Physicians are described as having difficulty relaxing, failing to take vacations, neglecting their families, and chronically feeling that they are "not doing enough" (Gabbard, 1985). The compulsive character traits of physicians not only influence their work habits, but impair marital relationships as well. Physicians and their spouses have been observed to postpone gratification and rationalize such delays as temporary when, in actuality, they serve to avoid emotional intimacy. Consequently, marital discord, often covert, prevails (Gabbard & Menninger, 1989).

The compulsive traits (doubt, guilt, exaggerated sense of responsibility) described by Gabbard (1985) may be stress- or fatigue-induced derivatives of highly valued qualities such as intellectual rigor, conscientious-

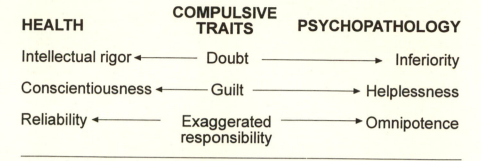

HEALTH	COMPULSIVE TRAITS	PSYCHOPATHOLOGY
Intellectual rigor ◄———	Doubt ————►	Inferiority
Conscientiousness ◄———	Guilt ————►	Helplessness
Reliability ◄———	Exaggerated responsibility ————►	Omnipotence

Figure 6.1. The Interface of Compulsive Traits between Health and Psychopathology (after Gabbard, 1983)

ness, and reliability. Alternatively, these traits may reflect pathological feelings of inferiority, helplessness, and omnipotence. Thus, one sees that compulsive traits may, depending on consideration of other personality dynamics, be the ragged edge of basic health or the partner of despair (Figure 6.1).

A dynamic formulation of addiction in physicians is feasible through an integration of the developmental concepts of self psychology (Kohut, 1971), with the cultural "idealization" of the physician and the pharmacologic "power" of intoxicating drugs. Using the concepts of self psychology, we appreciate the infantile mental structures of a "grandiose self" and an "idealized other." With empathic nurturing and optimal frustration these early views of the self and others are transformed as follows:

infantile grandiose self *evolves to* mature adult self-concept
("I'm Superman" *evolves to* "I'm worthwhile")

idealized other *evolves to* realistic acceptance of others
("You are God *evolves to* admiration, respect, values)

When the necessary empathic matrix between the developing child and the parental figure fails as a result of abuse, neglect, or overprotection, the infantile structure continues to exert undue influence on adult functioning. A continuing search ensues for perfection in others and in oneself.

Perhaps for some, the idealized vision of the physician answers this quest. A "cure" through achievement and success is pursued, but ultimately fails. The dysphoric experience of disappointment and failure leads to feelings of guilt, depression, anger, and anxiety. The physician (as well as others) so dynamically situated will discover, by accident or choice, the change of mental state characteristic of intoxicating substances, and will find "rewards" in alcohol and drug induced states to be beyond that experienced by the ordinary social drinker or casual drug user. The vulnerable physician not only experiences the usual brief euphoria but finds anesthetic relief for chronically unsettling feelings of guilt, shame, anger, or anxiety. Yet, the reinforcement is extended further through the capacity of alcohol and drugs to prop up or reinflate the early infantile feelings of grandiosity and idealization (McClelland et al., 1972). This sequence is diagrammed in Figure 6.2. When alcohol or drugs accomplish this much for any one individual, the reinforcement properties of the chemical are magnified, and continued use becomes an increasingly compelling experience. Such dynamics are fertile soil for the development of an addiction.

Physician Suicide

A study conducted jointly by the American Medical Association and the American Psychiatric Association (AMA Council on Scientific Affairs, 1987) found significant differences between physicians who died from natural causes and those who committed suicide.

About one half of the physician suicides had made a threat of suicide within two years of their death; 34% of the suicides had a drug abuse problem at some point in their lives, compared to 14% of the controls; self-prescribing of a psychoactive drug had occurred in 56% of the suicides, but in only 22% of the controls; and alcohol-related problems during the final two years of life were significantly more common in the physician suicides. Emotional problems prior to age 18 were significantly more common in the physicians who committed suicide, as was a family history of alcohol abuse and/or mental illness.

An estimated 90 physician suicides occur per year (AMA Council on Scientific Affairs, 1987), which is comparable to the rate among white males over age 25 (Rich & Pitts, 1979).

In the AMA–APA study, women accounted for 9.2% of suicides (women constitute 13.4% of the physicians population). The average age at death in this study was 49.3 years. Sixty-nine percent were married at the time of suicide. Professional and financial losses were significantly more common to the suicide group.

A profile of the suicide-prone physician has been drawn from this study (AMA Council on Scientific Affairs, 1987). Among the factors noted are:

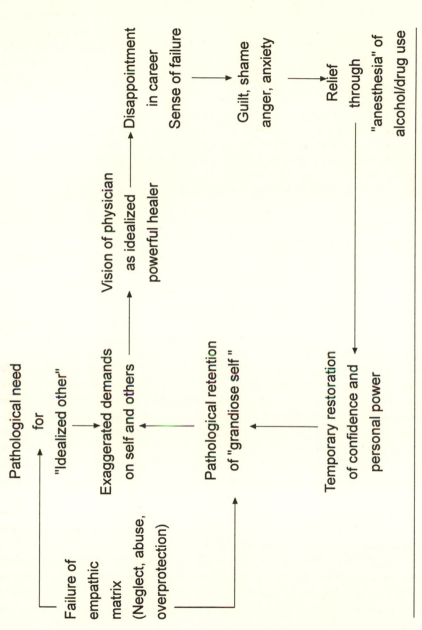

Figure 6.2. A Dynamic Formulation of Physician Addiction

- Physicians in danger of suicide often signal their intentions
- The physician is likely to be aware of emotional problems and may seek treatment
- The danger of suicide remains during treatment, and it is important to guard against the belief that the physician-patient is less endangered than any other psychiatric patient
- Suicide may be motivated by the desire to escape mental pain
- Depression is a major risk factor
- A history of physical and mental health problems is common
- The suicidal physician may self-prescribe medications, and a history of drug abuse may have been reported
- The suicidal physician is likely to exhibit social problems related to alcohol
- A difficult childhood and troubled family of origin are common

This chapter concludes with the case histories of two recovered physicians. Those histories are written in the physicians' own words and convey the impact of their experience with addiction and their struggles to recover.

PHYSICIAN A

I was born in a large city in the southeastern United States. I was the second of two children in a middle- to upper-middle-income family. My father was a professional, and my mother a homemaker. My recollections of my childhood are of a very happy home, where my parents got along well and were extremely functional individuals. I found them to be warm, loving, and affectionate parents. Typically, we had breakfast and dinner together as a family.

In elementary school and junior high, I was an average student. My parents were very supportive, and I have no recollection of their ever being critical of my grades. I was a poor athlete and remember quite vividly the pain of always being the last one selected for the team, as well as being the slowest whenever asked to run. Looking back at old photographs, I realize that I was an attractive youngster, but at the time, I never felt that this was the case. One particularly painful experience occurred when I went out for football in tenth grade. Unfortunately, the school I attended was the state champion and they took winning seriously. I remember how hurt I was when I was in the first group of players to be cut.

With the exception of the football incident, high school was fairly unremarkable. I turned into a good, but not great, student, and I started dating with an average amount of success. I did not use any drugs or alcohol, though we did have alcohol in our home and, on occasion, I tasted my father's drink in the evening when he came home from work. He never had more than one.

I went to a large state college and joined a fraternity. While I drank beer on occasion, I have no recollection of ever getting drunk. My first quarter in school I had a good time, and my grades showed it. I remember feeling, upon receipt of my first quarter grades, that I would never get into medical school with grades like these. Consequently, I dedicated myself exclusively to the pursuit of academic excellence. I started studying every day. On weekends, I had dinner at the fraternity house at 5:00 P.M., went to the library at 6:00 P.M., and studied until 11:00 P.M. On Friday nights, I frequently studied until 2:00 A.M.; on Saturday from 9:00 A.M. until midnight, and on Sundays from noon until 9:00 P.M. I had virtually no social life, but my average went from a 2.3 to a 4.0.

During my premedical education, in a comparative anatomy class, I had my first exposure to drugs. I had a friend who was a veterinarian. One day I asked him if he had anything that would help me study. He gave me a couple of tablets of methamphetamine, and it was an incredible experience. After having taken just 5 mg, I sat down and studied with an ease I had never known before. I actually felt that amphetamine was the greatest drug ever discovered, and the world needed to know about it. I continued to take single, small doses of amphetamine when studying for exams during the balance of my undergraduate career, as well as in medical school. With the exception of a single isolated experience of trying marijuana, I had no other drugs.

Upon completion of my training program, I entered the military. Here, a new pattern of drug use started. I might go several weeks to several months without using anything, but would then binge, merely to experience the "high" of the drugs. At the end of my first year, an astute departmental chairman realized that I had a problem. He had me see one of the base psychiatrists and, for the first time, I acknowledged to another individual that I had a drug problem. I developed a wonderful relationship with my psychotherapist, and, while under his care, I did extremely well. Despite good intentions, however, he had little knowledge of substance abuse, so when I left the service the following year, no aftercare program was established.

I moved to a different city and started in private practice. I remained clean for the first year. Once again, however, I had patients hand me unused portions of amphetamine prescriptions, and I started using again. Within a very short period of time, I was back to writing bogus prescriptions. Typically, I would go from a couple of weeks to a couple of months without using any drug, then binge for a week or two. While I always started with a small dose of a drug, I escalated the dose very quickly so that it was commonplace for me to take 30–50 mg of amphetamine a day. For the first time, I experienced blackouts, and I became aware that the drugs were impairing my functioning. In addition, I found that when I stopped using drugs, I became extremely sleepy and depressed. In order to deal with this, I started taking tricyclic antidepressants a couple of days before I would end my binge. They definitely helped.

Three years after relapsing, I realized that I had again developed a serious drug problem. I started seeing a private psychiatrist, hoping that things would go as well as they had the first time. Unfortunately, this was a totally useless experience. Fear began to creep into my life. I realized that I had a monkey on my back, and I didn't know how to deal with it. Although I had never used alcohol in an abusive fashion, I began attending a local A.A. group. I found that I was openly welcome, and this seemed to be very beneficial. I remained clean for about six months. I stopped attending the A.A. meetings, and shortly I was using again.

While my wife had been aware that I had a drug problem, I had been able to disguise my drug use. Now, however, she became aware immediately of any time that I took a psychoactive agent. Clearly, even small doses were having a marked effect on me. A few close associates also started to pick up on the changes and could tell when I was using. Three years after the A.A. experience and my continued bingeing, I again sought the help of a local psychiatrist who had expertise in substance abuse. Despite the strong recommendations of my medical society's impaired physicians committee, I adamantly refused an inpatient treatment program. After several relapses under the care of my psychiatrist, I finally entered an evening outpatient program. My hope was that this program would be unnecessary. Unfortunately, one month after completing my evening outpatient program, I was bingeing again. I binged monthly for the next three months and then was able to go four months without taking any drug. After a brief binge, I then went seven months drug-free, only to relapse around Thanksgiving. I contacted the psychiatrist who had helped me get into the outpatient program and told him I was having trouble again. I started seeing him regularly, but relapsed shortly after the first of the new year. We agreed that if I relapsed again, I would go into the hospital. One month later, the expected happened.

For the first time in my 19-year history of taking drugs, I realized that I had a very serious problem that needed to be dealt with. I knew, for the first time, that I could not afford to relapse again. After being in the hospital for just one week, I entered an intensive outpatient program. I took a leave of absence from my practice. The most important thing, however, was that I needed to close all the back doors of escape that I had successfully used on so many previous occasions. As painful as this was, I realized that it was necessary for my own well-being to notify people in positions of authority that I had a drug problem. I voluntarily surrendered my DEA license and notified all state boards where I held licenses of my problem. I also notified all hospitals where I had privileges.

After two months of intensive treatment and the establishment of a good aftercare program, I was allowed to return to work. This also was very difficult, because my associates were not altogether supportive.

I am pleased to tell you that now, more than three years after going into treatment, I remain drug-free and feel that I have been accepted fully back into my practice. I got my DEA license back when my treating physicians felt that it was appropriate, and I was lucky enough to retain hospital privileges at all hospitals where I had previously held privileges. I have an active practice and seem to have regained the respect from the community that I had prior to going into treatment. I have been similarly fortunate in my personal life, as my family has remained intact.

PHYSICIAN B

When I was asked to tell my story, I felt honored. I have struggled for about a year to write of my experiences. During this time, feelings of joy, fear, and intense grief have been evoked. I hope my efforts will give understanding to those who have never battled addiction, and hope to those who continue to strive to overcome their disease.

I was born in Houston, Texas, in the mid-1940s to a middle-class family; I was the oldest of five children. My parents had a traditional relationship in that Dad worked outside the home and was the undisputed leader. Mom was a homemaker and a sometimes reluctant follower. We lived in the country with few neighbors and no children my age near us. When I was three, my brother was born. Just before his third birthday, he suddenly died of acute epiglottiditis. I remember feeling shocked and sad, but also secretly glad he was gone because of his competition for Mom's attention. His death had a dramatic effect on our family. We abruptly stopped going to church. My parents didn't enter a church for the next 15 years. Dad became withdrawn. I believe he blamed himself, Mom, and God for my brother's death. He became an agnostic.

When I was seven years old, Dad took a government job, and we moved between Texas and California numerous times. I was in three different second grades in two states. I remember being told how well

I adapted to the moves, but I remember how lonely I felt. A sister was born next. Two years later, my youngest sister arrived. After several more moves, we were transferred to the Pacific Northwest. My brother now joined the family.

Dad's job required that he travel a lot, so, often, he was not home. Even when he was physically present, he was emotionally absent. Mom was the one who provided a semi-stable home, and I felt love from her. I also saw her being physically and emotionally overwhelmed by almost complete responsibility for the care of me and my siblings. Probably, I was given more responsibility than was appropriate, but I ran with this idea. I became an overresponsible "hero" child. Soon, I felt almost equal duty for my sister's and brother's care. I started taking my sisters to church with me and making all arrangements for their care. I helped Mom with the cooking. I began sewing clothes for myself, Mom, and my sisters. I felt like my childhood was over. I was 12 years old.

About this time, I started having terrifying, recurrent nightmares, in which a pair of adult concrete ducks from my grandparents' backyard came to life and chased me. No matter how fast I ran, hid, or struggled, I'd be caught. The ducks would then peck at me and beat me with their wings until I felt on the verge of death. Just as I was dying, I awakened, terrified, sweating, trembling. Sometimes this dream came nightly.

I began a pattern of binge eating or severe dieting to control my weight. I started to think about inducing vomiting. Food became a coping tool for my inward fear and anger. I developed a very distorted body image and always felt that I was grossly obese. The truth was I just developed rapidly. By 14, I had the majority of my height and weight. But I began to hate my body, especially my hips. I stood in front of my bedroom mirror, crying, because I wanted to take a knife and cut the fat from my hips. Then, I would berate myself for not having the courage to act. I started having fantasies about torturing myself and my father. I started inflicting physical pain upon myself. There were never any outward burns, cuts, or bruises. No one suspected, no one knew.

By junior high school, I had learned the arts of isolation so well that I would not speak for hours, except at school. I was especially silent around my girlfriends, because I felt so inferior. Talking was too risky; someone might find out who I was. Except for being "shy," I think I appeared well-adjusted and very successful. Routinely, I made all A's in class, even in honors classes. I was active in track and field sports and even placed in city wide competitions. By 16, I was playing violin in the city youth orchestra, which was just one step below the professional symphony. I "ran" with the fine arts crowd and never was in trouble. I was very active in church. I was always the obedient daughter.

During my middle teen years, I began to be more aware of Dad's emotional abuse of Mom. Routinely, he berated her or told her and us she couldn't understand anything. Each parent independently pulled me aside, told me their side of the conflict, and pressured me to side with them. I felt a gulf of torn loyalty and conflict. Mom responded with passivity laced with cryptic aggression and anger. I saw Mom's coping mechanism as superior, so I copied her. I also accepted Dad's belief of female inferiority. I remember vividly asking Dad for money for college. I was told there was minimal money for me because money had to be saved for my brother's college education. He was seven years old.

My beliefs about the second-class nature of women were also shaped by the ultraconservative church I attended. The message seemed to be that females were created inferior and were meant to be dominated by men. Also, my vision of God was one of anger, authority, judgment, only somewhat modified by love and acceptance.

After high school graduation, I went to a local college for two years. During this time, I became engaged to a man I had met three years before at a National Science Foundation summer study program. My junior year, I left home and moved to the midwest to join him at school. We were married later that year. Just before our marriage, I had my first bout with major depression. I expected superhuman accomplishments of myself, teaching my own violin students and helping my husband with his church. I became suicidal and had several well thought-out plans for ending my life. I was 21 years old. It took two to three years to climb out of that deep, dark, oppressing pit. During that time, I tried to go to church, looking for peace, guidance, but I only sat in the pew maybe 20 to 30 minutes, then I had to leave. I felt so angry at God for abandoning and betraying me during my depression. Then, I felt angry at myself for being angry at God. During that recovery time, whenever I recalled the intense feelings of hopelessness and despair, I shook with fear, cried, and swore I would commit suicide before I repeated the experience. While this internal conflict was going on, I finished college with honors and entered a medical technology training program.

Early in my marriage, conflict began. I tried to rely upon my new husband as the main source of my security and self-esteem. I had few friends and was encouraged not to talk about our marital problems. My feelings of isolation continued.

Then, my husband decided to enter medical school. That rekindled my desire to become a physician. I had always considered myself too ignorant to be able to become a doctor. But, I applied, and I was accepted. The following year I started. Medical school was a very difficult time with both of us. Besides keeping the house, my first year I worked and took call almost full time as a med tech. My sophomore year, I worked half-time, but was pregnant with my daughter. She came two weeks early; two weeks before finals. The end of my junior year, I became pregnant again, hoping another child would solidify our marriage. This pregnancy triggered Graves' disease (hyperthyroidism). In an attempt to save the pregnancy, I accepted only conservative treatment. I lost the pregnancy in the second trimester. Into my senior year, my hyperthyroidism continued, and I went into congestive heart failure and was hospitalized. Finally, I had I-131 therapy and stabilized. Around that time, my youngest sister, who had had a near fatal trauma, came to live with us.

I began to realize I was unhappy with my learned passive-aggressive behavior, and I started to become more assertive. (I don't know if it is possible to survive medical school without some assertiveness.) In direct response to my changes, my husband began to abuse me verbally. With my medical problems, I was very volatile. I almost filed for divorce, but I felt so responsible for my marriage and child that I decided to continue with the marriage.

Following graduation and after my second I-131 treatment, my marriage seemed to improve a little. But there was intense fighting between my sister and husband, which I didn't understand. Then, I became pregnant with my son at the beginning of my intern year. When I was six months pregnant, we moved to the midwest and started a family practice together in a small rural town. I felt inadequate as a physician and inferior to my husband–partner. I also doubted my very worth as a person and my adequacy as a wife and mother. I felt intense guilt for pursuing my dream of practicing medicine and not being a full-time mother.

Some time into my second or third year of family practice, I started to use drugs occasionally. During the late 1970s, professional drug samples of controlled substances were freely left at the office with minimal control. I started having severe tension headaches and occasional GI problems. I rationalized that it was okay to self-prescribe and medicate because I treated my patients with the same medications. I intermittently used minor tranquilizers, Darvon, and codeine. Occasionally I used injectable Talwin. I also started to drink more. I still was drinking only socially. Around this time, I underwent major surgery and lost a lot of weight. I finally thought I looked good. The reality was I was very underweight. To keep from going back to my normal weight, I used diet pills occasionally.

Also during my fours years in family practice, I had two more cycles of major depression and again became suicidal. There was a bottle of Brevital I planned to use in the office safe. But, during the worst nights I could never remember the combination. That probably saved my life. My husband became more abusive verbally and started becoming physically abusive. (It wasn't until treatment that I recognized that hitting, slapping, and shoving were physical abuse. I thought that, since I had no major bruises or fractures, it was not abuse.) I remember vividly how, at times, I wanted to leave the marriage but simply could not. I was so emotionally dependent upon my spouse that I even had fantasies of homelessness and destitution at the prospect of being without him because I couldn't support myself and the children. I didn't realize my part in the dysfunctional relationship; I thought my husband was the sole source of unhappiness and happiness. I was too afraid and suspicious of psychiatrists to seek help. No one knew my internal hell—perhaps some suspected.

Finally, I realized that something had to change if I was going to live. So, I acted on my long held desire to become an anesthesiologist. In 1980, I began my residency. I began to feel some self-confidence and started to see that I had real talent for this area of medicine. My depression lifted. I did not use drugs or drink during my first year. During the second year, my marriage began to deteriorate again. I reverted to using moderate amounts of alcohol and started to take some narcotics and minor tranquilizers from the operating room. Six months before completion of my training, my husband filed for divorce. The legal proceedings dragged on for almost two years. During this time, my youngest sister told me that she had been raped by my husband eight years earlier. I also discovered he had raped a deaf girl who had lived in our home. I was so enraged, I wanted to kill him. I became depressed again. My divorce was finalized in 1983, but because my husband had had primary responsibility for the children for about three years, he received custody. My world fell apart. I truly didn't know if I had anything to live for without my children. My drinking and drug use were still erratic.

With great fear, about one year later, I married my second husband whom I had known for almost eight years. My life started to stabilize, and I didn't use any controlled substances from the operating room. I ordered some codeine and muscle relaxants from a medical catalogue and for a couple of years occasionally used them to help me sleep. To add to the feelings of loss over my children, my second husband and I couldn't conceive. So I tried artificial insemination for almost a year without success. During this time I was completely clean.

In 1987, while giving an anesthetic, I lost an eight-month-old baby in surgery. My attorney advised me not to talk to anybody about the mishap. Some surgeons stopped requesting my services. I felt isolated in the operating room and unsupported by my own department. This reinforced my established pattern of isolation, and about a year later, I was routinely using drugs stolen from the operating room; mainly potent narcotics. At that time, this was the only way I knew to control the raging fear and anger within. After about a year of fairly regular use, my tolerance and usage increased until it became obvious I had a problem: I was addicted.

Finally, I was observed using in the summer of 1990, and I was reported to the state board. My medical society had an intervention for me. For two to three hours I lied, rationalized, and denied that I had a drug problem. Finally admitting that I was chemically dependent was one of the hardest things I have ever done. The next week was horrible. I felt overwhelmed by shame, guilt, and fear. Familiar thoughts of suicide plagued me, and I almost gave in to them. But, with the support of my husband and family, I decided to enter treatment. I chose life.

I'm sure that treatment is both similar and different for everyone. I will try to share my experience. The best description I can find is *absolute terror*. I felt isolated and distrusting of everyone, especially men. It was the second week into treatment before I could gather enough courage to start to share my story. I remember thinking that I'd much rather be beaten physically than talk about my thoughts and feelings and share details of my drug use. I shook with fear for eight hours after that group session. When I began individual sessions with my psychiatrist, I began to realize that he wanted me to become vulnerable. In the past, vulnerability had meant betrayal, abuse, and harsh judgment. I felt close to the edge of the well of psychosis. The best way I can describe it is that I felt that if I trusted completely again, I would die emotionally. I have vivid memories of being awake most of the night before the sessions, hyperventilating, and having premature ventricular contractions. These feelings remained this intense during the sessions and up to two to three days afterward. Gradually, and agonizingly slowly, my fear began to subside. I began to realize that I would not be judged, condemned, or taken advantage of. I began to learn that it was physically and emotionally safe to share my thoughts and feelings and to be assertive. After six years of marriage, I finally decided to give complete trust to my husband. Fairly recently, my husband and I were assaulted and robbed. Afterward, I felt the old familiar fear, anger, hypervigilance. I realized that the intensity was the same as it was one year into recovery. It took 12 months for my fear to come *down* from the assault level.

About three months into therapy, I began to recall a childhood "spanking" with intense fear. As I remembered more details, I realized it was a severe beating that I had "forgotten." Then the childhood duck nightmares began to make sense. Because of similar experiences with my brother and sister and fragments of other memories, I know there were more. But I don't remember them.

By talking to my aunts, uncles, and cousins, I began to see a more complete family picture. I began to see a very dysfunctional family in which emotions were not expressed, females were devalued, and children were verbally and physically abused. I also saw familiar patterns of religious fanaticism: expected perfection and severe judgment.

Also, gradually, I began to realize my own part in the dysfunctional relationships. Previously, I had been very overresponsible, but I saw that I was underresponsible in being good to myself. I began to release feelings of responsibility for others' success and happiness. I'm continuing to learn assertiveness, especially with men. Gradually, I'm feeling equal and not inferior to men. I'm learning that emotional sharing and self-disclosure can have great rewards. I'm learning to accept myself as I am, physically, emotionally, and spiritually. For the most part, my self-hatred has evaporated. I try to accept myself as a struggling child, and I try to nurture myself. I'm learning to accept my mistakes and not expect perfection of myself.

Lastly, I've come to see addiction as a multifaceted disease. I realize I may have inherited predisposing genes. My early experiences certainly taught me to survive by isolation and withdrawal. Finally, when these learned defenses failed, drugs helped me to cope.

Addiction has started to become a positive factor in my life instead of a negative one. Recovery and the 12-step program are teaching me a kinder, gentler, better way of living. I am truly happier now than I have ever been. I hope that my story has been of help.

CHAPTER 7

Nurses

The prevalence of alcoholism and drug dependence in registered nurses (RN's) can only be estimated. There are approximately 1.7 million RN's in the United States, and 97% of these are women (Sullivan, 1987). Among certified registered nurse anesthetists, the percentage of males is higher—38% (Norris, Pierson, & Waugama, 1988). It is useful, therefore, to use data on the prevalence of alcohol abuse/dependence and drug abuse/dependence in women in order to estimate impairment in the nursing profession.

The Epidemiologic Catchment Area (ECA) study of the National Institute of Mental Health determined, through community surveys in five different areas of the United States, that in the month prior to the interview (one month prevalence) 1.6% of women and 6.3% of men had symptoms of alcohol or other drug abuse or dependence (Regier et al., 1988). Based on these data, at least 27,200 nurses are currently chemically dependent. The numbers would be higher if lifetime prevalence rates were calculated. For example, 5% of women met criteria for drug abuse/dependence at some point in their lifetime (Helzer & Pryzbeck, 1988). The peak age for substance abuse in women is 18 to 24 years. Nearly 5% of women have drug and/or alcohol related disorders during this time period, with nearly equal rates for drug (2.4%) and alcohol (2.3%) problems (Regier et al., 1988).

Basing the prevalence of substance use disorders in the nursing profession on the rates for women in the general population most likely underestimates the extent of drug and alcohol problems for nurses.

First, there are male nurses, and the rate of chemical dependence could be expected to be higher among them than among female nurses, based on the fact that the ECA data indicate alcohol abuse/dependence to be five times more common in males and drug abuse/dependence two times more common in males. A higher risk for substance abuse among male nurses has been documented in clinical studies (Norris, Pierson, & Waugama, 1988; Sullivan, 1987).

Second, there is some evidence that women's drinking patterns may be converging with men's. For example, one study found that college women consumed more wine than men in 1985, a reversal from a 1977 survey. In the same study, the annual amount of beer consumed by women increased by 34% between 1985 and 1988, and fewer women were reporting abstinence in 1985 than in 1977 (Mercer & Khavari, 1990). Also, in adolescence, it has been determined that girls are as likely to use alcohol as boys (Thompson & Wilsnack, 1984).

Third, the nurse is exposed to and handles a variety of drugs with addictive potential. A nurse not only dispenses medications (thus having an opportunity for diversion) but also has contact with numerous physicians, any one of whom may become a source for obtaining prescriptions.

Fourth, a career in nursing exposes one to a great many stressors. All professions involve significant stress, and the stress on women in nursing is great. Considering the shortage of RN's in the United States, the loss, underperformance, or detrimental performance of perhaps tens of thousands of nurses marks chemical dependence as a crisis for both the public and for the nursing profession.

CHARACTERISTICS OF NURSES WHO BECOME CHEMICALLY DEPENDENT

How do nurses who develop an addiction differ from their colleagues without a substance use disorder? One of the strongest findings from the few studies available is that the chemically dependent nurse has a history of better than average academic and career achievement. Bissell and Haberman (1984), in a study of 100 alcoholic nurses, found that most had been in the top one third of their class; held demanding, responsible jobs; had advanced degrees; and had been recognized as excellent nurses long after heavy drinking had started. In a comparison of chemically dependent and non-chemically dependent nurses, Sullivan (1987) reported that each group was comparable in obtaining baccalaureate degrees (43%) and doctorate degrees (1%). Over 50% of each group had received academic awards or honors, but the chemically dependent nurse was less likely to be currently employed in nursing.

Family histories differed significantly between the two groups in Sullivan's study. The chemically dependent nurses were more likely than non-chemically dependent nurses to come from a home where there was heavy drinking, to have an alcoholic family member (62% versus 28%), and to have parents who died from alcohol abuse (16% versus 2%) or drug abuse (5% versus 0%). The chemically dependent nurses were more likely to report a family history of depression and reported a greater likelihood of having assumed parental roles in their families of origin (48% versus 22%).

Health is another differentiating variable between the chemically dependent and non-chemically dependent nurses. The former were significantly more likely to report a personal history of depression, were more likely to have been hospitalized in the past five years, and reported that physical health problems had interfered with their job. Sexual problems, including history of incest, molestations, out-of-wedlock pregnancy, and body image problems were more common in the chemically dependent nurses.

The chemically dependent nurses were more likely to be divorced and less likely to be currently married or to have children. They were more likely to have married an alcoholic spouse. Male nurses were significantly more likely to have a history of chemical dependence than female nurses (Sullivan, 1987). Homosexual preference was reported by 13% of the chemically dependent nurses.

SUBSTANCE ABUSE PATTERNS

Early onset of alcohol or drug use, for example by mid-adolescence, is known to increase the risk of subsequent alcohol or drug-related problems and/or psychiatric problems (Schuckit & Russell, 1983). Whether such findings hold true for those entering the nursing profession remains to be studied. However, senior student nurses (ages 21 to 23) had established regular drinking patterns (two or more drinks per week) in the majority of students surveyed (Haack & Harford, 1984); 18% had established a regular drinking pattern prior to age 18. In this sample of student nurses, 13% reported that alcohol-related problems had interfered with their work or school performance.

Nurses with a history of chemical dependence reported initiation of substance use with alcohol followed by marijuana with progression to a variety of both illicit and legal drugs (Norris, Pierson, & Waugama, 1988). This pattern of early alcohol and marijuana use followed by the addition of other drugs is similar to patterns of drug involvement reported among adolescents in our society (Brooks, Whiteman, Gordon, & Cohen, 1989).

Clinical studies suggest that alcohol is the most frequently occurring problem substance for nurses. It is common for alcohol to be the first drug of abuse with additional drugs, especially prescribed drugs, to follow (Elaine B., Claire M., June S., & Janet A., 1974). Bissell and Haberman's (1984) study of 100 nurses found that 62% were addicted only to alcohol, 23% were addicted to both alcohol and a nonnarcotic, and 15% were addicted to both alcohol and narcotics. In a smaller sample of nurses treated for drug abuse (Levine, Preston, & Lipscomb, 1974), 50% of the nurses were addicted to alcohol, and the alcoholism always preceded use of illicit drugs. Overall, opiates were the most favored class of drugs among this sample of nurses. Sullivan (1987) reported that among a large sample of chemically dependent nurses, 43% were exclusively alcoholics, 32% were alcoholic and addicted to other drugs, 23% were addicted only to narcotics, and 2% were addicted to other drugs.

Nurses with a history of chemical dependence, despite exceptional exposure to addicting medications, are most likely to become alcoholic, at least initially. A substantial number develop subsequent dependencies, but most often to legal drugs (especially narcotics) rather than "street drugs." Early patterns of substance use reported by nurses are similar to general patterns of adolescent drug use in our society.

STRESS

The stress on nurses and the etiological contribution of stress to the development of a substance use disorder involves consideration of both the specific stressors of nurses' roles and work environments, and the stressors intrinsic to being female, a consideration justified in a discussion of nursing, because the majority of nurses are women.

The frequency of drinking and the volume drunk increase in women with higher educational backgrounds. Employment also increases alcohol consumption in women (Parker, Wolz, Parker, & Harford, 1980). Nurses, employed, educated, and most often women, are put at increased risk for alcoholism by these two facts alone. Additional stress accompanies the role of women with children in our society—whether married or single. A recent study (Hochschild, 1989) found that married working women take on a "second shift" upon returning to the home. These middle-class employed women worked an average of 15 hours per week longer than men. This work involved domestic duties such as meal preparation and child care. Men may participate in these duties, but usually choose their assignment to mesh with other interests, while women are left to do what has to be done now. Fatigue is certainly one result, but also a covert strain develops within the marriage. The single, employed mother may face more overt problems, which compound an already high degree of stress. For example, in a representative sample of over 700 families, the children of single working mothers were more likely to show symptoms of anxiety, depression, or conduct disorder than children in intact families (Cohen, Johnson, Lewis, & Brook, 1990).

A substance use disorder in women differs from that in men in several important respects. These differences have been most carefully studied in alcoholic women. Women begin drinking at a later age than men. Nevertheless, they develop alcoholism more rapidly than men and enter treatment at about the same average age as men (Blume, 1986; Piazza, Vrbka, & Yeager, 1989). The same finding holds true for women heroin addicts, in that they become addicted more rapidly than men (Hser, Anglin, & McGlothlin, 1987). Although pathological drinking time is shorter for women, their rates of medical complications, such as liver disease, hypertension, anemia, and gastrointestinal hemorrhage are comparable to those of men (Blume, 1986). The mortality rates for female alcoholics exceed those for males, and, in one study, life expectancy was decreased by an average of 15 years (Smith, Cloninger, & Bradford, 1983).

Alcoholic women are more likely to have co-occurring psychiatric disorders. Sixty-five percent of alcoholic women (compared to 46% of alcoholic men) have an additional psychiatric disorder in the course of their lifetime (Helzer & Pryzbeck, 1988). Other studies have found abuse of amphetamines, sedatives, and tranquilizers more common in women alcoholics (Blume, 1986), and, in a study of cocaine abusers, women were more likely to develop major depression and showed a slower recovery from depression than men (Griffin, Weiss, Mirin, & Lange, 1989).

Further sources of stress include the facts that women are more likely to be divorced when they enter treatment or are more likely to be living with a man who is also addicted (Blume, 1986). In addition to higher rates of divorce and separation in alcoholic women, they also report less social support as children and adolescents and describe existing relationships as less satisfying than nonalcoholic controls (Schlit & Gomberg, 1987). The role of an addicted man in the life of a chemically dependent woman is further illustrated in a study of over 500 heroin addicts. The female addicts, unlike the males, were commonly initiated into heroin use by a male, usually an addicted male sexual partner (Hser, Anglin, & McGlothlin, 1987).

Chemically dependent women are stigmatized to a greater extent than men (Blume, 1986). Both alcoholic and nonalcoholic women feel that social attitudes are more negative toward alcoholic women and toward intoxication in women than toward men. In addition, women believe that the effects of maternal alcoholism are worse than those of paternal alcoholism (Gomberg, 1988). Women bear a burden of greater social stigmatization from substance abuse, develop dependence and medical sequelae more rapidly, are initiated into drug use more commonly by a sexual partner, and are more likely to have less social and marital support, and more co-occurring psychiatric or drug problems. Consideration of such findings, combined with the specific stressors endemic to nursing, enables us to appreciate that the chemically dependent female nurse bears substantial burdens as the recovery process is undertaken.

SPECIFIC STRESSORS

Fatigue is a stress intrinsic to clinical nursing. Nighttime shifts and erratic schedules have been considered factors in substance abuse (Norris, Pierson, & Waugama, 1988). Nurses often pursue further education and/or maintain a home in addition to their demanding work schedule.

Responsibility/accountability for patient care is a constant demand put upon nurses, who spend more time with patients than other health care providers. They are expected to detect changes in the clinical condition, assess clinical needs, and make judgments on whether a change in treatment plan may be necessary. Further, there is a covert expectation that the nurse is to comfort the patient, allay fears, assure behavioral compliance, and, perhaps, keep the patient "happy" if at all possible. Nurses are, therefore, in the giver-caretaker role; this constant sense of responsibility combined with the demands of caretaking is a stressor endemic to clinical nursing.

Physician-domination of the hospital or clinic environment may be stressful for nurses. The problem of responsibility without authority can lead to feelings of impotence. Relationships between physicians (both male and female) and nurses can be competitive, condescending, authoritarian, or demeaning. Conscientious professionals strive to avoid these dynamics, but they remain a reality in many instances and contribute to work-related stress.

Access to drugs may be considered within the category of stressors because easy availability sets up a conflict situation. Nurses count, dispense, and stock drugs. Wasted drugs can become part of a personal supply, or drugs can be diverted from patients. Nurses also have access to physicians who may too readily provide a prescription.

Exposure to death and illness remains stressful, even with years of experience. A tide of human misery, suffering, and folly flows without ebb across the daily charge of the nurse. Clinical detachment or hardened demeanor are evidence of this stress, not immunity from it.

In today's health care climate, *"down-sizing"* of hospitals, and *cost containment* are additional stressors. A National Nurse Survey conducted by the Service Employees International Union found that workloads were outpacing salary increases. Seventy percent of nurses reported that staffing levels were often inadequate. Nurses also reported having less time with patients, doing more non-nursing chores, and being given assignments for which they were not qualified (Noble, 1993).

And, as indicated above, nurses may be mothers, *sole providers* for a family, and be striving to balance *career and child care responsibilities*.

PAIN: A FINAL COMMON PATHWAY TO STRESS

The diverse stresses that impact a nurse may ultimately be experienced as pain: psychic and/or physical (Hutchinson, 1986). Somatic complaints are common in the history of many nurse addicts (Hutchinson, 1986; Levine, Preston, & Lipscomb, 1974). In the latter study, historical antecedents of addiction were assessed, and nurses were found to have had a high rate of surgery during childhood or adolescence. Nurses had an average of six surgical procedures, and half of their numerous hospitalizations preceded drug abuse.

With the experience of pain, physical or emotional, the nurse may justify to herself the initiation of self-medication. Hutchinson (1986) has described a process of justifying, bargaining, and denying as follows:

> The nurse justified the drug or alcohol as necessary to alleviate pain and to help in daily survival. With bargaining, a nurse made intrapersonal deals: "I can take these pills from the doctor, but if I ever take (steal) drugs from the unit, I'll quit." A while later, "I'll never use on the unit." And even later, "I need these drugs to get through the shift, but I'll never take drugs from a patient in pain." As the drug habit increased, some nurses not only took medication from patients in pain, but some, after they took the Demerol or Dilaudid, went so far as to inject narcotic vials with sterile saline to keep the narcotic count accurate.
>
> Denial was manifested by the nurse's ignoring the consequences of such behavior: "I am a nurse. I know what I'm doing. I can quit whenever I want to. I can handle this." (p. 199)

RECOGNITION

Salient signs of impairment are listed below. Many of these cues appear in the nurses' self-reports:

1. *A history indicating a somatic orientation and/or intense involvement in medical treatment:* Manifestations may include somatic symptoms, excessive sick leave, frequent doctor appointments, seeing several doctors, and numerous requests for prescriptions.

2. *Absenteeism and tardiness:* calling in sick, especially before or after days off; arriving late or being absent from floor without good reason; last-minute excuses.
3. *Decreased job performance:* medication errors increase, poor record-keeping; poor relationships with patients; inefficiency; nurse's clinical reports do not correspond to others' clinical observations.
4. *Patient complaints:* patients complain of brusque, indifferent care or lack of attention; patients complain of not receiving adequate medication when a particular nurse is on duty.
5. *Suspicion of drug diversion:* nurse volunteers to be med nurse; narcotics count frequently off; appears euphoric following absence from floor; vials frequently broken or tampered with.
6. *Emotional/behavioral changes:* labile, unstable, withdrawn, defensive; poor staff relationships; eats alone, avoids coworkers; changes in mood and behavior that are uncharacteristic of past behaviors.
7. *Evidence of chemical use:* pin-point pupils (opiates); alcohol on breath; flushed face; unsteady gait; slurred speech; tremor; excessive use of breath fresheners; wears only long sleeves (to hide needle scars).
8. *Interpersonal problems:* increasing severity of marital conflict; parenting problems mounting (children acting out); broken friendships.

Such manifestations may alert coworkers and supervisors to the possibility of impairment. No one incident should be taken to assume chemical dependence. A pattern of changed behavior and performance must be documented and conditions other than substance abuse ruled out, for example, other psychiatric disorders, neurologic syndromes, endocrinopathies, or effects from legitimate use of medications.

Below are case histories of two nurses presented in their own words. These histories illustrate pathways to addiction and the interaction between physical and emotional problems and substance use. They also provide a glimpse of the interface between professional role and chemical dependence.

NURSE A

I always wanted to be a nurse, even as a young girl I wished about that. Without money I couldn't even hope, though, but with my grandparents' help I was able to go. It was only LVN school, but I didn't care. I graduated LVN school in 1968 and was very happy. After an unhappy marriage and two young sons, I realized I needed more education if I was to provide a good life for my children. I started college in 1975, taking only two courses at a time. I started nursing school in 1978 and finished in 1980.

I never intended to become addicted to drugs. It just happened.

I developed diabetes in 1981, but never really accepted it. I wanted to be like everyone else in my family and my friends, and having diabetes meant too many changes, so I just ignored it. Sometimes, I took my medicine and sometimes not. I developed severe diabetic headaches and was given Tylenol #3's, which helped some. Then a friend got me started on marijuana, which I loved. The combination of codeine and marijuana was really great. I used that for a long time; when my prescription of #3's ran out, and I couldn't get them renewed, I just started giving my patients regular Tylenol and I took the #3's myself. No one was the wiser.

That went on for a long time, and I never thought much about it. Then one day, a patient asked for pain meds but refused the Demerol I offered. I knew that a brand new C-section patient needed something stronger than Tylenol plain. I really had had a bad day, and I hated to waste the Demerol, so I hid it and took it home. I didn't take it for a while; I didn't know what to do with it. I knew it was wrong, but I knew taking the Tylenol #3's was wrong, too. About this time, my pregnant sister came to live with me. I took care of five people besides my sons and myself. The stress was too much, and I was having a hard time sleeping and resting. That is when I started taking the Demerol. At first, just 75 mg at a time, but that was enough, but when I could, I took a lot more—sometimes 300 mg—boy, it was great!

I didn't realize how unhappy my two sons were; I didn't care. I knew I couldn't abandon my sister and her kids. So, I ignored their complaints. But the stress was really mounting. I was unhappy, so was my sister, and so were all the kids. Finally two of the kids went to Arkansas. That was better, but my children were still unhappy, and so was I. I just kept taking the Demerol and codeine and smoking marijuana. It helped to mask the problems at home.

Then I started having problems with my ex-husband. He wanted my youngest son. No way. I didn't know that my son wanted it more than his father, but he did. In July, a letter came from a lawyer about a change in custody. I drove to a distant city and demanded that my son come home. I had a big fight, almost was arrested, but I did get him back. Two days later, I had a heart attack. I was really scared. I thought the drugs had caused it—plus all the stress. I lied about the drug abuse and the stress, but I know they knew about the stress. That made me scared for quite a while. I was started on Isordil and a nitro patch for chest pain. The combination gave me severe headaches, so I started taking codeine, and within just a week I was back to Demerol, morphine, and codeine, plus anything to get me a high.

I lost custody of my own son while in the hospital with the heart attack. This is when the depression started up with a vengeance.

I had been diagnosed with depression before, but fought it off. I thought it was just because of the diabetes. Now, I was diabetic, a heart patient, and a drug addict. What a mess. I couldn't stand the fact that I lost my son, too. I wanted to be dead. I tried fighting, but I really didn't care. I forced my sister out, and my son joined the Navy. I was finally alone, which I thought I wanted, but really didn't. I was lonely, very lonely. My other sister talked me into moving in with her so she could take care of me.

Soon I was taking care of her, plus all my bills and hers, too. Now, I was even more miserable. I took more and more drugs to balance my life. I was really hooked; I couldn't stop. I felt sick, tired, depressed, suicidal, and paranoid about the drugs I was taking.

In the meantime, my oldest son was discharged from the Navy because of a heart problem. My younger son moved to Italy. I felt so alone. I wanted to die.

More and more drugs was my answer. I was asked about it numerous times at work. I know they were wise, but I couldn't stop now. I tried suicide several times. A 10 cc overdose of insulin seemed the only answer, but I just couldn't do it. I was scared to live and even more scared to die. Two days later at work, the inevitable happened. I was the subject of an intervention at work. I was so hurt and embarrassed, what was I to do? Hospitalization was the only choice I had. I couldn't lose my license. I had worked too hard. I thought of suicide again, but I still couldn't do it; I was still too scared of death.

I was hospitalized in March, but my rehabilitation was hampered by the hospital I chose. I knew the nurses as friends and former colleagues. My doctor had been a student at the hospital where I had worked. I was miserable. I felt I had no privacy or confidentiality. Student nurses I knew and taught were now my caretakers; I couldn't work or talk. That's one reason I shut down during treatment.

I also was made to feel stupid about issues from my childhood. The psychologist said I was sitting on my pity pot and not concentrating on recovery issues. But here at this hospital, I have learned that these same issues are what are keeping me sick. My psychotic father has kept me sick. My ex-husband is keeping me sick, also.

Accessibility of drugs is another problem. It is just too easy to steal them. I know that if I hadn't been so weak and stressed out, so depressed and sick, I might not have gotten in trouble. If I had been able to ask for help, maybe I would not be here now. Eight years ago, I saw a psychologist for depression. If I hadn't been embarrassed to be there, too proud to ask for help it might have been different. I just don't know. I am so glad this has happened. I'm not scared of life now. I'm glad to be alive and ready to get on with my life.

NURSE B

My great-grandfather was an alcoholic, and my grandmother was a nurse, as was my mother. My grandmother spent many years in and out of state hospitals being treated for depression. A friend once called it "genetic insanity," and the more I reflect on it, the more I think he was correct.

I grew up in a very abusive home environment, physically at times and emotionally always. My father was into anger and control. What he said was law, and no other opinion mattered. My mother was very passive and went through life as if she had no other choice. This feeling must have been communicated to me, because all of my life I felt trapped. She was totally unwilling to make any change in our situation, and if the one person in your life who is in a position to make a change chooses to remain helpless, how is a powerless child to see any hope for a different future?

At 14, I made an independent decision to run away. My parents must have identified this, or I told them. I have a very poor recollection of childhood events. I ended up in the office of a pastoral counselor. We all went a few times, although my father continued to admonish the counselor to "do something about her." Apparently, the situation was not progressing to my father's satisfaction. In the last session I had with the doctor, he told me that my father would not let me come back anymore. He wanted to know if I was still planning to run away. I told him I was, and he said he wanted to explore some alternate plans. He agreed that my situation was very bad and that he understood my reasons for wanting to leave. He told me I was very bright, and he thought I was tough enough to stick it out for three more years. At that time in my school system the option existed of graduating a year early if you completed all 20 credits required for graduation. Since I was already in advanced Math and English (the only accelerated classes at that time), I would be able to take Senior English my third year in high school. I said I would do it and left with very mixed feelings. I felt he really cared, but I also felt as if my father had defeated me once more. It was this feeling of hopelessness for any change in the future that was to continue to permeate my life and my choices.

I registered for seven classes that fall and started high school. I was very depressed, and when someone offered me marijuana to smoke it seemed only natural to accept. I proceeded to spend the next three years stoned on a daily basis, and in spite of it all, remained on the A Honor Roll. In my third year, when all my friends were juniors, and I was ready to graduate, I missed the interaction of seniors applying to different colleges and making their choices. My father had graduated from the same college I would also attend. Period. No question about it. There was also no question but that I would be accepted because of my grades. They were not a cause for pride, they were expected. So in this way, also, my ability to free myself from their expectations was limited. I was very tired and even more resigned to my fate at 17 than I had been at 14, probably from a combination of stress, fatigue, and pot.

The summer before I was to start college, my father had a heart attack and then open-heart surgery. Looking back on it, I realize that my parents used the money they had saved for college on my father's surgery. At the time, however, no one discussed it with me. One morning, two weeks before I was to leave for college, my father told me to get dressed and took me to his bank. Once there, he made me co-sign papers on a ten thousand dollar student loan. I was 17! Needless to say, I was extremely upset and, to make matters worse, he used his tired old line of "he was doing this as a favor to me." If I was depressed before, this certainly kicked me over the edge.

That fall, I started college as an undecided major. I lived in a dorm with a lot of "social" girls and probably because of my own unfriendliness and low self-esteem, I had few friends. By this time, I had started having blackouts. I also became very preoccupied with how much money different occupations paid. I was very interested in archeology, psychology, and business, yet I felt completely convinced that I could not make it in a field without some "edge," but at least I could make it in a field where I had some prior knowledge (because of my mother and grandmother), so I picked nursing as my major. Also, the people graduating in those other fields were not making any money, and archeology and psychology seemed to require graduate degrees. Not only was I unsure that I had what it took to earn a Master's degree, but that loan would be due when I graduated with my Bachelor's degree. All things considered, I made a "safe" decision, but was utterly miserable with it. To continue drinking and drugging to dull my misery seemed perfectly reasonable to me.

The actual nursing part of my Bachelor's program was the last two years. I realized that the party climate at college was interfering with my grades, and I did not want to go through nursing school stoned. I moved back home and stayed with my mother a few months. She had divorced my father after I left, for which I was murderously angry with her for not having done it sooner when I begged her to. She had remarried and was having a great time without kids around, since my sister had graduated from high school. Due to bad attitudes on both our parts, we could not get along. However, I stayed in town and finished my degree. I was 21.

At that time, I was limiting my drinking and drugging to weekends. This was a pattern I was able to continue for several years because I was terrified of being "stoned" on duty. For one thing, I knew I had experienced blackouts in the past, and I was counting my drinks in an effort to avoid repeats. In addition, supervisors were always telling me that I was doing a good job and giving me greater responsibility. (If they only realized how little I knew!) Of course, the physicians I worked with, with few exceptions, were rude and overbearing. Although this environment was emotionally difficult most of the time, I felt perfectly at home and really had no frame of reference to expect anything different.

After I had been a nurse for three years, I was gradually able to see the reward inherent in being "the best." Before that time, I did a good job and was in charge a lot but did not receive many benefits of management.

At the time, I was working for a Director of Nursing who went to a great deal of trouble to mentor me. I was the relief Charge Nurse in the ER from 11 to 7 and also was the Relief Supervisor the other days from 11 to 7. I felt woefully inadequate, but I came to know what it was about me that other people respected. I had the talent to make a good decision in a crisis and pull the rest of the staff with me. This is fairly rare in nursing, when you consider that 95% of nursing is following physicians' orders and Policy and Procedures. The other 5% of the time, you are on shaky ground. If it is the middle of the night, especially in a private hospital with no house staff, somebody has to make a decision, even if it is wrong, and proceed from there. Many times, it is a clinical crisis such as major trauma overloading your ER. Priorities have to be set and people need to remain calm.

In those kinds of crises, I felt as if I were standing in the eye of a hurricane—time slowed around me and I could see the problems and the possibilities. Whatever decision I made cancelled those other possibilities, and I could act in a deliberate and confident manner that helped people around me. When the physician eventually became involved, he was usually pleased that all he had to deal with was his part of the crisis instead of the disorderly results of a team not focused efficiently.

The down side of all this was that day-to-day realities never worked very smoothly. People in real life do not do what you tell them to do. I did not surround myself with people who valued me as much as I was valued at work. The intense pace also wore on me. I became frightened from the frenetic pace and night hours. I was drinking, but I had quit using pot. It slowed down my reflexes for a long time after using it. I was also aware of the negative consequences of being involved in something illegal as a member of the hospital management team. At that time, I was using tranquilizers prescribed by a friend of mine. This seemed a perfectly reasonable solution to my problems of fatigue, nervousness, and sleeplessness.

The rest of my story can be heard at any A.A. group in any town. I continued using tranquilizers and drinking until my first psychiatric hospitalization at the age of 28 for attempted suicide. Even after that hospitalization, I continued taking them, although they were now prescribed by my psychiatrist. He did not even object when I told him I was still drinking on a daily basis despite my tranquilizer and antidepressant medication. I eventually quit all my medication in order to become pregnant. Although I had some trouble quitting, it was not too difficult, probably due to the fact that I had reduced my use so drastically. My husband could not quit, so we started to go to A.A. and Al-Anon. Eventually, we divorced when our child was one year old, and I was devastated to learn that my problem with alcohol and tranquilizers was me. My using was not way out of control at that time, although it would have become so in time. I was hospitalized with severe depression and, while there, started with A.A. for myself. It has been almost four years since I had a drink or any other mind-changing chemical. I do take an antidepressant. These last four years have been difficult in many ways but my moods no longer hold my life hostage. I work in a health care management setting but not in a hospital. I had left and returned to a hospital several times in the past, but I feel this time that my self-esteem is sufficiently high so as to prevent me from returning to an environment so destructive to me.

CHAPTER 8

Pharmacists

Impairment among pharmacists was recognized as early as the 19th century. In 1888, the trade journal *The Apothecary* reported as follows:

> I don't think the temptation to give way to dissipation is greater in the drug business than in any other profession, but it is a fact that while the employing druggists are, as a rule, men of more than average sobriety and of excellent moral character, the drug clerk, as a class, has two great and besetting vices—tippling and opium eating . . . . Perhaps confinement and the long hours first induce the drug clerk to resort to stimulants. Several with whom I have talked tell me that where they are obliged to do day duty and respond to night calls as well, they suffer from insomnia and get into the habit of taking a narcotic to produce sleep. (Karabensh, 1988)

Today, the pharmacy profession provides a constructive example of responsiveness to the problem of impairment among pharmacists. In 1979, the first state program to aid impaired pharmacists was established in Indiana. The second state program was formed in Texas in 1981 and assisted 50 pharmacists in its first year. By 1991, there were 46 state programs in existence. The American Pharmaceutical Association has the policy that pharmacists should not practice when subject to impairment from drugs, alcohol, or other causes, and that pharmacists and pharmacy students should be subject to means of detection for impairment and should have available opportunities for prevention and treatment (Sheffield, 1991).

CLUES TO IMPAIRMENT

The physical or emotional manifestations of alcohol or drug abuse in the pharmacist will be no different from other professionals. The impact within the family and community is similar to the list provided for physicians (see Chapter 6).

Clues specific to the profession include (Sheffield, 1991) often late, absent, or ill; decreased work performance or patterns of overworking; prescription errors; patient complaints; filling illegal prescriptions; poor record-keeping; frequent trips to the bathroom; frequent job changes; mood changes, especially after being away from the work site for a brief period of time; inaccessible to the employer or patients; deterioration in appearance; change in the way coworkers and patients are treated; seen taking drugs at work; odor of alcohol on breath.

RISK FACTORS

Exposure. Pharmacists use relatively few "street" drugs. Only 1% of pharmacists in recovery from an alcohol or drug addiction had been addicted to cocaine (Bissell, Haberman, & Williams, 1989). In a survey of over 300 New England pharmacists, 2% reported current cocaine use and that usage was at a rate of less than once per month. Five percent reported current marijuana use, with 3% using marijuana once a month or more (McAuliffe, Santangelo, Gingras, Rohman, Sobol, & Magnuson, 1987). More recently, higher rates of street drug usage were reported in a sample of women pharmacists in recovery. Marijuana had been used by 57%, cocaine by 43%, LSD by 25%, and heroin by 9% (Sheffield, O'Neill, & Fisher, 1992).

Whether exposure to drugs increases the risk of abuse and dependence in pharmacists is uncertain. In one sample (McAuliffe et al., 1987), 2.3% of pharmacists and 3.9% of pharmacy students reported drug dependence. It is likely that these figures understate the problem, since 9% of pharmacists and 25% of pharmacy students reported at least one adverse drug-related experience (e.g., falling behind at work or school, worry about using too much, poor grades, less that optimal patient care, etc.), and 48% of pharmacists and 62% of students reported using a controlled substance without a prescription (McAuliffe et al., 1987).

Exposure seems to shape the pattern of substance abuse in pharmacists. For example, the percentage of impaired pharmacists who are alcoholic only is lower than that found in other health-care groups. Approximately 21% of pharmacists are alcohol dependent only, meaning that about 80% are drug dependent primarily (Bissell et al., 1989; Sheffield et al., 1992). Pharmacists also have a lower rate of intravenous drug use than other health-care professionals, reflecting, perhaps, their unfamiliarity with using syringes (Bissell et al., 1989).

Stress. It is difficult to compare stress across professional groups. Studies on stressors experienced by pharmacists are not available. Pharmacy is a profession where an error could be life-threatening, and mistakes are not acceptable. Many pharmacists work in high volume dispensaries, and the need for sustained concentration, efficiency, and exactitude can be reasonably considered stressful.

Personality. Studies of personality variables in pharmacists are not available. Pharmacists, as with other health professionals, have extensive knowledge of drugs. The pharmacist's knowledge of drugs may lead to a false sense of security concerning self-medication. As Sheffield (1991a) points out, "they know all about drugs and believe they are too smart ever to get hooked" (p. 8). In one study (Bissell et al., 1989), pharmacists, compared to other health professionals, were observed to be more scrupulous in reporting their behavior, more guilty, and more willing to own up to their imperfections.

Genetic/familial factors. As in most examples of chemically dependent professionals, a family history of alcoholism or other addiction is common. In a predominantly male sample, 55% of recovered pharmacists reported a parent who had been alcohol or drug dependent (Bissell, et al., 1989), and in a female sample of recovered pharmacists, 48% reported a chemically dependent parent (Sheffield et al., 1992). In a general survey of pharmacists and pharmacy students, 22% of pharmacists and 35% of students reported a family history of substance abuse (McAuliffe et al., 1987).

PHARMACY STUDENTS

Pharmacists do not demonstrate higher rates of chemical dependence than other health professionals, but the contrast between graduate pharmacists and students merits concern. A survey from New England found 3.9% of pharmacy students in contrast to 2.3% of pharmacists reporting drug dependence, despite the fact that the years of exposure were much less for the students. Students reported significantly greater use within the past year of marijuana, cocaine, stimulants, and tranquilizers and significantly greater lifetime use of marijuana, cocaine, hallucinogens, and opiates (McAuliffe et al., 1987). In another large survey of pharmacy students, 88% reported using alcohol, 41% marijuana, 15% stimulants, and 13% cocaine (Tucker, Gurnee, Baldwin, Sylvestri, & Roche, 1988). Drug use in students is greater among younger students, American students, and those who do not attend religious services (McAuliffe et al., 1987).

The pharmacy profession has responded to the threat of substance abuse within its ranks. Prevention programs for students have been established (Giannetti, Galinsky, & Kay, 1990); the American Association of Colleges of Pharmacy has acknowledged its responsibility to address substance abuse (Giannetti et al., 1990), and state boards of pharmacy have levied surcharges to licenses to support impaired pharmacist programs (Sheffield, 1991b).

PHARMACIST A

One of the hardest tasks I have had in recovery has been to reflect on my life and try to see where the problems began. I have asked myself, "Why is this even necessary?" I believe it is, because when I hear others in recovery tell their stories, I feel much more a "part of." I can relate their lives to my own.

I find that my memory of my childhood serves me poorly. No unique events stand out as damaging or traumatic. All I remember is that I was extremely quiet and rarely caused problems. I was the "model child" in the neighborhood, and in school I had learned that all I felt inside must stay inside. I never was aware that I needed to talk about my feelings, and my recollection was that my parents never asked.

As adolescence came, I appeared very stable, but my inner feelings were in turmoil. Because of my quiet nature my social skills developed more slowly than those of many of the other kids. I remember being so afraid of the children my own age in school. For some reason my self-esteem told me that I was less than they were. They had friends and I didn't, or so it seemed. I was becoming emotionally fragile and never talked about it. I remember my elementary school teachers' telling my parents that I was "too quiet," and I just never caused any problems. I believe they saw this as a good quality in me rather than a liability. I was an easy kid to rear.

As I grew into later adolescence, the fear did not go away. Fear of failure, of people, and unfamiliar territory created an atmosphere of emotional deficit within me. My feelings of being different intensified. Emotional pain became an everyday burden. My withdrawn nature wouldn't allow me to approach girls, so they approached me. This is how I dated, but my male ego was not encouraged by this at all. If others had not taken the initiative, I doubt I would have had any friends.

I did find some relief by being involved in church for a brief time. I became easily disappointed due to my tendency to have expectations high above what reality could deal me. The politics of church became disappointing to witness, so I left that scene and opted for loneliness instead. Actually, there was a small network of friends in my life at all times. They were always very loving and accepting of me, not that they shouldn't have been. Others never gave me any reason to think what I did. I seemed to have so much going for me, and friends used to be baffled about my depressed nature and low self-esteem.

The family physician prescribed Elavil for me, hoping to make me feel better, but I never noticed any positive effect from what were to be complete and thorough trials of just about every antidepressant available. I spent several years looking for a chemical to fix my emotions.

In college, I chose pharmacy as my course of study. I knew that my interest was in the sciences. The problem was most degree plans required a foreign language. I had struggled with foreign languages early on in college so I chose the only degree plan which did not require it: That was pre-pharmacy. My decision was based on fear of a particular challenge—Spanish. As it turned out, I loved pharmacy school and did quite well with my studies. I graduated with high honors. However, all was still not well within, as my fears continued.

During my later days in college, my search for relief from my emotions became obsessive. Through my studies in pharmacy, I discovered which drugs might offer me some kind of relief. I became curious about one particular class of drugs, the benzodiazepines, thinking that these drugs might be worth a trial. Soon I had in my possession, from a college friend also in pharmacy school, four Valium tablets. One would have thought I had four gold coins. I pondered how to best take one and, when I did, I experienced that feeling I had been wanting for so long. I thought I had found the solution, a way to kill the misery. I was certainly not aware of what was to lie ahead for me. The next 12 years of my life would be a period of drug addiction, unhappiness, and depression like I never dreamed possible. It is a miracle that I lived through it. Before it was to come to an end, for what I hope to be for the rest of my life, I would experience combining alcohol with drugs that could have killed me. I put needles in my arm to obliterate my pain, only to wake up to more pain. I became a slave to drugs and to the behavior to acquire them. My life was completely controlled by the compulsion to acquire and consume downers. I never was interested in stimulants of any kind, except caffeine, which still remains a problem today, even in recovery.

I was married for eight years during this time. My ex-wife never knew me clean and sober. She saw me through one treatment, and I was to do it two more times after the divorce before I could claim any success at all with recovery.

After my third and last treatment, I was fired from my job because I admitted to the theft of controlled substances. I had been well respected at my job, and it was a painful event for my employers to have to fire me. It was, however, a blessing, because it helped get me into aggressive action. At this point, my recovery became serious to me and being unemployed gave me an opportunity to concentrate on my most immediate needs.

If I may, I would like to share some of my experiences as an addict and then as a recovering addict. Being an addict represents a misery otherwise unobtainable. I would experience the type of fear that only an addict could endure. I would experience a hopelessness toward life that even today frightens me when I remember how it was. The desperation and guilt would rob me of any form of quality of life, which is why I am amazed that I survived that period in my life. Being employed as a pharmacist made access to all my drugs of abuse very easy, and I was never caught in the act of taking anything, whether putting it in my mouth or my pockets. I hear of addicts who spend thousands on their habits, mine cost me nothing, but it cost my employers plenty. My expense was in the pain of knowing what I was caught up in and not being able to stop. Somehow, through all of this, I was able to maintain enough accuracy in my work never to cause serious harm to any patient. I have heard it said that God works in mysterious ways. I could go on about my experiences as an addict, but why? What is important is that I am drug free and successfully working as a recovering pharmacist in a hospital pharmacy. When interviewing for the job I presently have, I was able to experience what honesty could bring: freedom from guilt. I shared with the pharmacy director my experience as an addict and my resulting treatment and recovery. I had only four months of clean time, but something gave them a confidence in me to hire me. I believe today, almost two and a half years later, that I am a good employee and pharmacist. I share my active role in recovery with supervisory people at work, and I have received from them nothing but encouragement and support.

PHARMACIST B

My personal account of drug dependence is a long-lived affair, with many people crossing my path during my drug years and many people ultimately being affected.

I was an up-and-coming professional with a broad range of ideals, none of which included drug use. I accepted a position as the director of a pharmacy in a small hospital, a one-man operation. I was new, in a small town, with my family still living in the city. I was bored and lonely and having problems because of my newfound responsibilities, and one evening I decided to "take something" to help me sleep.

This is my first recollection of the underlying problem brewing. Sure, over the years prior to pharmacy school, I had experimented with a wide variety of controlled substances, including alcohol. Each experience seemed to be more gratifying than the one before. I was popular with my peers, the "life of the party," and life seemed to get better and better. I didn't have any problem with the law, and my life at home was holding together very well. I continued to experiment with drugs through college and into professional practice.

There is something about being alone in a new town and having access to all the mind altering chemicals one could possibly ask for. In addition, I did not have another professional looking over my shoulder. I did the controlled substance inventories in the pharmacy, since I was the only pharmacist on board. I rarely saw the pharmacy board inspector, and when he turned up at my door, it was for the usual handshake, the "How are you today? Can I see your P&P manual? Your reference library?" and another handshake, and off he would go.

In retrospect, I really wish I had someone to share my professional experiences. Of course, we all have those classes in pharmacy school that talk about drug dependence and, being students, we listen to what we want to hear. Only those people with low moral characters, with life-threatening illnesses, with constant excruciating pain, or those living on the streets have serious drug problems, right? Wrong! I told myself, "It can't happen to me," I am a trusted professional with much to look forward to, a promising career, a young family, respected in the community.

After that first night, taking that sedative to help me sleep, the ease of taking medication off of the shelf became too much easier. I worked day to day with constant interruptions; phones, customers, meetings, etc., and to take an antianxiety agent in the middle of the day became common for me. It appeared to take the edge off my stress and gave me the false impression that I was handling even the most difficult situations with ease. One dose a day turned into two, then three, then four, and on and on.

I began combining antianxiety agents with Talwin and barbiturates and, during a particularly low point early in this period, I would have a "small drink" at lunch to once again help take the edge off, which accentuated the drug "high." This became a daily routine for me, I took just enough to quiet my nerves, after all, I was "experimenting" with these products and since I had not recognized any negative effects, I must be doing all right.

One day, a patient was admitted to the hospital with a prescription for Dilaudid and Brompton's cocktail (a mixture of cocaine, morphine, and antiemetics). Since I didn't have the Dilaudid or the necessary products to make the Bromptons, I asked the family to bring the medication from home. Due to some recent controlled substance "shortages" on the nursing units, I decided to keep the products locked in the pharmacy. The patient was suffering from leukemia and was in his last days. He lived two days and died, leaving me with 200 Dilaudid 4 mg tablets and 16 ounces of Bromptons that had not been properly inventoried and were sitting on my shelf.

Now I had controlled schedule II drugs in my possession, nontraceable and in sufficient quantities to really get where I wanted to go. I began taking small quantities, which turned into larger quantities and, before I knew it, I "needed" the products to keep me going. I used and used and, one day while in a stupor, I decided to drop the remaining Dilaudid down the sink. That I did; I'm not sure why I did it, but it was the wisest thing I had done up to that point.

With all this "experimenting," as I called it at the time, I was not caught, no one seemed to suspect my wrongdoings, and it appeared I had beaten the habit. I should have learned a valuable lesson from this exercise—about ethics, professionalism, and quality of life—but what I seemed to learn was how I had done some serious drugs for two years, it didn't cost me a dime, I had no run-ins with the law and I didn't get caught.

I moved on to a larger city, once again picked up where I had left off in a pharmacy. This time it was a two-man operation, but rarely did I see the other pharmacist. I was face to face with the public every day and had some anxieties about working with these complaining people. I began ingesting small amounts of antianxiety agents with similar effects that I have already mentioned. Although I did not last at this position long, I had *again* developed a "taste" for the drugs, and I was off and running.

My next experience came in a one-man store. Again, little supervision, no one checking controlled substance inventories, and I began thinking about how I could get away with sneaking a dose or two. This job was extremely pressure filled, with daily problems, staffing shortages, and money shortages with the organization all seemed to build into a peak that I could do little about. I was also experiencing some difficulty at home, and this is what probably pushed me over the edge.

One day I decided to experiment with some Dilaudid. I tried a small dose with little effect and, by the end of that evening, had ingested 20 mg. The Dilaudid had upset my stomach so I laid off for a week. Next, I was into morphine and the rest is history.

I became hooked on the morphine. I would come to the pharmacy in the morning and have my first dose by 10:00 A.M. and repeated the dose every two hours. I had developed a system, and very ingenious one at that, where I could "hide" the missing drugs from surveyors, if necessary. I became progressively edgy, deceitful, paranoid, and angry, all of those warning signs that come with drug use and abuse. The most concerning thing about it all was I soon learned I was hooked, I "needed" the medication to function "properly" day to day, and I was using a much larger amount than I could possibly cover.

I was at the end of my rope, my family was very close to leaving me, my job was crumbling, my self-esteem was at rock bottom, and even my friends and the old "life of the party" image had faded. I had serious thoughts of suicide, but the thought turned my stomach since it would have a lasting effect on my family and that is one thing I didn't want my kids to live with the rest of their lives.

I finally decided, after much pain and suffering, to turn myself in, to admit defeat, to walk away from the best job I had ever had, and to see what life would have in store for me.

I called the pharmacy board, entered a drug treatment program for protection, and almost immediately my life began to turn around. I had a reason to live, my attitude began to change, I became very involved in my recovery, and I was open and honest, which was something I had not been for years.

Being straight and sober I began to make friends. I found I could actually have a good time with people without being "stoned." I made a commitment to attend daily A.A./N.A. meetings for 90 days (incidentally, after 16 months of sobriety, I continue to attend at least two meetings a week). I learned through these meetings, reading of the A.A. Big Book, talking to other narcotics abusers and people in other recovery programs, that what I did was wrong but this did not make me a bad person, just one out of control and unable to handle life on life's terms.

After 16 months of a nightmare, I am more comfortable with myself than I have ever been. I have definitely turned my life around but not without experiencing a great deal of pain and anguish. My license, although not suspended, has some restrictions. My job searches are a day-to-day effort for me (once potential employers find out you are an alcoholic or drug addict they tend to close their doors). If I practice pharmacy, by Board order, the pharmacy must be informed that I am a recovering addict. Therefore, I have not applied at pharmacies, since I prefer my background to kept as confidential as possible.

I have applied for jobs that two years ago I wouldn't have even considered, such as medical sales and pharmaceutical sales.

CHAPTER 9

Attorneys

Serious problems face the legal profession: negative public image; high cost of legal services; the bottom line orientation of law firms; and personal stress, such as heavy caseloads and insufficient personal time (Hoffer & Macleod, 1988). Professional stressors that affect the attorney include lost cases, noncompliant clients, critical clients, excessive paperwork, disputed fees, and unpaid services (Krakowski, 1984).

In a randomized study of over 200 attorneys working in urban law firms, one third were "completely" or "quite" satisfied with their work, while one third were "somewhat satisfied," and the other one third "dissatisfied." The demands of the profession—80% of attorneys work between 50 and 70 hours per week—take a toll on personal lives. Approximately 70% of attorneys were dissatisfied or only somewhat satisfied with the way their work affected their family, social, and personal lives. At the level of the family, the two most commonly reported effects of professional stress were being irritable, argumentative, or verbally abusive; or being withdrawn, detached, or preoccupied. Reflective of the dissatisfaction with professional life was the surprising finding that 35% of attorneys are not sure or definitely do not want to remain in the profession (Hoffer & Macleod, 1988). In a recent poll by *California Lawyer* magazine (as reported in *The Wall Street Journal*), 70% of lawyers said they would start a new career if possible (Stevens, 1993).

Compared to research on physicians' health, studies of lawyers are quite uncommon. Recently, data on the prevalence of depression in lawyers or depression and alcohol problems have become available.

A study on the prevalence of major depression among occupational groups found that the rate of major depression among lawyers during the year prior to the survey was 10% or three-and-one-half times the expected rate based on a comparison with the general population (Eaton, Anthony, Mandel, & Garrison, 1990). A study (Benjamin, Darling, & Sales, 1990) of Arizona lawyers found that prospective law students did not differ from population norms in regard to the incidence of depression. However, by the end of the first year of law school, 32% reported depression, and 40% reported depression when surveyed near the end of the third year of law school. When surveyed two years after law school, a 17% incidence of depression was found. These findings are similar to the observations of increasing levels of depression in medical school and the early years of residency.

A random sample of lawyers in the state of Washington (Chiles, Benjamin, & Cahn, 1990) found that 17% were depressed as measured by the Brief Symptom Inventory (Derogatis & Melisaratos, 1983), and 12% were "problem drinkers" as measured by the Michigan Alcoholism Screening Test (Selzer, 1971). Six percent of these attorneys were both depressed and had alcohol problems, yielding a prevalence of 23% with depression and 18% with alcohol problems.

Concern about alcohol use increases as an attorney's career advances. For example, concern about one's alcohol use was reported in only 8% of pre-law students, but in 15% of first-year law students, 24% of third-year students, and in 26% of alumni (Benjamin et al., 1990).

Concern about drinking does not necessarily indicate that a problem exists. Nevertheless, the trend of increasing concern over the years noted above is paralleled by greater prevalence of alcohol problems as years of practice increase. An alcohol problem, as measured by the Michigan Alcoholism Screening Test, was reported by 18% of attorneys in practice 2 to 20 years and by 25% of those in practice over 20 years. This difference was statistically significant (Benjamin et al., 1990).

CLINICAL SAMPLES

An inpatient alcoholism treatment unit reported on 12 lawyers who were admitted within a one-and-one-half year period (Frances, Alexopoulos, & Yandow, 1984). Of these 12, two (16.6%) were women, six were currently married (50%), and five were divorced (41.5%). The average age was 48 years. In addition to alcoholism, 42% had major depression, and 42% had a personality disorder. One third of the lawyers also had a history of drug abuse. Seven had liver disease, and seven had evidence of organic mental changes. The lawyers in this sample were forced into treatment, usually by employers. Six (50%) were unemployed at the time of admission. The lawyers were perceived to be resistant to treatment, to have a poor prognosis, and to evoke negative feelings in the staff.

A review of 19 lawyers admitted to a psychiatric hospital (Nace, 1992, unpublished data) determined that 88% were alcohol dependent, 10% were drug dependent, and 53% had a diagnosis of major depression or dysthymia. Thirty-two percent were both depressed and alcoholic, and 32% were diagnosed with a personality disorder. Seventy-nine percent of the lawyers were currently married, 32% had a history of divorce, and only one had never married. One third had legal problems, which were mostly DWI charges. The average age was 39.5 years, and 21% were female. Half of the lawyers were noted to be resistant to treatment. As with the sample reported by Frances, Alexopoulos, and Yandow (1984), nearly 50% had a primary relative with a history of a substance use disorder.

The two clinical samples of lawyers in treatment are separated by 10 years. Currently, lawyers are presenting for treatment at a younger age, and the percentage of women lawyers seeking treatment may be increasing. In the more recent sample (Nace, 1992, unpublished data), lawyers seeking treatment were referred by their families or were self-referred compared to employer pressure as reported by Frances, Alexopoulos, and Yandow (1984). In both samples, "dual disorders" with depression and/or personality disorder were common, and both samples were notable for treatment resistance.

IDENTIFICATION OF THE IMPAIRED ATTORNEY

Several factors make identification of the substance abusing attorney difficult. Most attorneys work in small law firms, which, unlike large organizations, do not have formal supervision or disciplinary mechanisms. An attorney's work is mental and not subject to immediate observation. Attorneys work in a highly individual manner, with wide latitude as to how they handle a case. Nevertheless, their work and behavior are observable to judges, partners, office staff, and clients. The description of the manifestation of alcohol or drug abuse in the family setting of physicians applies as well to attorneys.

Some specific indicators of substance abuse in attorneys are (Crosby & Bissell, 1989):

- failure to appear in court
- failure to file required legal notifications
- borrowing from clients' trust funds
- slowness in processing mail, dues, bills, etc.
- missed deadlines
- unanswered phone calls

Less specific but common indicators include (Crosby & Bissell, 1989):

- decline in quality of work
- office staff complaints
- verbal abuse of office staff
- client complaints
- frequent disruption of office schedule
- absence with elaborate explanations
- alcohol on breath
- observed intoxication, mood swings, unusual irritability, drowsiness

The identification of an impaired attorney and the facilitation of treatment are greatly enhanced when a state bar association has an organized program to assist lawyers. The Michigan State Bar has established a Lawyers and Judges Assistance Committee, which provides assistance to lawyers and judges with personal or professional problems (Wolf, 1991). This program has provided assistance to over 1,000 lawyers, law students, and judges in its first year of existence. The essential features of the Michigan program include:

1. a 24-hour telephone hotline
2. a diagnostic initial evaluation
3. statewide treatment referral assistance
4. referral to a network of recovering judges and lawyers
5. referral to a network of women in the law profession
6. crisis intervention
7. provision of information on substance abuse, mental health, and stress to members of the legal profession, students, and their families.

Within the legal profession, grievance committees are established to determine appropriate disciplinary action when an attorney violates the Rule of Professional Conduct. Attorneys appearing before grievance committees have a high probability of being chemically dependent. Recent recognition by grievance committees of addiction as a disease has facilitated a switch from punishment or banishment to rehabilitation (McShane, 1992).

The American Bar Association has recognized that addiction can play a role in misconduct, but also that addiction may play a role in defending an impaired attorney. For example, alcoholism may be considered a mitigating factor if successful rehabilitation has been demonstrated since the period of misconduct. Five factors have been described, which, if present, enable alcoholism to be a mitigating factor in cases of attorney misconduct: "(a) The lawyer is affected by alcoholism; (b) Alcoholism is a cause of the misconduct; (c) The lawyer is recovering from the illness; (d) Recovery has arrested the misconduct, and the misconduct is not likely to recur; and (e) Evidence clearly establishes these facts" (Carroll, 1992, p. 269).

Attorneys now have available programs of probation and monitoring similar to other professional groups, yet the existence of assistance programs is not widely appreciated within the profession (Sales, 1989). Outcome studies of the impact of these programs are not available, but it is reasonable to assume that a combination of treatment and monitoring will protect the public, preserve careers, and save the lives of many attorneys.

ATTORNEY A

By the time I reached law school, alcohol was already the focus of my life. It seemed to be the one thing that took the edge off an unhappy relationship or a less than satisfying pay period where my commission pay was not enough to meet my obligations. (I worked as a clothing salesman on commission.)

When I entered law school, I had no idea how the level of stress would be increased. No longer was I one of the brightest in my college class; rather, I was lumped together with extremely smart people who graduated from the finest schools in the country.

On top of this self-imposed pressure was the obvious indication that those who were my classmates did not need to work to pay their way through law school. Nowhere was this pressure more exemplified than when I pulled up in the law school parking lot to see the latest model BMW's and various other expensive vehicles.

As I began law school, I attempted to employ a pattern that I used in college: drinking only on the weekends. This scheme did not last long, and soon I was drinking wine at home with the justification that it relaxed me. By two months into law school, I was back to drinking over a whole bottle an evening. By then, red wine was the choice.

As my time in law school increased, so did my drinking. Weekends were a blur, beginning with happy hour on Friday and ending with a tired Sunday evening. This was my time to release my stress and work pressure.

During this time, I was working at least one job in the evening. I was not retaining much from the law books I was reading; however, that was easy to rationalize since I was going to law school full time and often working two jobs at the same time. After all, I deserved to drink.

Early morning classes, the 8 A.M. variety, were often missed due to drunkenness from the night before. In fact, I recall missing over half of my 8 A.M. classes in the second semester of my first year. It was little wonder I was hustling to get notes for those missed Contract classes. Surprisingly enough, my first year grades were not bad, placing me in the middle of my class.

The second year of law school clearly brought out the most traditional episodes of my alcoholism. Not only were classes missed, but I attended various social functions only to get sloppy drunk. Another time, I passed out at a school dance, leaving my date from out of town completely humiliated.

Towards the end of my second year, I met a woman in law school who I thought was my match. We were intense and spent our evenings together. By now, while working at the clothing store where I had worked for several years, I began to drink at work, but limited it to the last hour before closing time.

This young woman I was dating advised me that she thought I drank too much, and I let her know I could cut down. But I never did. One thing led to another and my drinking coupled with her dishonesty resulted in a traumatic breakup, which ended in a predictable depression. My drinking did not let up.

Somehow, though, I weathered that depression, which was, of course, intensified with increased alcohol use. By the start of my third year, I knew my drinking had to be cut. It was affecting my life and, without some sort of change, I was in trouble. I started limiting drinking to weekends and began a running program with a friend. For a while, this regime worked.

Shortly into my last year, I met my wife. We began dating, but I was being rivaled by her interest in her former boyfriend. My feelings of insecurity resulted in increased alcohol consumption. Fortunately, I did not create any irreversible conduct that would end this romance.

Drinking on a daily basis came back by late fall with drinking at work right before closing time becoming a regular practice. I had also learned a new method of drinking; that is, having mimosas (champagne and orange juice) for breakfast on the weekends. My drinking, I believed, had stabilized in terms of there being no serious incidents to destroy my wonderful relationship. After all, we were going to get married.

Inside though, the stress and pressure were mounting. I could not find a job, and the bar exam was coming up. I drank my way through the summer following law school with a couple of glasses of wine at lunch and several beers or gin-and-tonics on the plane home from San Antonio each day. (I was working a job that required me to go back and forth between Dallas and San Antonio each day.) Not only was I doing the daily plane schedule, I was attending bar review courses almost every evening.

The bar exam approached rapidly, and I was still looking for a job. I got lucky. An old insurance firm was in the market for an associate, and I fit their need.

The bar exam arrived. Three of us went to Fort Worth to stay for the three days of the exam. Day one went all right; day two was different. I could not relax. I bought a bottle of wine and promptly drank it all. The wine coupled with a railroad track behind my hotel room kept me up all night.

The next day of exams was miserable. I barely managed to keep my eyes open, and I was unable to answer one entire question of twelve total essays. I was sure I flunked.

My drinking was out of control, but I did not want to face what I already knew. I realized each day that I would drink. When I got up in the morning, I faced the mirror and fought how I could overcome drinking. By night, defeat had set in, and there was no fight left. Drinking was a way of life for me. The only question left was how soon during the day I would start.

My new job was highly stressful and, of course, the drinking went right along with it. I managed to avoid drinking during the day and, in fact, joined a health club where I worked out at lunch. But, when it was time to go home, my pattern was set: a stop at the 7-Eleven for two tall cans of beer for the drive home and a large bottle of wine for the evening.

While I did adhere to a fairly rigid schedule of avoiding drinking at lunch, the rules changed when I was out of town on business: No one knew me well, so I could have some alcohol at lunch. I would return to the out-of-town deposition sufficiently relaxed, but looking forward to the five o'clock whistle and happy hour. A Friday flight return home would provide plenty of reason to get all the alcohol I could "respectably" consume.

Drinking was the primary focus of my life, but my fiancée did not challenge me. She too enjoyed an occasional glass of wine, but was not addicted.

Somehow, I passed the bar exam and was licensed in November, 1985. On the other hand, my first job was going downhill fast; I was thrown to the wolves with little or no direction but with regular criticism. Little wonder that this job fed my already well developed insecurities. By February, 1986, I was asked to leave the firm.

With my wedding less than a month away, with no job and nothing to do, I started drinking in the morning with mimosas to beer, then ending with wine.

As luck would have it, I landed a job. It was miraculous in light of the fact that I needed two mimosas to get through the interview. Nevertheless, following my honeymoon, I had a place to work.

This phase of my life is a large blank. I did continue drinking, and it got worse with regular drinking at lunch. In fact, at least three days a week, I went to a nice little French restaurant to drink my regular three to four glasses of wine at lunch. It was no wonder my credit card bills were ridiculously high, with $40 to $50 lunches.

Sometime during this period, my elevator started downward. My performance at work began to suffer, our credit problems began, and I became involved with my secretary, who claimed she had magically self-helped and cured her own addiction to crack. (Given my active alcoholism, it is no surprise that I believed her.) She, of course, became my drinking partner, since by now my wife did not want to participate in my demise.

It was also during this time that I faced irrefutable evidence of my alcoholism. A routine liver function study test for life insurance revealed elevated liver enzymes.

I attempted to limit my drinking to weekends to battle these test results. New tests showed improvement, but the conclusion was obvious: Quit drinking or suffer serious health consequences.

The elevator dropped a few more floors. Soon the walls began to close in. The money and credit began drying up, and I could no longer live my jet set alcoholic life style. My affair with my secretary became public, and my job was in jeopardy. My wife left me, and I was all alone with the only friend I thought I had left, a bottle of wine.

With the assistance of my wife and my brother, I made it to a recovery program. I completed rehab still in denial. The turning point came when I asked my wife if she thought I was an alcoholic; she replied in the affirmative and stated, "But I still love you." That provided the impetus I needed.

Soon, I readily acknowledged my alcoholism and came out of denial. When presented with an appropriate situation, I had little trouble in talking about my recovery.

During this time, I attended a Lawyers Concerned for Lawyers (LCL) meeting and heard for the first time the term "grateful alcoholic." What a contradiction in terms, like "military intelligence." But how wonderful when you finally understand what the "grateful alcoholic" was explaining and sharing. I, too, became a very grateful alcoholic.

Since the acknowledgement of my denial, my life has continued to get better. No longer do I consistently act on impulse. My personal life has improved through honesty and growth. My wife and I are closer than ever before. She cared so much for me that she, too, gave up drinking. Just seven weeks ago, we shared the birth of our first child, a beautiful baby girl.

I have been sober now for over three-and-one-half years, with no relapses. Nevertheless, I am humble enough to know that it would only take one drink to start back downhill. I have a commitment *not* to return to drinking.

The theme of my life revolves around the Serenity Prayer, which I keep conveniently in my pocket. That theme and my commitment have kept me sane, secure, safe, and, of course, sober. Without the recovery program, I fear what would have happened. I will be forever grateful to my new way of life.

ATTORNEY B

Things started out pretty normal. I was born in Austin and raised in a middle-class family. At a very early age I was taught that I must be successful and go on to some sort of a professional life. The American dream was to be my life story.

On one side of the story was an above-average, all-American boy growing up in the suburbs. I was successful as a student, a starter on the football team, and one of the "in crowd" on the local high school campus. The other side of the story was a scared young man constantly battling to suppress feelings of inadequacy and low self-esteem. I always felt that I was different and out of place. The conflict arose from contradictory messages from my parents; on one hand I was a failure, not good enough, a constant disappointment to them, but on the other hand they demanded perfection, excellence, and achievement that they could be proud of. All the while they reminded me that they doubted I would make it; and this induced me to try even harder. I can't remember any time in my childhood I didn't feel that I must be perfect, but at the same time I felt doomed to failure. Even when there was a real success on my part, such as scoring high on an achievement test or making the varsity football team, instead of recognition or praise, my parents would ignore the success and point out some area of my life they found unacceptable or a failure. I never felt right, but the belief was if I tried a little harder I would succeed in winning their approval. It never came! I was endlessly pulled closer then pushed away. I never felt loved.

As I entered the teenage years a tremendous tug-of-war took place in my life. On the outside I was the son that all parents wanted to have, and on the inside I lived in fear that I would be found out to be no better than the rest. Then one fateful summer night I tried alcohol for the first time. I got drunk and felt a release from the secret fear that had gripped me all my life. The secret fear was that all the world, my friends and everyone I knew, would discover what I and my parents knew— that I was a failure and not good enough. You see, there were many real successes on my part that my parents never acknowledged, but other people did and that made me feel "right" and "good" and "loved." But, I always was in terror that I would be found out to really be a failure. As a result I would lose that desperately needed acceptance from others I had learned to substitute in place of what I really needed from my parents. Approval from others was all I had. Surely I would die a disgrace if I lost that too. At times the fear was all but paralyzing. From then on whenever I drank, I drank until I was drunk. For when I was drunk or high on drugs there was no fear, no conflict, only one side, only one person, and he was good, right, successful, and loved. He was confident and in control. He had no fear. At least that was the illusion. But, alas, the illusion lasted no longer than the alcohol or drugs. To escape the fear I needed ever increasing amounts taken closer and closer together. Soon I was trapped in a continuous state of intoxication—reality was no more.

Upon graduation from high school, I entered one of the more elite colleges to prepare myself to become a lawyer and a productive member of society. I became an excellent student, a college football player, and rewarded myself almost every evening with a good drunk. Being of above-average intelligence, I soon realized that daily morning hangovers might have a detrimental effect on my academic performance. I was delighted to discover that marijuana and other street drugs relieved my anxieties and left me with a clear head in the morning. Besides, it was 1969 and all normal college kids were doing what I was doing. Drugs and alcohol became a daily part of my life. As I graduated from college and went on to law school there was a constant and steady increase in the amount of drugs and alcohol I used every day.

Soon I graduated from law school, and the exciting world of the high-powered trial attorney lay before me. The only problem was that the same fear that had gripped me all my life, that I was not what I appeared to be and that I would soon be found out, increasingly fed my need for more alcohol and drugs. The two sides of the story were very clear. Side one was a very successful young trial attorney with a vigorous practice; a wife, a child, and a law partner who was a state political official; a rising star who was the president of his local bar association. Side two was an unhappy and scared man desperately trying to hide his alcoholism and drug abuse and fighting a battle to get out of bed each morning and continue to be what he was not. The stressful practice of trial law only served to magnify to a new level those same childhood fears of inadequacy and discovery as a failure. Only in place of my parents' approval I had put the approval of my peers and the desire for financial success as proof of my worthiness. The nature of the practice of trial law is that every day brings a report card with your very public grade—every trial is won or lost, every success is yours as well as every failure your responsibility. Long ago, I had learned how to cope with the fear of failure or the humiliation of actual failure—alcohol and drugs. I continued to apply that lesson in my life.

Then in 1980 a "miracle" occurred. I discovered the perfect drug, cocaine. Now I was able to feel no fear, work harder than ever, with almost no risk of discovery by my peers or my family. That each day it took more and more to continue the deception was only a minor inconvenience. I wanted out but there was no way I could get out.

Finally, the inevitable happened. I could not work—I was gripped in the constant insanity of the use of cocaine. My law partner decided it was time to abandon the sinking ship. My wife and my child soon followed—there was a bitter divorce. Soon I lost my office, my home, and the rest of my material goods. Finally, I was caught misapplying a client's money in order to pay the bills. The State Bar took away my license for a period of six years. All through this agony I continued to deny that I had a problem with drugs and alcohol.

During the first year of my suspension I worked for approximately $700 a month planting trees at middle- and upper-class homes like those where I used to live. During the first year I was approached by an old friend who was now a member of the group known as Lawyers Concerned for Lawyers. Lawyers Concerned for Lawyers (LCL) is a peer assistance group that operates along the lines of the Alcoholics Anonymous 12-step program, but is limited to members of the legal profession. It is not an A.A. group, but a fellowship of recovering attorneys who help support one another. Its members are encouraged to regularly attend a 12-step group such as Alcoholics Anonymous or Narcotics Anonymous. He shared his story with me, and it was clear that his "side one" was the same as mine. However, incredible as it was to me, his "side two" was much different. He had found recovery, and he offered to show me how I could also.

So I walked into my first meeting of Lawyers Concerned for Lawyers in February 1989 and immediately felt the joy of hope. It was like being reborn to know that I was not the only lawyer with a drug and alcohol problem and that there was a way that I could recover. It was just icing on the cake to find out that other lawyers had been suspended or disbarred and through recovery had made it back to practice their profession.

Through the friendships I developed in LCL I was soon offered a job as a legal assistant. With the support of my friend and LCL, I filed an application to have my suspension reinstated to a probation basis. In the beginning this attempt was turned down by the trial court, which made it necessary to appeal to the Texas Supreme Court. In 1991, that court finally ruled in my favor and I was given a chance to present my

case in the trial court that had originally suspended me. My local grievance committee also allowed me to show them the facts of my recovery.

It felt like a Hollywood movie: the very same grievance committee
that had taken my license listened to me with open hearts and minds
and unanimously agreed to support me during my hearing in the District
Court. At the District Court an agreement was finally reached where I
was allowed to practice law on a probated basis.

Since August 1991 I have once again been allowed the privilege of
calling myself an attorney and representing my clients in court. For years
I could not call myself an attorney—I never appreciated what I had until
I lost it.

Today I remain in recovery by taking a few simple actions. I rigorously
work the 12 steps of my program. I try my best to apply those principles
in my everyday life and give what I can to others in trouble. In doing
so I have come to learn I can be one now, every day, in all areas of my
life. I have no fear of discovery, because the true me is always in the
open and visible to all. Without that secret fear there is no compulsion
to use drugs or alcohol. But most important, the fear has been replaced
by a spirituality of belief (not to be confused with a religion); a belief
that a Higher Power is always with me, guiding me, caring for me, and
loving me as I am. With this belief comes a feeling of acceptance of one's
self and a serenity in knowing that today's troubles all will end well. I
continue to pursue personal therapy because there I find extra help in
learning to understand my past and how it affects my feelings today.
Therapy also leads to new insights helpful in making changes in myself
that I have identified as desirable.

As sad as this story may sound, I look at it now as having been the
greatest thing that has ever happened in my life. What I lost was a
tragedy but what I saved was my life and sanity. Through the 12-step
recovery program that I learned about through the Lawyers Concerned
for Lawyers, life has once again become what it was meant to be. I am
proud of my sobriety and my new relationship with the spiritual power
greater than myself. Honesty, an open mind, and willingness have been
restored to my life. There is only one side of my story now. The fear
and the hopelessness have been replaced with acceptance and serenity.
I am grateful for what I have today.

CHAPTER 10

Executives

Because business executives are among the most highly compensated professionals in the United States, the use of alcohol is highly prevalent in this group. A 1% increase in income has been found to produce a 2.5% increase in wine consumption (Duffy, 1983). Within each age and sex group, alcohol use is more common in those of higher social status than those of lower status (Cisin, 1978). In a survey of over 14,000 employees, college graduates had the highest prevalence (29.6%) of "at risk" drinking (Fielding, Knight, Goetzel, & Laouri, 1991).

A similar pattern has been found for substance abuse (illicit drugs or nonmedical use of psychoactive prescription drugs). A survey conducted in New York State determined that higher income groups were more likely to have abused drugs. For example, of those reporting annual incomes greater than $50,000, 46% had used an illicit drug, and 21% had used a drug in the six months preceding the survey. The comparable percentages for those in the $15,000 to $25,000 salary range were 31% and 13% (Frank, Marel, Schmeidler, & Lipton, 1984). Employees in the highest job classifications in a large Southwest city reported a 26% lifetime rate of marijuana use and a 16% rate of other drug use. These rates exceeded those of lower job classifications (Lehman & Simpson, 1990).

These data, however, do not tell us the prevalence of abuse or dependence for higher income groups, such as executives. As with physicians, there is little reason to doubt that executives develop alcoholism with at least the same rate as the general population. In the Frank, Marel, Schmeidler, and Lipton (1984) study, the highest income group self-reported a drug dependence rate of 4% compared to 2% for lower income groups. Substance abuse related problems were reported by 11% of the highest income group compared to a range of 8 to 10% for the lesser income groups. Recent anecdotal reports suggest that highly dangerous drugs, such as heroin, are gaining a "lighter image" within some executive circles (Treaster, 1992).

A study of managerial and professional employees with the Westinghouse Electric Corporation was conducted using detailed clinical interviews to assess DSM-III-R prevalence rates of alcohol abuse/dependence and major depression (Bromet, Parkinson, Curtis, & Schulberg, 1990). Lifetime prevalence rates for alcohol abuse/dependence were 16% for men and 9% for women. The one-year prevalence rates, that is, the presence of symptoms of alcohol abuse/dependence during the year prior to the interview were 4% for both men and women. The average age of onset for drinking problems was 25 years in both men and women. Only 5% of the men and 19% of the women had ever sought help for their problem.

In the above study, rates of major depression were high: For men, the lifetime and one-year prevalence rates were 23% and 9%; for women, 36% and 17%. Individuals with a history of depression were twice as likely also to have a history of alcohol abuse/dependence.

As with other achievement-oriented individuals, executive impairment from alcohol and drugs can be expected to derive from the permutations and combinations of availability, personality/temperament, stress, and genetics.

Genetic and personality/temperament factors have been discussed in Chapter 3. Is availability a factor in executive impairment? As noted above, alcohol use increases with higher income and is often part of the corporate culture (for example, lavish entertaining). What about drugs? Availability of drugs has always been considered an important variable for health professionals. Today, however, it is difficult to discern any less availability for other groups. Illegal drugs, for example, cocaine, marijuana, or heroin, remain quite accessible once initial exposure occurs. Networks of distribution are well established, and availability is forthcoming either through personal initiative to contact suppliers or by chance encounters, which commonly occur in clubs, private parties, or other social settings. Occupational standing or social class are not barriers to the illicit drug trade. In the same vein, prescription drugs are readily obtained. A respectable, well-attired individual with any one of a number of common complaints may find a physician who, perhaps too readily, will prescribe pain killers (codeine, propoxyphene or hydrocodone products), sedatives, tranquilizers (benzodiazepines and barbiturates), or diet pills. The executive, therefore, because of his or her position in society has the means to procure addicting substances, and because of the widespread availability of illicit drugs can readily have access to available channels.

Stress has long been recognized as a contributing variable to substance use disorders. In studies of employment, four types of job stress are commonly recognized: job competition, time pressure, dirtiness of work, and heaviness of work (Parker & Farmer, 1988). For executives, the first two factors commonly apply. Jobs with great responsibility, and which require excessive time involvement, have been found to predict frequency and quantity of drinking by both men and women so employed. Job competition is associated with alcohol consumption and alcohol abuse in men and alcohol abuse in women. Time pressure is associated with alcohol consumption in women, and "felt job stress" is related to alcohol abuse in women (p. 125).

INDICATORS OF IMPAIRMENT

Generally, the executive will manifest signs and symptoms of impairment from substance abuse that are similar to other impaired professionals. Arrest for driving while intoxicated, accidents, marital strife, spouse or child abuse, divorce, children with behavioral problems, medical complications, sexual indiscretions, embarrassing social behaviors, social withdrawal, and mood swings (e.g., fatigue to excessive energy) are commonly described. Gambling, extravagant spending, and financial problems are further signs.

> A young, highly ranked manager in a growing industry became dependent on cocaine. He kept the problem hidden from his wife and young children. To finance his growing cocaine addiction and to maintain his posh life style, he borrowed large sums of money from several banks. The loans were made by friends who did business with him on the basis of his reputation as a successful entrepreneur and his apparent assets. Eventually, job absenteeism, flawed performance, and the suspicions of his office staff prompted an intervention. He responded favorably to treatment and eventually made amends to the loan officers whose careers had been compromised by their flawed lending practices.

The impaired executive may present with problems specific to his corporate role. Failure to meet deadlines, breached contracts, ill-advised business decisions, and deteriorating work relationships are examples. A polarity in decision making may be observed, such as vacillation between impulsive decisions and a paralysis of the decision making process. As with other professionals, actual use of substances is not an uncommon means of detection during work hours: for example, odor of alcohol on the breath when arriving at work, intoxication at lunch, snorting or ingesting substances in the bathroom or behind office doors, bottles or drug paraphernalia in desk drawers or briefcase.

When depression is present, executives report the following four symptoms most commonly: exhaustion, poor concentration, irritability with colleagues, and withdrawal from colleagues (Bromet et al., 1990).

Speller (1989, p. 87) lists behaviors in executives that warrant concern. An intervention may be justified for executives:

- who become unpredictable and behave strangely and inappropriately
- who become easily overwhelmed and unable to manage intense and painful feelings, resulting in unpredictable and often violent emotional outbursts
- who become forgetful and lose track of flow and content of meetings
- who overreact to situations and lose their sense of humor or perspective
- who become suspicious and distrustful in their dealings with others in the firm
- who appear to lose touch with reality
- who become apathetic and pessimistic and lose their intellectual sharpness, political savvy, and good business sense
- who become indecisive and appear confused
- who lose all sense of perspective and misinterpret events in their environment
- who appear inappropriately intoxicated or hung over
- who have a large number of unexplained absences
- who appear tremulous, "shaky," and ill at ease

APPROACHING THE IMPAIRED EXECUTIVE

Attention to the drug- or alcohol-impaired executive is of vital importance to a corporation's functioning. Cohen (1984) has described six consequences of substance abuse for companies: absenteeism, illness, demoralization of the sober work force, theft, errors, and injuries. Often, treatment is initiated by an intervention that stipulates job jeopardy if an evaluation and subsequent treatment recommendations are not accepted. A study of over 100 opiate dependent executives determined that nearly one half accepted the need for treatment only when their jobs were clearly threatened (Washton, Pottash, & Gold, 1984). In that sample, outcomes were good for the 68% who completed recommended treatment. That is, they retained their jobs and were drug-free. Those who discontinued treatment early had poor outcomes. The importance of using the job as leverage was illustrated in this study, as successful completion of treatment was more likely to occur for those who knew their careers were on the line.

As with most chemically dependent individuals, executives do not self-identify as being alcoholic or drug dependent. Their denial defenses are in place, shielding them from awareness and acknowledgment of their disturbed behavior. In addition, guilt, shame, and an increasingly fragile self-esteem provoke even greater layers of defensiveness, which may manifest as aggressiveness, grandiosity, self-righteousness, or perfectionism. Some form of intervention is, therefore, usually necessary. The technique of intervention is described in Chapter 12, and a detailed manual on intervention is available (Crosby & Bissell, 1989). Sometimes, an expression of concern about drinking (or drug use) by a spouse, physician, or trusted colleague prompts the individual to seek either an evaluation or specific treatment. This is a natural process, but one that may be insufficient. The chemically dependent individual often ignores or scoffs at the implication of a problem. Or, if the advice is heeded, he or she may not be directed to health care professionals who are knowledgeable in assessing and diagnosing substance use disorders, and, thereby, be falsely reassured that there is "no problem."

> A 36-year-old investor was abusing cocaine and experiencing binges of intravenous drug use, which would last for two days. His wife and parents were alarmed and distressed. He reacted with anger and blamed them when confronted. Eventually, he was sent to a well-known physician in a distant city for an evaluation. A slight abnormality on his EEG led to the conclusion that the patient was experiencing dissociative states, not drug-seeking behavior. This interpretation further delayed the executive's accepting his need for substance abuse treatment. Further losses from his cocaine abuse eventually led him to accept the problem and to receive appropriate treatment.

More commonly, the chemically dependent individual tries to stop on his or her own. This may be successful for a few days or a few weeks, but eventually fails. Confrontation best proceeds gradually, with careful and consistent documentation of declining productivity or inappropriate behavior. Such preparation lays the groundwork for effective intervention (Schuster, 1993).

Participants in an intervention with an executive may include the individual's supervisor, the human resources director, the medical director, and spouse or appropriate colleagues. The chief executive officer does not have a superior, but input from a friendly and concerned board member, the medical director, and trusted staff will usually be sufficient. A professional trained in the intervention process should be used to help participants gather data that document their concern for their colleague. The professional "coaches" the team on how to express concern and assess any attitudes that might compromise the process. For example, a participant may feel punitive; or, alternately, feel guilty and not want to "embarrass" the executive. If these concerns cannot be modified, the participation of such an individual should be avoided. Once the intervention team has been educated and prepared psychologically, a meeting is scheduled with the impaired executive. A plan of action is proposed in advance. For example, a facility for evaluation and treatment are recommended; coverage for the professional's duties is arranged; and financial resources for treatment are assessed. In addition, consequences of noncompliance have to be established. Leave of absence without pay, termination, or demotion are possible options if a constructive, necessary course of action is not followed.

Return to work is associated with considerable stress for the executive. The returning executive needs time to go to therapy appointments, attend 12-step meetings, and develop a balanced life style. Support and direction regarding these issues is necessary from his or her superiors. Typically, the returning executive wants to compensate for his or her sense of failure and work harder than ever to make up for lost time. The executive often feels that he has to out-perform others, never make a mistake, and do extra work in order to regain and retain what he feels to be his lost status. Reassurances and support from management are crucial to precluding a destructive, obsessive work style. As recovery advances and the executive "matures" in his or her recovery, this initial process of anxiety and self-imposed demand for performance ameliorates. No doubt the perception that an executive or manager is under "pressure" to drink when entertaining clients or to appear collegial has been exaggerated. For example, a survey of business executives revealed that abstaining while others were drinking produced a positive evaluation, and having three or four drinks at a business dinner or getting drunk were perceived as negative. Similarly, solitary drinking after work in order to wind down was perceived negatively by these executive respondents (Shore, 1985).

Discharge planning conferences involving the executive patient, management, and treatment personnel, as well as training programs for supervisors on drug and alcohol problems have proven to be helpful in facilitating a successful return to work and the ability to go forth with career objectives (Machell, 1990).

EXECUTIVE A

Clearly, the most destructive interplay between my job and my addiction was the need for strict secrecy, an element certain to fuel my addiction. As a young chief executive officer and a user of crack cocaine, the potential consequences of discovery were extreme: termination, ostracization by my peers, and loss of community standing. Eventually, this pattern led to an alternative life and a progression into a dark underworld totally separate from my daytime "existence."

Compounding this pattern of secrecy was a life where friends, relationships, and business were intertwined in a complex and overly dependent structure. As the business succeeded and the pace of travel increased, the only time left for friendship and interpersonal relationships came in business settings. This left virtually no safe outlet to seek help for my addiction, and no relief from the pressures of business except my drugs. Essentially, I had accomplished complete isolation in a world of chaotic activity and constant interaction.

Business travel became the natural solution. Already, I was spending ten or more days per month on the road, often flying to two or three cities a day.

Repeated overnight stays in a strange city, anonymous and alone, provided the perfect vehicle for this pattern of secret addiction, and I became highly skilled at making "street buys." Eventually, I began to characterize cities not by the projects we were developing, but by how I made drug buys: Tucson became crack picked up at a Hispanic park; Phoenix, an aging bag handler who was trustworthy and quick; Chicago, a nerve-racking street buy with heavy police patrols. Alcohol and business meetings played a critical role in my pattern of crack cocaine addiction. Late evening business meetings provided the perfect forum for the drinking necessary to brave the anxiety of street buys. Often, during business meetings, one part of my mind planned how to acquire my drug even as I hyped multimillion-dollar syndications.

The high pressure, almost theatrical and performance nature of selling multimillion-dollar joint ventures fueled my addiction. First, I created an almost chameleon-like personality, interpreting the client's desires and concerns and selling the deal accordingly. In this environment, I quickly lost any real sense of self in trying to be all things to all people. Finally, the hype and adrenaline of almost daily performances created both an addiction of its own, in an effort to maintain this constant high, and an extreme need for release from the pressure. Cocaine served both these functions—all too well.

Not surprisingly, this world came crashing to an end. On a day in May, I walked into an Atlanta hotel, expecting to have breakfast with a board member and instead was broadsided by a professionally managed intervention involving my closest friends, business partners, board members, venture capitalists, and corporate attorneys.

Only the complete humiliation brought about by the total surprise of this act, and the ultimate threat of loss of employment managed to force me into treatment. That afternoon, accompanied by a professional interventionist and a substance abuse psychologist, I entered a psychiatric hospital and began what would be the most significant 90 days of my life. For that, I shall be eternally and forever grateful.

While the next 90 days brought much pain and many more hardships, I know now that each element was exactly as God had intended, and that only the path travelled could have brought about the miracle and transformation that God has bestowed upon me.

EXECUTIVE B

Making cold calls lugging 50 pounds of shipping equipment through the business district of downtown San Francisco, just trying to make ends meet! This probably doesn't sound like much if you're a strong male, but if you're a pregnant woman with toxemia this can be brutal. Why did I put myself through this?

That paragraph starts the beginning of my alcoholic thinking. I was a liberated woman of the eighties. After graduating from college, I worked as a chef on a private yacht. This is where I met my ex-husband. We stayed in the Caribbean for about nine months and then took another boat to Florida. Once back in the United States, I started looking for a job in advertising. The job market was tough on the East Coast, so I decided that I would move back to California and try my luck there.

Two months later I discovered I was pregnant. Having been told that I would never be able to have children, due to a serious operation five years before, I was in shock. I come from a Catholic background and felt that getting married was the "right" thing to do. I didn't realize that I would be responsible not only for having this baby but for providing for her as well. I quickly learned that I was having a baby but also marrying one.

Throughout the next five years I had to plot my career path to support a husband, two children, and a nanny. We all know today that this takes quite a sum of money, especially in California. I threw myself into warp speed. I changed my sales career to pharmaceuticals and proceeded to win every award possible in a two-year period of time. After the birth of my second "miracle" child, I started having a glass of wine every evening. I just needed it to calm down after a busy day and a grueling aerobics class.

My job took me away on business trips where I found myself increasing that glass of wine to drinks before dinner, wine with dinner, and shots after dinner. These drinking bouts with the boys seemed normal. Everybody got drunk. Why should I be any different? It got to the point that I would drink and party so much that by the time I returned from these meetings I could barely speak.

My drinking at home started to change. We would have rum and tonics before dinner now, wine with dinner, and B&B after dinner. On the weekends we would make either pina coladas or strawberry margaritas. I was drunk every day. But I needed it! My husband was a bum eating up any extra money we had. He had several sleazy encounters that I was aware of and probably an ongoing affair. Hell, I was successful, but bored with my career, and I had two wonderful kids. I wasn't an alcoholic, was I?

A job offer to go with an upstart biotech company was thrown in my lap. Wow, this would solve all my problems. I would make more money, travel more, and climb the corporate ladder more quickly. With alcohol as my fuel, I could do anything.

Within three months I was promoted to the Midwest as a regional manager. I would not be bored with my career for years to come. With this new position, I was responsible for entertaining on numerous occasions and was on the road 65% of the time. So, if I hadn't managed before to give my alcoholic mind enough reasons to hide in the bottle, I sure did now.

I moved from my hometown of 28 years and away from my family. I lived in the Midwest for three months, then later moved to Texas. I took over the losing region in the company. Finally I bolstered up enough courage to leave my husband. I went through four nannies in four months. So there I was raising a two-year-old and a four-year-old in a town where I didn't know a soul, traveling 65% of the time and trying to make a winning region out of a dog.

Any spare time I had, I spent drinking. While in the Midwest I drank B&B like water. I would take the kids to dinner and have about four or five cocktails while they ate. On business trips to New Orleans, I would get so drunk that I had no idea how I had gotten back to my hotel room. I still functioned. I slowly but surely turned the region around and started receiving accolades from upper management.

The drinking only got worse. After numerous times driving while drunk and feeling miserable the morning after I told myself "No more!" This was good for about one day. Then I would do it again and again. I got into a couple of predicaments with colleagues while on business trips and had to start covering up my drinking by ordering room service and drinking alone. I started to realize I no longer had control over my drinking.

I found myself not flying unless it was first class, where I could drink easily. Everyone drinks in first class! I never went out to dinner without getting drunk; and when you go out to dinner five times a week you're drunk a lot. I would never have less than four bottles of wine in the house or I'd become panicky. I wasn't a morning drinker except on the weekends. As soon as the workday was through, I would have happy hour that lasted until I went to bed.

Again, I was going to quit. I told myself over and over again, "When you get on that plane, don't drink," but when the flight attendant came by, I always did. This would set the pace for that trip. I started going over in my mind the consequences that would ensue if I continued to drink. I hadn't gotten a DUI, not yet! I hadn't let work suffer, not yet! I hadn't hurt my kids, not yet! I hadn't had any financial problems, not yet! The not yets kept ringing in my mind. I had admitted to myself that I had a drinking problem long ago, but I hadn't accepted it until one morning I woke up in my hotel room for the third night in a row not knowing how I had gotten there.

I have been sober for only one year, but after completing a rehabilitation program and becoming a faithful A.A. member, I know that I will not drink today!!

CHAPTER 11

The Recovery Process

This chapter discusses dynamic events that accompany the recovery process. Some occur early in recovery, that is, in the first 6 to 12 months. Other aspects develop throughout recovery but can be appreciated later. In this somewhat arbitrary division of "early" and "late" recovery dynamics, the process of ego maturation is paramount. In the early stages, strengthening of self-care skills (Khantzian, 1981) is emphasized, and in the later stage, emphasis is placed on maturation of defenses (Vaillant, 1971) and spiritual growth.

EARLY RECOVERY DYNAMICS

Pain and Shock

"I'm upset, humiliated, embarrassed, and mad. I wish it hadn't happened." These were the opening words in an initial interview with an opiate-dependent physician. His words capture the state of initial awareness of addiction. When confronted, or shortly after a successful intervention, the professional, who is now a patient and newly aware of his or her condition, undergoes two startling and "shocking" experiences. The first is predominantly cognitive in nature. With considerable rapidity—over hours or days—sequences, patterns, and consequences of substance abuse emerge. The rapidity with which this cognitive process develops contrasts sharply with the years of denial, repression, and avoidance. The suddenness of awareness versus the obstinacy of denial; the clarity of one's behavior versus the previous defensive fog startle the patient. "Why didn't I recognize this?" and "How could I let this happen?" are common responses.

A 58-year-old pharmacist, admitted for diazepam and alcohol abuse remained resentful and adamant about being "mistreated" by his referring colleagues. He searched fretfully for reasons why

129

others would think he had a problem. His distress produced head-aches and poor sleep. Over several days, the attending physician had obtained data from fellow pharmacists, who had arranged the initial intervention, as well as from his adult children. Observations of his impairment were simply and directly presented during rounds. A remarkable transformation took place. Astonished, the pharmacist saw the risks he had taken, how he had endangered his career, and tearfully expressed remorse over his, at times, indif-ferent care of his retarded child. The headaches ceased and his sleep returned to normal. He was able now to focus on the treat-ment process.

For those engaged in careers where mental activity is their strength, the suddenness of having been "blind" to their own behavior yields affects ranging from humiliation and anger to self-doubt and fear.

The second experience that affects the patient when denial falters is affective in nature. Whereas the entire recovery process is accompanied by increasing awareness of one's feelings, this early, initial appreciation of one's chemical dependence is characterized by staccato affect made particularly acute because the relief of alcohol or drugs is absent. The pain of acute shame, guilt, and humiliation require a sensitive clinical response. Well-meaning but false reassurances—for example, "You're being too hard on yourself"—should be avoided. The patient needs to experience these feelings but also needs to receive a sense of understand-ing and hope, as well. Anger or rage may develop. In some cases, suicide is a risk. For example, a surgeon in a small town, who was visited by an investigator from the state board of medical examiners, became overwhelmed by the awareness of his addictive behavior and threatened by the possible consequences for his practice. He shot and killed himself within 24 hours.

The initial affective storm experienced by patients early in the process of recovery is particularly difficult for professionals, who characteristi-cally value control and rationality. The discomfort of the unexpected and unwelcome affect commonly provokes craving for relief and may result in a relapse.

These cognitive and affective experiences, which occur in the initial and early phases of the recovery process, may not become integrated into a mature level of adaptation. They have been brought into aware-ness through a crisis, such as a well-conducted intervention, illness, accident, job loss, or family conflict. The increased awareness of the extent and consequences of one's substance abuse, accompanied by the emotional pain, lead one to admit the problem and comply with initial treatment recommendations (Johnson, 1973). But, it is unrealistic to expect that the dependence on and attachment to the substance can simply dissipate at this time. The dynamics of the disease of addiction (Nace, 1987) remain active and powerful. One usually finds that, as the acute feelings of guilt, shame, embarrassment, remorse, or humiliation subside, the mechanism of denial ascends. I recall my dismay many years ago, when a professor of psychiatry called to discharge his physician patient from treatment for a barbiturate dependence. I was assured by the professor that the addicted doctor had been so embarrassed by his need for hospitalization that he would not return to a pattern of future drug abuse. This commonsense assumption is a major error, but may be expected in those not well-acquainted with the treating of addictions. The same type of thinking operates in the professional patient. He or she has "learned a lesson." Professionals are characteristically quick learners, goal-oriented, and have high expectations that they can achieve what they set out to do. This legacy of expectation and experience fails them when they face recovery if they expect a quick "cure."

The process characteristic of early recovery is illustrated by a 37-year-old family practitioner:

> After an acute medical crisis precipitated by opiate withdrawal, the physician accepted his wife's urging and partner's insistence to receive treatment for his opiate dependence. Humiliated, embarrassed, and contrite, he went through inpatient treatment and signed an aftercare contract for continuing outpatient treatment, including monitoring by an impaired physician committee. Within days to weeks after returning to his practice, he began to let "outside" concerns erode his aftercare plans. He did not attend A.A. meetings regularly because patients' phone calls required a response. Competing demands for time, such as involvement with his children, further compromised sustained follow-through with psychotherapy and contact with his A.A. sponsor. The physician began to self-medicate, not with opiates, but with very small amounts of another compound with which no prior addiction existed in his case. In addition, injections of a nonsteroidal, antiinflammatory drug were self-administered and ultimately aroused the concern of his medical partners. He was once again confronted and acknowledged that he had initiated another course of self-medication, although not to the extent that an active addiction was established. He was fortunate to have the opportunity to process the evolution of this erosion in his treatment, all within the first six weeks following initial rehabilitation. The acute sense of failure and shame he experienced when he first became fully aware of the impact of his opiate dependence had not sustained his determination to work a recovery plan when competing demands for his

time developed. He had quickly slipped back into a pattern of self-medication, which harbored a poor prognosis if it had not been detected and interrupted.

This case is typical, in that it highlights the early struggle with acute cognitive and affective events that are startling and painful, followed by admission of a problem and intended compliance with a treatment regimen. What is not fully appreciated by the recovering patient at this stage is his or her need to totally grasp the seriousness of an addiction, the subtlety with which it makes further inroads into his or her life, and the importance of maintaining recovery plans as the highest priority, even at the expense of time with the family and the sacrifice of practice hours. Because of the constructive confrontation and interaction with recovering peers and treatment personnel, the physician referred to above regained his momentum for recovery and was able to establish the balance necessary to follow through successfully.

When Perfectionism Fails

Closely associated with painful awareness and affect is a profound sense of disappointment in oneself. Addiction represents the loss of the professional's valued attributes. In place of control, competence, and respect, loom chaos, failure, and disgrace. Personal expectations and public trust are now seen to be dashed. The disappointment over being chemically dependent is, in part, related to the stereotyped negative images of addicts and alcoholics. Disappointment is magnified by the possibility that what one has striven and prepared for—a successful career, security, and status—may now be lost. Yet, these factors, with all their social consequences, have less power than the internal injury to one's sense of self. The contrast between what one expects of oneself and the state of addiction disappoints more pervasively than does the potential for social decline. The profound sense of disappointment for the addicted professional lies primarily in the exaggerated self-expectations he or she maintains. These expectations are often seen as *perfectionism*, a term widely used to describe personality traits of physicians and other professionals (Racy, 1990).

Perfectionism has been attributed to character structure (Gabbard, 1985) and to social reinforcement (Millon, 1969). Physicians are the most studied group of professionals in terms of trying to understand perfectionism. Gabbard attributes perfectionism to the compulsive personality of the physician. The compulsive physician, plagued with feelings of self-doubt and guilt, works hard to overcome feelings of failure and to appease a considerable sense of responsibility. Millon (1969) proposes that inflated expectations and inflated self-worth derive from parents' modeling and feedback. As a result, personal beliefs about uniqueness and self-importance are formed (Beck & Freeman, 1990).

In addition to the contributing factors of perfectionism, the process of becoming a professional, for example, the socialization process for physicians, reinforces perfectionistic traits. The striving for a 4.0 grade average to insure acceptance into medical school is an example. The training years are highly demanding physically, mentally, and emotionally and require performance despite exhaustion. Fels (1991) describes "young physicians [as] overwhelmed by the godlike power with which they have been invested and by their underlying fear of its obverse-lethal power." Anything less than complete effort, failure to consider all diagnostic or treatment possibilities, or, worse, an overt error, can be lethal. Clearly, the demands placed on the physician throughout the training years and the pressure for high performance foster what may be considered a sense of exaggerated responsibility or perfectionism. Khantzian (1985a) describes another possible contributing factor to perfectionistic strivings—a failure to value oneself and the subsequent effort to compensate for self-esteem problems through excessive work. Feelings of being undervalued or uncared for may be transformed into efforts to care for others. This effort, although often effective professionally, cannot be expected to heal one personally. Thus, "success cures" (Khantzian, 1985a; p. 250) can carry one only so far and, perhaps, renders one more vulnerable to chemical dependence.

Apart from the possible etiologic role of partially compensated self-esteem problems, is the impact on self-esteem for such professionals when their addiction becomes manifest. The professional whose work has been, at least in part, an effort at self-repair through caring for others can be profoundly disappointed in himself or herself when the "failure" is realized. The professional identity is compromised, but, even worse, the fear of being inadequate now seems to be verified. Professionals are, therefore, vulnerable to a profound decline in self-worth, self-esteem, and self-regard as they face their dependence on alcohol or drugs and the consequent failure of their perfectionistic strivings. Table 11.1 summarizes the factors contributing to perfectionism.

Hypertrophied Defenses

Thus far, a description has been presented of the affective and cognitive turmoil experienced by the professional patient during the early stage of recovery. However, the remorse, shame, guilt, and humiliation

TABLE 11.1
Determinants of "Perfectionism" in Professionals

- Compulsive personality structure ("Exaggerated sense of responsibility" [Gabbard, 1985])
- Overinflated self image (Millon, 1969)
- Compensation for self-esteem problems (Khantzian, 1985)
- Assumption of significant responsibility
- Demands for high performance

may fail to stimulate constructive change (see Self-Care Skills on p. 136). Instead, defenses reemerge to shield one from a continuing awareness of past behaviors, current or future consequences, and the attendant painful feelings. Denial returns. The return of denial is perplexing to those unfamiliar with the dynamics of the addictive process. Denial returns because it blocks the painful, conflicted experience of substance dependence from consciousness. One is, therefore, better able to attend to and focus upon "important" matters, such as career, productivity, and financial concerns. We know, of course, that this defense ultimately fails, but its initial economy is impressive.

Denial also returns in the interest of preserving the chemical dependence. It is a daunting task to face discontinuance of alcohol or drugs when uncertainty abounds as to whether one can cope without substances, or whether one really needs to live with such a "deprivation." Further, the awesome spector of not being able to quit alcohol or drug use confronts the chemically dependent individual. This amalgam of doubt and fear is resolved nicely by denial—"I'll go about it differently in the future." Denial preserves the "acceptability" of continued alcohol or drug use. The threat to the addiction engendered by intervention and confrontation not only opens up the possibility of addressing one's dependence through an initial lessening of denial, but also stimulates powerful affect, which in turn may restimulate a need for denial.

Along with denial, additional defensive forces may appear. Narcissistic defenses, such as self-sufficiency, grandiosity, and perfectionism are commonly noted. The professional thrives on conceptualizing himself or herself as being in control, self-sufficient, and ultimately responsible. The process of recovery threatens this self-conceptualization as intellect, control, self-sufficiency, and pride fail. The painful affect, which accompanies awareness of the addiction and its consquences, may also compel a return to well-known, comfortable psychological positions. The latter include a rejection of the need for help from others (self-sufficiency), a belief that one can manage what needs to be done better than would-be helpers (grandiosity), and a determination to compensate for losses or humiliation by even greater achievement (perfectionism). Fears of appearing vulnerable are pervasive.

Dr. L. sought out a mental health worker, as he was feeling terrible about being hospitalized for alcoholism. He subsequently complained that he was ignored by the worker. More likely, the physician was not forward in requesting a chance to talk. He acknowledged that he had felt humiliated about his need to seek someone and doubly humiliated when he perceived that there was no interest in him. This experience recapitulated early childhood experiences where he was largely ignored by his parents. Although he was adopted by his grandparents, who nurtured him sufficiently, he recalled that until age five or six, he screamed and cried if someone tried to hold him.

Another example of defensiveness about feeling vulnerable was demonstrated by a physician through his interaction with an activities therapist. He wanted help in developing leisure time skills, but he felt the therapist did not respond to him or was not able to give him the help that he wanted, and he was disappointed, then angry. He was further angered when she suggested that he talk with the nursing staff that evening. He resented this, because the nursing staff were of a lesser educational level than he, and he thought they could not understand his life experiences. He avoided asking for further help, because he felt rebuffed by the therapist, after taking the "risk" of asking for help. Throughout the rest of the course of treatment, he described having a "personality conflict" with this therapist and remained harshly critical of her. Similarly, the vulnerability issue came up when his marriage was probed by the social worker. He spoke in derogatory terms of the social worker, but later was able to acknowledge that he had been threatened by the truth of the revelations that came out in marital sessions.

The combination of denial and narcissistic defenses often leads to a rupture of the recovery process and is a prelude to relapse. Alertness to this process and an appreciation of the "need" for this process will enable the clinician to support and confront such developments. Reminders of past experiences, appreciation of the patient's fears of being "vulnerable," and acknowledgment of gains already established are helpful approaches to a lessening of defensiveness. One physician kept a list of all the losses he would experience if he returned to drug use. He kept this in his office desk and read it over several times a week. It served not only as a "warning" but stimulated appreciation for what he had gained.

The next section addresses a process, which, when developed, provides a stabilizing influence throughout the vacillating stages of early recovery.

SELF-CARE SKILLS

The patient with a substance use disorder begins treatment in a regressed condition. Regression refers to the utilization of defenses that are less mature than expected in capable, achievement-oriented adults. "Immature" defenses include acting out, denial, somatization, and passive-aggressive behaviors, in contrast to higher level "neurotic" defenses, such as repression, reaction formation, intellectualization, and rationalization. The "mature" defenses are, of course, optimal and include altruism, humor, suppression, and anticipation (Vaillant, 1971). The regressed psychological condition of the chemically dependent patient is a function of several factors. First, the rapid, predictable, pleasurable reinforcement of the drug overpowers and erodes one's capacity to delay gratification or endure frustration (Nace, 1990). Second, the chemically dependent person is threatened by the loss of control over substance use and, accordingly, reacts defensively. Third, the chronic use of alcohol or drugs compromises neuropsychological functioning and impairs information processing, judgment, and decision making (Bean, 1981).

An example of the importance of dealing with repression and pathological defenses is provided by Dr. G. This patient was the youngest of four sons. By the time he was five years old, his three older brothers had been killed; two were killed in World War II, and another died of leukemia. (Interestingly, the patient became an oncologist.) The deaths of the three older brothers led Dr. G's parents to idealize these children. Dr. G could never live up to their images. The parents became overcontrolling and derogatory, because he was not what the other children had been in their idealized memories. He tried hard to please them but, in order to survive, had to become a "pathological liar." For example, during his adolescence, he lied to his parents about where he had been because they refused to allow him to see certain girls or friends. He became a "con man," as he put it, because he found that if he told the truth he would be punished, but if he lied things were safer. He was successful in his medical career, but found that, as his career developed, he actually became more and more unhappy. Ultimately, he had marital problems, divorced, remarried, and, subsequently, suffered addiction and depression. He made a serious suicide attempt, and this precipitated treatment. He was unable to ask for help in a direct way, and thereby expose his psychological vulnerability. This was graphically illustrated by his claiming that he had a malignancy. In fact, prior to his being admitted to the substance abuse program, he had submitted false pathological specimens to another treatment facility, indicating that he had a fatal disease. His nearly fatal disease actually was major depression. Later, he was able to see that his impairment in asking for help had led him to his distorted use of medical knowledge both in trying to ask for help (submitting malignant specimens and claiming they were his own) and subsequently devising a carefully calculated dose of medicine as part of a suicide gesture.

The initial approach to such an amalgam of cognitive dysfunction and psychological regression is to separate the patient from further substance use. Whether this is best accomplished in an inpatient or outpatient setting is discussed in Chapter 12. The task of sustaining abstinence depends in part on providing information to the patient that is relevant to his condition, establishing an alliance that facilitates engagement in appropriate therapeutic modalities, and fostering long-term involvement in 12-step programs. In order for these endeavors to be accomplished, however, a substantial strengthening of specific ego functions is necessary. Specifically, initial attention to the ego functions of self-governance (Mack, 1981) and self-care is necessary (Khantzian, 1981).

Mack (1981) considers self-governance to be a group of functions within the ego system that have to do with "choosing or deciding, with directing and controlling" (p. 132). Self-governance implies a capacity to be in charge of oneself while also being receptive to influence from individuals or groups—that is, to be responsive to and to integrate input from one's social field as one experiences the ability to choose and act. The ego function of "self-care" is best considered a derivative of the more global and encompassing functions of self-governance. Accordingly, to Khantzian (1981) self-care as an ego function includes such skills as judgment, reality testing, and an appreciation of danger or vulnerability.

Deficiencies in self-governance/self-care functions are observed in clinical work with professional and nonprofessional patients alike. They are not necessarily secondary to drug or alcohol use, but can occur outside periods of substance use. The probabililty of relapse increases to the extent that these ego deficiences are not addressed. At the clinical level, the ego functions of self-governance/self-care are strengthened by addressing impulsivity, initiative, and isolation.

Impulsivity is a widely recognized characteristic of substance abusing individuals. Risk-taking and novelty seeking behavior traits are a basis for typologies of alcoholics (Cloninger, 1987; Knight, 1937). On the other hand, the stimulating and disinhibiting effects of drug use foster impulsiveness. A reciprocal relationship exists between ego functions and the pharmacologic impact of intoxicating drugs. In the absence of alcohol and drugs, impulse control and other self-care skills improve. Ego deficiencies, although aggravated by substance use, are often primary to the substance use. This circular relationship is illustrated in Figure 11.1. Impulsivity as one manifestation of this ego deficiency requires confrontation and redirection. For example, a young physician went on her first pass with her husband. When she arrived home, she decided not to continue with treatment. Her husband called and asked what to do. The patient was persuaded to return and complete the substance abuse program, which she did. Another example is a male physician who, after a year of no drug use, found alprazolam tablets in a jacket. He took two and discarded the remaining few. He was dismayed by his behavior and the sudden urge to use the drug when it unexpectedly became available. Others report overeating, driving at high speeds, reckless spending, and abrupt career decisions. These examples occur in the absence of alcohol or drug use and are best modified through individual or group therapies.

A dentist, who was in successful recovery for over two years, was dismayed by his apparent inability to cut back on coffee drinking, which reached 12 to 15 cups a day. Periodically, he binged on food and was upset by transient weight gains. During the first year of his recovery, he considered these problems "trivial" relative to his prior problems with alcohol and prescription drugs. As he gained confidence in maintaining abstinence, he was able to focus on other areas, including his inability to resist using coffee and food excessively. These problems, although not as dangerous as his prior addictions, affected his self-esteem and prompted a mature and productive effort on his part to strengthen his self-care skills.

A major strategy in modifying impulsiveness is to build upon the principles used to quit alcohol and drug use—for example, recognize the "impulse" as early as possible, avoid situations (if possible) that might promote the impulse, and attempt to identify possible reasons for the emergence of the impulse. Along with identifying and understanding impulse formation, the establishment of cognitive techniques to manage impulsivity is essential.

A useful cognitive behavioral technique is a modification of covert sensitization (Ashem & Donner, 1968; Cautela, 1967) and is referred to as "play your tapes." Each patient is instructed to imagine ("create a videotape") consequences of drinking or drug use, which he or she would not ever wish to reexperience. Adverse consequences of behavior other than alcohol or drug use can be utilized as well. A vivid imagining of painful memories is necessary. These "tapes" are then "stored" in memory and recalled whenever the individual is confronted with the impulse to drink or use drugs. This process pairs aversive remembered experiences with the impulse that signals the onset of undesired behavior. The paired association assists in extinguishing such impulses. The power of the technique "play your tape" lies in the utilization of one's own personal, painful consequences and is not dependent on theoretical or potential consequences.

A second clinical manifestation of self-care deficits is a failure of initiative. A readiness to take action is integral to working a program of recovery from a substance use disorder. Passivity and delayed action are examples of relapse behaviors—that is, behaviors that foreordain the return to substance abuse. A pharmacist complained of his procrastination over obtaining continuing education credits. Documentation was due in one month, yet, for a year, he had failed to take the initiative to obtain these credits. A physician from a distant city was to arrange his on-call schedule so that he could return for several therapy appointments within one day. The plan was to return for such appointments monthly. He waited for weeks before clearing his schedule and apologized for his tardiness in making plans.

As with impulsivity, passivity and a lack of initiative are reinforced by substance abuse. Alcohol and drugs are powerful reinforcers because they provide a rapid, predictable, and pleasurable change in affect. The usual and customary rewards we receive from work, school, task completion, or relationships are delayed and are experienced only after considerable expenditure of effort and time. The ingestion of drugs or alcohol is accomplished with little expenditure of effort, yet is accompanied by a powerful, immediate experience of gratification. Patients can identify with this process when it is described as "being spoiled" by substance abuse. Natural "highs" (for example, receiving a paycheck, getting a good grade, or receiving praise) require initiative and action over time. The sense of gratification is more subtle, but more enduring.

The failure to initiate good self-care behaviors is well illustrated in many professionals by their inattention to signs of stress in their lives. A physician who had recovered from a relatively brief but intense bout of alcohol dependence became depressed years later. He recognized the symptoms of his depression and after several weeks went as far as to look up the telephone number of a psychiatist he had seen years earlier. However, he never got around to making the call and, six weeks later, was both drinking alcohol and injecting meperidine. Treatment was initiated when he was found unconscious in a laboratory.

Lack of initiative contains elements of passivity, dependency, and a relative inability to experience oneself as a center of responsibility, particularly in relation to self-care behaviors. It is not a pervasive deficit, as professionals necessarily demonstrate considerable initiative in many areas of their lives. Yet, they, along with other substance abusing patients, commonly manifest this ego deficit in uniquely personal areas of their lives.

A third manifestation of deficit in the ego function of self-governance/self-care is the isolation of the chemically dependent patient: isolation from interpersonal influence and from one's affective experience. The chemically dependent person often describes a lifelong pattern, preceding substance abuse, of interpersonal and emotional isolation. Although such descriptions are often vague, they convey the end product of a number of possible contributing variables: for example, isolation may be an expression of narcissistic pathology characterized by defensive self-sufficiency and grandiosity; or it may reflect the above described lack of initiative and subsequent inhibition of action. It is commonly observed that substance use facilitates interpersonal interaction and may serve to overcome, in part, this particular expression of ego deficiency. Eventually, substance abuse results in interpersonal isolation, as the individual's behavior becomes intolerable. Thus, we again find a reciprocal relationship between substance abuse and the expression of ego weakness in the area of self-care skills, with one fostering the other (Figure 11.1).

The correction of a longstanding sense of isolation in a physician occurred through continuous, albeit begrudging, attendance at A.A. meetings. This surgeon continued to attend A.A., in spite of a disparaging attitude toward the optimism, spirituality, and camaraderie of A.A. groups. He knew that he needed A.A. to stay clean and sober and did not want to risk his professional standing through another relapse. About two years into recovery, he was able to acknowledge and describe a shift in his attitude. Cynicism concerning the tolerant philosophy of A.A. was replaced by a growing appreciation and gratitude for the constancy of the A.A. members' relatedness. Defensive narcissistic structures, such as self-sufficiency and grandiosity, which had aided the longstanding interpersonal and emotional isolation, gradually eroded through the constant and corrective experience of sincere human contact.

Another manifestation of isolation is isolation of affect. This is commonly seen in professionals who disparage affective experience in favor of the cognitive and intellectual. To some extent, this may be learned behavior secondary to prolonged professional training. But, in addition, the ground for such learning is usually laid through blocks in affective development (Khantzian, 1981). A physician gave her history of amphetamine abuse, which had existed intermittently over five years. She intended to do something about it when assuming a professional role of advanced responsibility. Although her husband urged her to seek help, she delayed (lack of initiative) for several months before contacting a recommended source. She further delayed acting on subsequent recommendations. Gradually, she faced her addiction. She did not know if she felt depressed, yet she described many symptoms characteristic of depression, and acknowledged that amphetamines "did something" for her and made up for something she was lacking in her life. Unable to

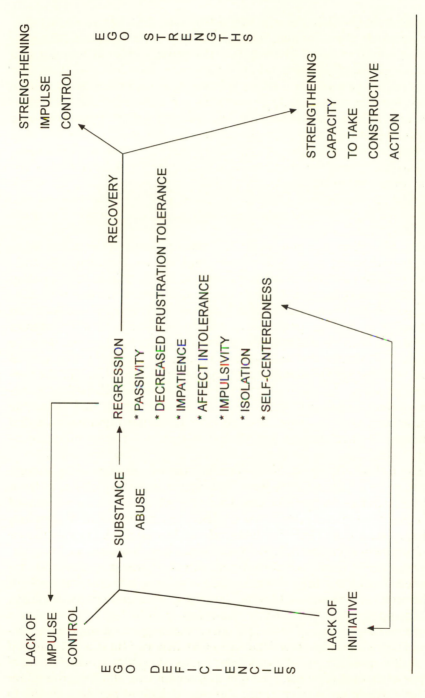

Figure 11.1. The Relationship between Ego Deficiencies in Self-Care Skills and Substance Abuse

describe how she felt, she was necessarily isolated from significant aspects of her experience. This isolation further contributed to her failure to initiate help-seeking behaviors, as she found it difficult to bring her vague dysphoria into focus.

The importance of overcoming isolation is illustrated in the wisdom of 12-step programs, which commonly urge people to "keep coming back" and reminds members that "no one can do it for you, but you can't do it alone."

LATE RECOVERY DYNAMICS

Coping with the Legacy

After two years of sobriety, Dr. C was reviewing his recovery with me. He mentioned that, from time to time, he had the feeling that he was "damaged goods." A referring physician had sought consultation from another specialist. Although Dr. C had had no contact with this physician for several years, he immediately thought that he had not been consulted because of the fact that he had a history of drug addiction. He realized that his thinking was a product of continuing shame and self-disappointment and that his past history was unlikely to be in the minds of those with whom he now had a respected professional association.

The themes of shame, guilt, and loss resound across the recovery. Early in recovery, the chemically dependent patient often feels caught between a regrettable past and a hopeless future. With support, treatment, and successful coping without drugs or alcohol confidence increases and denial lessens. Losses can be faced as one regains confidence and a sense of future. One then is able to look more clearly at and inventory the losses that have occurred. For some, career opportunities have been lost or compromised. For others, relationships with a spouse or children are lost. Health or financial status may suffer, as well. Grief work may be necessary. At the least, a process of understanding and appreciation of losses is necessary, not in the interest of dredging up emotional pain but for the focus such a process provides on current effort and achievement and for the antidote it provides against euphoric recall (Johnson, 1973) of drug or alcohol use.

Guilt is often a factor in an individual's decision to begin treatment. Typically, something "bad" has occurred that precipitates a crisis. In the throes of this crisis—for example, legal, occupational, familial—the patient is motivated to make changes and accept help. Guilt is prominent at this point in time. Guilt spurs compliance with treatment, but does not necessarily lead a person toward accepting his or her powerlessness over alcohol and drugs. Too often, when the initial crisis has resolved, guilt may be relieved, but an acceptance of the need for continuing treatment is missing.

Feelings of guilt extend, of course, into the later phases of recovery, as well. However, a treatment experience that teaches the disease concept of addiction and the "unmanageability" of one's life as a result of addiction does much to relieve guilt. Guilt is dealt with further when Steps 4 and 5 of A.A. (See Table 14.1) are completed (Kurtz, 1981).

Guilt and shame are intertwined, but shame is likely to replace guilt as the predominant emotion as recovery proceeds beyond the initial stages. My impression is that professionals have a particularly consuming sense of shame. Professionals have high expectations of themselves, are ambitious, perfectionistic, and expect to be highly functioning. These attributes crumble in the face of dependence on drugs or alcohol. Vulnerability is exposed, and vulnerability is necessarily an acknowledgment of personal limitation. According to Kurtz (1981), feelings of shame derive from perceived limitations or "shortcomings." Kurtz's (1981) valuable essay distinguishes between guilt and shame: Guilt results from a violation or transgression, from an exercise of power or control, and leads to a sense of wickedness of being "not good." Shame derives from a failing, a lack of power or control, and leads one to feel inadequate and "no good."

Kurtz (1981) provides an instructive metaphor on this distinction: "on a football field, there are two kinds of boundaries: side-lines and end-lines. The side-lines are containing boundaries: to cross them is to 'go out of bounds,' to do something wrong. The end lines are goal-lines: the purpose of the game is to attain and cross them. One feels bad (guilty) when one crosses the side-line, the restraining boundary. Feeling 'bad' about the goal-line (shame) arises not from crossing it but from not crossing it, from failing to attain it" (p. 6).

Guilt, then, hovers over the professional's performance. Recovering professionals often express that they "can't have a bad day." They believe that they are automatically suspected of relapse if anything goes wrong at work, or if they appear unkempt, or if they become irritable or angry.

A pharmacist who was substituting in the operating room worried about the handling of a variety of addictive substances he did not ordinarily encounter in his regular assignment. A large part of his concern was that he not make any mistakes and that he be able to account for all of the drugs because being in recovery would make him a suspect if anything were missing.

After being in recovery for a year, an alcoholic physician felt "bad" (guilty) that he had spent so little time with his young son during his drinking days. Although the boy was doing well in school and at home, this physician felt his son might need counseling to overcome some possible harm that the alcoholic environment had caused. A brief but competent family evaluation indicated that the boy did not require treatment, and the recovering physician felt less guilty.

Shame can provide continuing motivation for recovery goals: A married physician described with a sense of poignant shame a comment by his wife: She described being at a restaurant with a friend and wishing that she had a normal life with her husband and that they could go out socially without the embarrassment of his drinking. The physician-patient remembered this comment by his wife and remains moved by it, and it was, according to his account, a turning point in his decision to pursue treatment.

A crucial aspect of later recovery is the shift from guilt-focused material to the issue of shame. Accepting shame is accepting one's human limitations, a process so well conducted by the program of Alcoholics Anonymous. Kurtz (1981) emphasizes steps 2, 6, 7, and 10 as particularly helpful in dealing with shame. The idea of being limited and accepting one's limitations is a powerful counterforce to the more primitive drives of perfectionism observed in chemically dependent professionals. Therapists should feel comfortable with their professional patients as themes of shame emerge. The ability to bring forth such material is indicative of personal growth. A sensitive process of reflection and reexamination conducted by the therapist will further the process of developing self-esteem and the acceptance of limitations.

Integration

The later stages of recovery are a time when the experience of addiction can acquire perspective in one's overall identity. The contributing factors in one's life that led to the development of an addiction can now be better understood. Identity is no longer limited to denying one's substance dependence, nor does one view oneself totally in terms of being an "alcoholic" or "addict." Sobriety is stable, and roles are reestablished.

The integration of both the experience and the consequences of substance dependence occurs through two simultaneous, complimentary processes. One or the other of these processes may dominate in a given individual, but optimally, both show development.

First, a strengthening of ego functions takes place. Earlier, the point was made that the substance abusing patient is often regressed when treatment begins. A strengthening of ego functions can be expected as toxic substances are withdrawn and nutritional and physiologic states return to normal. As important as such organic processes are, the major stimulus for ego growth is the need to resist the urge (craving) for further alcohol or drug use. Each patient faces a crossroad when his or her best intentions interact with the feeling of a need, desire, or wish for a return to the euphoric, sedative, or stimulating effects of drugs. This crossroad may be encountered several times a day. One goal of treatment is to help the patient understand that such craving is part of the disease of chemical dependence and what to do about it (Nace, 1987). Nevertheless, no amount of education or therapy will remove those moments. Successful recovery depends, then, on enduring the discomfort of "not having what I want when I want it." This experience, which may be brief or extended, infrequent or moment to moment, becomes the paradigm for strengthening the ego in the area of affect recognition, regulation, and tolerance (Khantzian, 1981). Craving has to be recognized, rejected, and coped with.

The experience of craving may range from the purely cognitive (such as the idea of having a small glass of wine with dinner), to somatic sensations, including taste, odor, or increased autonomic nervous system activity, to strong affective reactions ranging from anxiety to compulsions. The ego is strengthened by experiencing craving successfully; that is, without succumbing to use of any drugs or alcohol (Nace, 1982). For, by so doing, the individual tolerates uncomfortable affect, avoids acting out, puts into action cognitive techniques such as "play your tapes" (p. 239), and breaks out of interpersonal isolation by calling a sponsor or openly discussing his discomfort with others. The successful repetition of this process of tolerating frustration stimulates a shift from such "immature" (Vaillant, 1971) defenses as acting out, somatization, and passive-aggressiveness to higher levels of functioning including humor, suppression, anticipation, and altruism. The gradual maturing of ego functions is usually apparent after six months of abstinence and becomes "integrated" over the first few years of recovery.

The second developmental process in the integration phase of recovery is that of spiritual growth. Spirituality is rarely addressed in clinical settings, and most physicians and other mental health professionals receive little or no training in the concepts of spirituality.

The patient with a substance use disorder commonly, but not invariably, enters treatment in a state of alienation from earlier religious experience. Loss, suffering, guilt, and shame all contribute to the alienation. Alcoholics Anonymous and Narcotics Anonymous, through their 12-step programs, deemphasize dogma and the orthodoxy one might associate with formal religion. Thus, participation in a 12-step program is

often more acceptable and better tolerated than a return to or an introduction to formal religion. This is not to imply that establishment of or
return to a specific religion is not indicated. In fact, I have known several
patients who avoided 12-step programs in favor of their church or syna-
gogue affiliation. For many people, the teachings of a specific faith
strengthen the process associated with recovery. Such individuals may
not affiliate with A.A. or N.A. because they find them too "loose" or
liberal in thinking.

Most patients, however, acquire an appreciation of major spiritual
themes through their involvement in A.A. or other 12-step programs.
The spirituality of the A.A. program may be understood as a series of
overlapping themes (Kurtz, 1989). The first spiritual theme is *release*.
Release refers to the "chains being broken," that is, a freedom from the
compulsion to drink. An attorney, who had been in psychotherapy for
nearly a year, finally agreed to my recommendation to attend A.A. His
decision to try A.A. occurred during a time when his family was out of
town, and he realized that his vulnerability to return to alcohol use was
growing. His appreciation for his vulnerability at this moment motivated
him to try A.A. This proved to be a remarkable event for this man, as
he experienced, for the first time in decades, freedom from the urge to
drink. He was astonished by this sense of release, had not expected it,
but welcomed it. He became a regular participant in A.A. Certainly, this
experience is not the norm with regard to the rapidity and clarity of
experiencing *release*. Nevertheless, it is a possibility and most often develops over time.

A second theme of spirituality is that of *gratitude*. Gratitude may derive
from the feeling of release and the appreciation that one can *not* drink
(mastery) rather than *cannot* drink (prohibition). Gratitude emphasizes
an awareness of what one has, rather than what one does not have.
This theme is reinforced strongly in Alcoholics Anonymous through the
intense focus and value on sobriety. Kurtz (1989) points out that the
words "think" and "thank" share a common derivative. Thinking leads
to remembrance, and from remembrance an attitude of thankfulness or
gratitude may develop. For the person in recovery, gratitude is linked
to not drinking or not drugging and the process of telling one's story
at A.A. and hearing others' stories links the concepts of "think" and
"thank."

A third theme is that of *humility*. Humility is the acceptance of the
reality that one is limited. Earlier, it was mentioned that the ability to
experience one's limitations is an important part of the early recovery
process and fosters spiritual growth. The fact that it is acceptable to be
limited, to be simply human, is yet another form of release encountered
during the recovery process.

A fourth theme described by Kurtz (1989) is that of *tolerance*. Just as one in the early stages of recovery has learned to tolerate his or her limitations and "powerlessness" over alcohol or drugs, tolerance for differences among others develops. The emphasis on tolerance helps in the breakdown of isolation so common to the chemically dependent individual. It must be apparent that the processes of ego growth and spiritual growth go hand in hand, and any attempt to fully separate the two would be artificial.

These themes of spirituality are very similar to the healing process in the mystical traditions described by Deikman (1982). The process of healing and psychological growth, according to Deikman, involves renunciation, humility, and sincerity. These attributes and processes are common to the traditions of non-Western religions.

Renunciation, according to Deikman (1982), is an attitude and does not imply that one is to give up worldly possessions, but rather that one relinquish or renounce one's *attachment* to material possessions. This process assists in relinquishing desire, which is integral to the chemically dependent person's need to experience release from cravings for alcohol or drugs.

A second healing theme in the mystical traditions is that of *humility*. According to Deikman (1982), humility is "the possibility that someone else can teach you something you do not already know, especially about yourself" (p. 81). Humility is the opposite of pride and arrogance, which are part and parcel of the narcissistic defense structure. The importance of overcoming pathological narcissism has been discussed. The ability to achieve humility can be expected to go a long way toward modification of pathological narcissism. To achieve humility, one must first accept one's "powerlessness over alcohol" (or drugs) and one's limitations in this regard. From that initial, crucial process of acceptance of a very specific limitation, tolerance and an acceptance of the broader range of limitations of ourselves and others can develop.

The third spiritual process common to mystical traditions is that of *sincerity*. Deikman describes sincerity as referring to "honesty of intention" (p. 82). The practice of sincerity is not only a moral issue, but has functional significance. This is readily apparent in one's attempt to cope with alcoholism or drug dependence. Sincerity of purpose is minimal, and perhaps lacking, during the compliance phase of recovery, but has matured by the time the acceptance phase is reached. If one sincerely accepts one's limitations in regard to alcohol or drug use and the "unmanageability" of those experiences, recovery and personal growth are likely to follow.

Clinical experience documents that the sincere man or woman who works the 12-step program of Alcoholics or Narcotics Anonymous integrates processes of renunciation and humility, as well as gratitude and tolerance. This process occurs over months or (more likely) years. No doubt it is subject to fits and starts and is far from a smooth continuum. Yet, profound testimony to these changes is available at A.A. meetings daily and is also backed by easily witnessed constructive changes in behavior.

CHAPTER 12

Matching the Patient to Level of Care

To facilitate the recovery process, appropriate treatment planning is essential. The first step is to decide whether placement is to be inpatient or outpatient. This chapter offers guidelines for that decision.

A treatment setting for an impaired professional should be a program with experience in treating professionals. A glance at the Yellow Pages of nearly any community's telephone directory reveals numerous alcoholism and drug abuse treatment programs. Random selection of a treatment facility is inappropriate. Guidance may be obtained from clinicians familiar with substance abuse treatment, from state or county impaired physicians committees, from state nursing and pharmacy associations, and from local or state bar associations.

The following features should be sought in a program:

- reputation for, and experience with, the treatment of professional patients
- leadership, preferably by a psychiatrist certified in addiction psychiatry by the American Board of Psychiatry and Neurology or a physician certified by examination through the American Society of Addiction Medicine (ASAM)
- multidisciplinary treatment team that includes registered nurses, licensed chemical dependency counselors, social workers, and activities therapists
- integration of the programs of Alcoholics Anonymous and Narcotics Anonymous into the treatment plan
- medical and psychiatric assessment for each patient
- program organized specifically for family members
- full spectrum of care levels
- variable lengths of stay based on clinical need
- continuous evaluation of treatment outcome

In planning treatment for professional patients, the following may be appropriate at some time for some individual patients:

- referral out of state (or out of the local community)
- placement on inpatient status
- extended absence from professional role

At times, referral away from local treatment resources may be desirable. This is often determined by patient preference. Inpatient treatment may be desirable for many patients, but it is not the only option unless appropriate criteria are met. Professionals often do better by starting with inpatient treatment, despite the fact that they are usually socially stable (a variable often mitigating against inpatient placement). The reason for this is that inpatient placement may allow the patient to free him or herself from the demands of and concerns about professional responsibilities and enable a focus on his or her own treatment needs. Length of stay also should be individualized. Only rarely is it necessary to recommend four- to six-month absences from professional activity. It is preferable to have a plan allowing the professional patient to phase back into professional work gradually. The pacing of return is determined by the patient's ability to give priority to continuing treatment in the face of a return to professional demands.

CURRENT INDICATIONS FOR INPATIENT TREATMENT

Four clinical domains (summarized in Table 12.1), either alone or in combination, may indicate the need for inpatient treatment. These domains represent acute states and include:

1. *Medical or psychiatric disorders caused by substance abuse.* The medical disorders caused by alcoholism are well-known and widely described (Nace & Isbell, 1991). When these conditions are acute (for example, pancreatitis) or when further drinking poses a risk (for example, bleeding from esophageal varices in a patient with cirrhosis), inpatient treatment is mandated in order to interrupt alcohol use effectively and provide stabilization.

Psychiatric disorders that arise from alcohol or drug abuse include any of the organic brain syndromes described in DSM-IV (APA, 1994). Of these disorders, delirium, delusional disorders, withdrawal delirium, simple withdrawal, idiosyncratic intoxication, and hallucinosis are the most likely to require inpatient treatment. Not all cases of withdrawal require hospitalization. The severity of the withdrawal syndrome (antici-

TABLE 12.1
Clinical Domains Indicating Inpatient Treatment of Addiction

I. Medical or psychiatric disorders caused by chemical dependence
   A. Medical conditions (e.g., acute pancreatitis, withdrawal seizures)
   B. Organic Brain Syndromes (e.g., delirium tremens, hallucinosis, severe withdrawal)
II. Medical or psychiatric disorders independent of chemical dependence that are adversely affected by alcohol or drugs or that compromise the person's ability to utilize treatment
   A. Medical conditions in which significant exacerbation is likely if chemical dependence is not treated (e.g., diabetes)
   B. Psychiatric disorders in which there is likely to be significant exacerbation if chemical dependence is not treated (e.g., bipolar disorder)
   C. Medical or psychiatric disorders that impair the patient's ability to utilize chemical dependencetreatment (e.g., cirrhosis, psychosis, severe personality disorder)
III. Environmental conditions that compromise a safe undertaking of treatment in an outpatient setting
   A. A home or other living setting with actively addicted individual(s)
   B. Chaotic, dysfunctional family environment that undermines treatment goals
   C. Intense interpersonal conflict that compromises treatment
IV. Manifestations of chemical dependence that deter safe, timely treatment in an outpatient setting
   A. Extreme denial and treatment resistance
   B. Potentially harmful alcohol- or drug-driven behavior
   C. Inability to abstain on outpatient basis

pated or actual) determines whether inpatient treatment is necessary. Idiosyncratic intoxication is questionable as a valid syndrome; but if violent behavior with amnestic episodes occurs, hospitalization is certainly indicated. The other syndromes—intoxication, alcohol amnestic disorder, and alcohol dementia—are not in themselves indications for inpatient treatment. The behavioral, social, and psychiatric implications of these disorders must be assessed for each patient.

2. *Medical or psychiatric conditions that are independent of substance abuse but are adversely and actively affected by alcohol or drug use and impair the ability to undertake treatment.* For example, an exacerbation of a seizure disorder, uncontrolled diabetes, or failure to comply with medical treatment.

Psychiatric disorders can follow the same route, in that a patient with bipolar disorder may fail to comply with a medical regimen. Similarly, depression can be acutely exacerbated by heavy alcohol or other drug use.

A 37-year-old professional woman with a chronic history of dysthy-
mic disorder and suicidal ideation experienced periodic relapses of
binge drinking. Initially, drinking seemed to relieve her depression,
but as her alcohol use extended over several days, her depression
deepened. A serious suicide attempt by carbon monoxide poison-
ing was the result of one binge.

Patients with significant psychopathology (including severe personality disorder, bipolar disorder, and psychosis) may not be sufficiently
compliant to utilize outpatient chemical dependence treatment modalities. Inpatient treatment is necessary to resolve or stabilize the acute
psychopathological conditions and to engage the patient in the recovery
process.

3. *Environmental conditions that compromise a safe undertaking of treatment
in an outpatient setting.* At the simplest level, treatment may not be available in a given geographic area, and inpatient placement is the only
available modality.

More complex, clinically, is the situation where other family members
are actively addicted and do not support efforts to seek treatment or
fail to provide a "safe" environment for the family member seeking
treatment.

Other situations likely to necessitate initial inpatient treatment are the
potential for physical or sexual abuse, chaotic families that undermine
treatment efforts, and intensive interpersonal conflicts that interfere with
the patient's ability to focus on chemical dependence treatment. Further,
some professionals and executives are so driven by achievement or compulsive attention to their spheres of influence that they cannot free the
energy and attention necessary to interrupt alcohol or drug dependence.
When such career pressure, self-imposed or not, is operating, inpatient
treatment may be necessary to break the hold of compulsive and controlling work demands.

A 55-year-old, self-employed businessman accepted his internist's
recommendations for alcoholism treatment after early cirrhosis was
diagnosed, but he could not find the time to start treatment. When
his tremors precluded his ability to use the telephone, he finally
accepted inpatient care for detoxification. After three days, he left
the hospital prematurely and failed to attend a scheduled evening
outpatient program. Time and travel were again the factors inhibiting treatment compliance.

4. *Manifestations of alcoholism and drug dependence that deter safe, timely
treatment in an outpatient setting.* This domain addresses the dynamics of
the disease of addiction in contrast to the above domains, which ad-

dressed medical and psychiatric complications, comorbid conditions, and family and environmental contingencies.

Specifically, the defense mechanism of denial and other expressions of treatment resistance may require the intensity of an inpatient treatment milieu to arrest substance use and drug-driven behavior in a safe and timely manner. Patients manifesting extensive treatment resistance often need the blend of support and confrontation provided on a 24-hour basis in an inpatient setting to overcome attitudes and affects associated with facing chemical dependence. Fear of stigma, guilt and shame, losses, lack of confidence about being able to stop drinking, and uncertainty as to how to cope without drugs are the building blocks for the fortress of denial, which is so destructive for the chemically dependent patient.

An inpatient unit with a multidisciplinary treatment team can create an intensive therapeutic milieu suitable for significant defense modification. If further morbidity is to be arrested, the chronic relapsing patient may benefit, indeed require, an extended period of treatment in such a unit.

Modification of defenses goes beyond overcoming initial denial, because denial is a layered process. Initial denial can be lessened or overcome as the patient is confronted about his or her experience with alcohol and drugs and as an understanding of addiction is gained. In other words, the alcoholic patient "admits" he or she is alcoholic. But, the second layer of denial (not well-appreciated by most alcoholics in early recovery) is an unawareness that one is vulnerable for relapse. The continuing attraction of alcohol and the experienced need for alcohol is often minimized by the patient, who wants to believe he or she is now well. If experience with subsequent relapses does not penetrate this layer of denial, pathological narcissistic defenses may be operating, and a longer inpatient stay may be required. Even deeper is denial of the affect and meaning associated with the losses and consequences of one's history of chronic addiction. This level of denial is best untouched in the early stages of recovery and can be treated with psychotherapy as a painful past becomes integrated with a sober future.

Modification of defenses addresses more than denial. Defense modification is an effort to lessen the reliance on narcissistic defenses such as grandiosity and self-sufficiency. An intensive inpatient milieu can break down the walls of self-containment and enhance the patient's responsiveness to the social field. The social field of an inpatient unit includes the staff and other patients. This rich interaction, on a 24-hour basis, confronts the patient with his or her characteristic style of relating and promotes altered behavior. As self-sufficiency ("I don't need anybody") and grandiosity ("I can do this myself") are lessened, therapy and 12-step programs can become more influential.

The modification effort also includes a strengthening of certain ego functions. Some alcoholic patients fail to recover because they are unable to identify, regulate, and tolerate strong affect (Khantzian, 1981). When faced with anger, frustration, and disappointment, the affect is experienced as unbearable—or at least highly undesirable—and is discharged through behavior (for example, drinking). An inpatient treatment experience stimulates affects, including frustration and anger. The observations of other patients and the constructive interaction with staff provide a mirror for the patient, which may reflect previously unrecognized defenses and behavior patterns. The patient learns, through day-by-day experience, that feelings can be identified, regulated, and tolerated without the use of alcohol. Along with specific coping skills, a sense of mastery is gained.

Impulsiveness and passivity are commonly observed in an inpatient milieu. The containment provided by the inpatient structure allows safe exploration of precipitants of impulsiveness and the possibility of learning alternative behaviors. Often, poor self-care skills are manifested in failure to complete assigned tasks, poor hygiene, poor eating habits, disregard of medication schedules, reckless use of exercise equipment, and inattention to scheduled activities. As the patient's behavior patterns become apparent, usually within a matter of days, the expectations of staff and peers and supportive confrontation begin to alter these behavioral deficits. A strengthening of ego functions can be expected in a relatively brief period of time, as both passivity and impulsivity are countered and modified by exposure to healthier models of behavior.

The use of an inpatient unit for defense modification does not overlook the fact that the bulk of such modification occurs over months and years of outpatient treatment, including use of 12-step programs. The role of the inpatient unit is to discern the areas of functioning that are most likely to compromise the recovery process and to provide the patient, as well as the outpatient staff, with a cognitive map for focused follow-up care.

In addition to their resistance to treatment, some chemically dependent patients—despite sound intentions—cannot obtain an initial foothold on sobriety while living in their usual environment or in an environment unprotected from alcohol or drugs. Conditioned responses and cravings undermine their efforts to discontinue using. Under such circumstances, the patient's best interests are served by inpatient placement, so a stable start to abstinence can be obtained.

OVERARCHING VARIABLES THAT INFLUENCE TREATMENT PLACEMENT

The decision of whether to conduct treatment in an outpatient or inpatient setting necessarily will be guided by consideration of the following four variables: acuteness, ability, safety, and stabilization.

Acuteness refers to a need for urgent intervention and implies actual or potential severity. If a clinician determines that the conditions in any of the domains discussed earlier are acute, inpatient placement should be favored.

Ability refers to whether or not the alcohol-dependent patient has the judgment or capacity to assume the responsibility inherent in outpatient care. Patients unable to achieve an alcohol- or drug-free state or those sufficiently impaired by medical or psychiatric disorders, which preclude their ability to follow an oupatient regimen rationally and predictably, require inpatient placement.

Safety for the patient and others is a paramount concern when selecting treatment options. If exhibited behavior is clearly unsafe or further use of alcohol carries a high probability of deterioration, safety considerations may dictate inpatient treatment.

Stabilization refers to the process whereby the acuteness or the complexity of the clinical presentation is resolved so that the patient can be expected to comply with outpatient treatment. Stabilization may be accomplished on an outpatient basis. Whether or not stabilization requires inpatient or outpatient placement can be determined by assessing the acuteness, safety factors, the ability and resources of the patient, and the demands placed on the patient by his or her environment.

THE CURRENT GOALS OF INPATIENT TREATMENT

From these previously discussed domains—acuteness, ability, safety, and stabilization—a simplified statement of the goals of inpatient treatment is derived:

1. treatment of withdrawal states or other acute organic brain syndromes
2. stabilization of medical and psychiatric conditions
3. refinement of medical and psychiatric diagnoses
4. modification of defenses through lessening of denial—that is, acceptance of Step One of Alcoholics Anonymous ("We admitted we were powerless over alcohol—that our lives had become unmanageable.")

5. assessment of family and family education
6. establishment of long-term treatment goals

ADVANTAGES OF INPATIENT TREATMENT

When inpatient treatment is used to address the full spectrum of a patient's needs, beyond acute medical or psychiatric conditions, some very specific benefits are derived. Further research is necessary to determine whether these benefits can be obtained as effectively through outpatient or other less costly approaches. Among these benefits is protection from continuing alcohol and drug use. Treatment cannot be effective as long as the patient continues to use.

Second, inpatient treatment enables the patient to be removed from his or her usual environment and responsibilities and, as a consequence, to be in a position to attend exclusively to his or her problem with alcohol or drugs. The usual distractions of everyday life that may support the patient's denial are eliminated by hospitalization.

Third, inpatient treatment provides a more concentrated and intense treatment experience than can be attained in outpatient settings. Such intensity is often necessary to break down denial, enabling the patient to gain an understanding of the disease concept of chemical dependence.

Fourth, inpatient treatment provides conditions necessary for the task of strengthening the ego. The chemically dependent patient is regressed. He or she is functioning with limited impulse control and a diminished capacity for adequate self-care. The inpatient milieu provides an auxiliary ego. The patient often needs these external controls until the internalization of self-care processes can be accomplished. A well-designed and well-functioning inpatient program provides consistency, instills a sense of responsibility, modifies impulsivity, discourages passivity, teaches the ability to delay gratification, assists the patient in gaining a sense of patience, offers healthy modalities for relaxation and normal regression, and provides a model for self-care behaviors. The external controls in an inpatient environment enable the patient to avoid alcohol or drugs. The support provided by the staff enables the patient to learn that feelings of frustration and acute need for relief can be tolerated, delayed, and directed into healthier forms of expression than that provided by the immediate gratification of alcohol and drugs.

Fifth, keeping the patient in treatment has always been a major focus of chemical dependency programs—an appropriate goal because length in treatment correlates with positive outcome (Smart, 1978). Inpatient treatment increases the likelihood of a patient's remaining in treatment. Outpatients can quit treatment simply by not showing up, and high attrition rates in outpatient settings have been documented (Baeklund, Lundwall, & Shanahan, 1973; Seixas, 1983). For an inpatient to quit treatment, a discussion of that decision is required with staff and peers, a process that often exposes faulty judgment and promotes reasoned reconsideration.

Sixth, patients often need to be removed from an environment where alcohol and drugs are available and use is reinforced by living conditions or through interpersonal associations. Inpatient treatment provides an opportunity to contain the patient in a safe environment, and thereby interrupt impulsive behavior and continued substance abuse.

The inpatient setting provides an intensive treatment milieu that may not be available on an outpatient basis. A skilled multidisciplinary team interacts with and observes a patient over each 24-hour period. The patient's characteristic defenses become understood by staff and patient alike and are subject to modification through confrontation and intense self-examination. Interaction with peers better enables each patient to judge his or her degree of progress toward recovery.

ADVANTAGES OF OUTPATIENT TREATMENT

Outpatient treatment should be utilized if the clinical conditions are suitable for a less intense level of care. There are distinct advantages to outpatient placement when treatment goals can be accomplished in such a setting:

1. *Lower cost.* Expenses are reduced by 50 to 75% for most outpatient programs. Financial hardship to the patient and his/her family often is avoided and often limited insurance benefits for inpatient treatment are preserved for emergency use.

2. *Treatment can be extended.* The financial feasibility of extending treatment over a period of months is increased by utilization of outpatient programs. The patient and family are able to endure more easily the less intense outpatient approach. The time and energy put into treatment is spread over weeks and months, and as progress is experienced, this investment of time, energy, and resources is appreciated.

3. *Recovery process can be integrated with family life and life style.* Outpatient treatment confronts the patient with the task of facing elements of family and personal life style that may compromise treatment goals. The necessary changes are then worked on and supported by the treatment team. The importance of finding leisure time activities that are free of substance use or that minimize relapse potential is confronted immediately. Family members may need to alter their drinking, as well as learn patterns of communication that foster trust, autonomy, and minimize

dysfunction. Progress in these areas can be evaluated day by day as the patient experiences his personal milieu.

4. *Recovery process can be integrated into professional role.* Outpatient treatment allows the patient an opportunity to evaluate the impact of professional life style, work elements, and assumption of responsibilities on his or her efforts not to drink or use drugs. The impact of the professional role on substance use can be appreciated day by day. The struggle over time allotment is confronted immediately. This confrontation enables the patient, with the help of the staff, to establish the priorities necessary for a successful recovery. The chances of having a lesser role in an organization or incurring a sense of wariness from colleagues is reduced when treatment is able to continue while the patient maintains his or her professional obligations.

5. *Reduction of stigma.* Stigma associated with treatment unfortunately still exists and can be expressed in many ways including extreme forms such as loss of job or being passed over for promotions or other sources of professional achievement and gratification. Assuming the patient can be stabilized safely in an outpatient setting and has the ability to follow a treatment plan, a lengthy absence from work can be avoided.

In Appendix B a schedule for inpatient and outpatient treatment, as well as a family program, is provided. The inpatient schedule may also be utilized by outpatients in a day hospital program.

CHAPTER 13

Specific Treatments

The treatment offered in organized outpatient and inpatient rehabilitation programs (see Appendix B) provides a core of knowledge, both cognitive and affective, and points the patient toward abstinence and recovery. Group process and milieu dynamics predominate at the expense of individual needs. The importance of meeting individual treatment needs is emphasized in this chapter, which outlines the use of psychotherapy, medication, and monitoring. These specific treatments add to and complement the structured approach of rehabilitation programs.

Before embarking on further consideration of treatment, it is necessary to introduce Miller's (1989) concept of "self-matching." Patients from a professional background can be expected to be sophisticated, discerning and, at times, subject to feelings of entitlement. They will expect that recommendations for treatment and their investments of time and money be justified. This challenge is effectively met by the concept of "self-matching." Self-matching does not mean that the chemically dependent patient simply chooses a course of treatment that suits his or her convenience. Rather, self-matching is a process of informed choice. The patient is provided with an array of options, and is given a description of each with an explanation of each one's potential benefit.

The clinician's opinion as to the advisability of any given option for this particular patient is of paramount importance. Guided self-selection is known to bolster motivation and improve compliance (Miller, 1989). Self-matching becomes a collaborative effort between the clinician and the patient and is an initial step in developing a therapeutic alliance. The professionalism of the clinician is communicated not only by the respect shown the patient through encouraging his or her participation in treatment matching, but also by the clinician's display of knowledge of each treatment option and its suitability for this particular individual.

Following is a brief review of the usefulness of psychotherapy, medication, and monitoring in the recovery process.

159

PSYCHOTHERAPY

Psychotherapy can play a critical role in the treatment of substance abusing patients (Woody, McLellan, Luborsky, & O'Brien, 1986). Individual psychotherapy with chemically dependent patients requires some specific behaviors on the part of the therapist (Nace, 1987):

1. *Active.* The therapist should be prepared to ask questions, provide answers, and intervene by involving family members or by utilizing a hospital. A passive stance in the interest of an unfolding of dynamically related material is called for only under specific circumstances, such as when the patient is not endangering his health by drinking or when the patient can tolerate the frustration of relatively little feedback from the therapist.

2. *Educative.* The therapist should be able to explain the disease of alcoholism or addiction to the patient. The characteristic responses, resistances, and experiences of chemically dependent people should be taught to the patient as therapy proceeds. Literature on alcoholism or drug abuse should be available for the patient to read between sessions. The patient's reactions to and understanding of the reading material can be explored in therapy sessions.

3. *Confrontational.* The therapist needs to be open with the patient about his observations. Patients who are drinking or using drugs but who keep therapy appointments need to be told of the risks to health and social functioning their behavior entails. They cannot be allowed to assume that they will get better simply by keeping appointments.

4. *Countertransference openness.* The therapist needs to retain awareness of his or her feelings toward the patient. If advice, recommendations, and treatment efforts are ignored or devalued by the patient, the therapist should explore these issues within himself or herself, and then explain these concerns to the patient. The therapist needs to avoid a build up of anger, disgust, or derision toward the patient. He or she should strive to communicate countertransference responses as tangible expressions of caring. Such openness helps patients appreciate their effect on others in a nonjudgmental setting. It also reveals the therapist as a real person, who is comfortable with his or her feelings and who is accepting of himself or herself as a less than omnipotent and less than perfect being.

These behaviors on the part of a therapist have as their purpose the termination of substance abuse and the consolidation of a relationship. The therapist is asking, indeed insisting, that the patient deprive himself or herself. It is necessary to be explicit about this: "The therapist must not sidestep his depriving role; instead he must freely acknowledge it and let therapy begin right there" (Tiebout, 1973, p. 6). With experience, therapists become more aware that chemically dependent patients will accept limitations, including abstinence from alcohol and drugs (Dodes, 1984). Active, open concern expressed by the therapist serves as an auxiliary form of self-care, temporarily complementing the deficit in self-care described in Chapter 10.

Khantzian (1988) delineates four functions of the therapist when treating substance abusing patients:

1. *Control.* Provided by such diverse techniques as monitoring urine drug screens, observing the taking of medication, and doing a structured review of the individual's life history and history of substance abuse.

2. *Containment.* Curbing the tendency to overdo; addressing and guiding the patient as impulsiveness and impatience are experienced.

3. *Contact.* A consistent and predictable availability of the therapist enlarges the patient's social field and lessens isolation.

4. *Comfort.* The "safe" environment of therapy fosters self-revelation and, thereby, lowers narcissistic defenses of self-sufficiency and grandiosity.

These functions are compatible with and, indeed, imply an active, sometimes directive role for the therapist. The utility of applying these "4 C's" (Khantzian, 1988), as well as confrontation and education (Nace, 1987) is further illustrated by "network therapy" for addiction (Galanter, 1993). In "network therapy," the therapist involves some of the patient's social system (for example, spouse, family members, coworkers, or friends) in the treatment process. Therapy sessions may involve such significant others in an effort to increase commitment to treatment and compliance.

It is in the first year of recovery that the therapist necessarily remains in such an active role and largely directs therapeutic efforts at themes related to substance abuse, including consequences of drug use, related relationship problems, and painful affects. A focus on a "core" issue in a patient's life has been shown to increase treatment efficacy (Luborsky & Crits-Cristoph, 1989). As abstinence is gained and maintained, the therapist's role and function can shift (Kaufman & Reoux, 1988). This gradual shift is illustrated in Figure 13.1.

The "early" and "late" phases of psychotherapy are diagrammed in Tables 13.1 and 13.2. "Early" refers to the first year of recovery but may be extended beyond one year if the patient continues to have relapses.

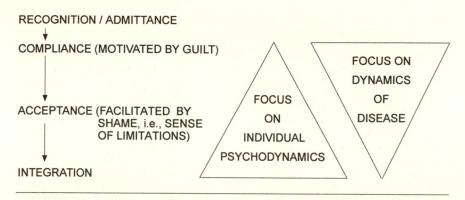

RECOGNITION / ADMITTANCE

COMPLIANCE (MOTIVATED BY GUILT)

ACCEPTANCE (FACILITATED BY
SHAME, i.e., SENSE
OF LIMITATIONS)

INTEGRATION

FOCUS
ON
INDIVIDUAL
PSYCHODYNAMICS

FOCUS ON
DYNAMICS
OF
DISEASE

Figure 13.1. The Focus of Therapy Changes in Parallel with the Recovery Process

Each phase has two core issues or goals, with the early phase being more specific in terms of goals—for example, abstinence from alcohol and drugs and development of specific ego strengths. The "later" phase of psychotherapy is more open ended in terms of goals—for example, spiritual growth and insight.

The themes outlined in early and late phases of psychotherapy can be addressed in either individual or group psychotherapy. Group psychotherapy holds a time-honored position in the treatment of substance use disorders (Zimberg, 1982). Over the years, group techniques have been adopted for substance abuse treatment (Brown & Yalom, 1977; Khantzian, Halliday, & McAuliffe, 1990; Nace, 1987).

The advantages of group psychotherapy for chemically dependent patients include a greater capacity to recognize denial. The tendency to minimize, rationalize, or deny one's dependence on alcohol or drugs is often apparent to the group as fellow members describe their alcohol and drug experiences. Patients see defensiveness more easily in others than in themselves, but gain greater self-awareness through these observations.

A second advantage is the ability to "keep the memory green." This expression refers to the importance of remaining aware of the consequences alcohol and drugs have had in one's life. Sharing experiences related to drug and alcohol use in a group provides a reminder of one's past and reinforces current commitments to treatment.

Third, substance-abusing patients have a reputation for being skilled manipulators. A group of such patients, therefore, can detect a manipulative process in a fellow member quickly.

Confrontation provides a fourth advantage. Chemically dependent patients can talk to each other in a way that is difficult for others to do.

TABLE 13.1
Early Phase of Psychotherapy: Two Synchronous Goals
Abstinence ⇆ Ego Strengthening

Abstinence	*Ego strengthening*

1. Understanding chemical dependence as a disease:
  a. Neurochemical effects of drugs
  b. Recognition of denial
  c. The altered and conflicted behavior that has been drug/alcohol driven
  d. Guilt and shame that are felt from being chemically dependent and from consequences of drug or alcohol use
  e. Understanding of craving
  f. The regressive effect of chemical dependence (impulsiveness, passivity)
  g. Loss of control, that is, the inability to predictably regulate the intake of alcohol or other intoxicating substances
2. Relapse behaviors
  a. Lack of honesty
  b. Less than full commitment to recovery
  c. Failure to keep treatment and recovery priorities primary
3. Avoiding cross addiction
  a. Abstinence from all intoxicating substances, not just those on which the patient was previously dependent
4. Accepting/grieving loss of use of alcohol/drugs
	1. Self-care skills
	  a. Ability to initiate behavior that interrupts relapse
	  b. Understand cause–consequence connections
	  c. Improved judgment
	  d. Improved reality testing
	2. Self-governance, same as 1 above plus ability to accept and respond to social field
	3. Affect recognition, regulation, and tolerance
	  a. Capacity to identify feelings
	  b. Ability to modulate responses to affect
	  c. Ability to endure or tolerate feelings without acting out

One patient can confront another with more vigor and certainty because his or her comments can be paraphrased by "I know, I've been there myself"; "I did the same thing myself"; "I learned I had to do things differently if I wanted to stay sober."

Fifth, the intensity of group therapy allows a wide display of feelings to unfold. The chemically dependent patient is in a setting where recognition of his or her feelings may be facilitated, and there is sufficient support to help each member tolerate strong affect.

TABLE 13.2
Late Phase of Psychotherapy: Two Synchronous Goals
Spiritual Development ⇆ Insight

Spiritual development	*Insight*
1. Gratitude: "I cannot drink/drug."	1. Decreased use of narcissistic defenses such as grandiosity, sufficiency, self-containment
2. Release: Freedom from compulsion to use drugs or alcohol	2. Process and integrate losses resulting from drug and alcohol use, for example, health, relationships, career, family, financial
3. Humility: The ability to learn about oneself through relationships with others	
4. Tolerance: Acceptance of limitations of others and of oneself	3. Explore and understand the meaning of chemical dependence in one's life; causal influences; psychodynamic factors
5. Renunciation: A giving up of attachments to things	

Sixth, a group may enhance the development of trust. Each group therapy session should add to the sense of trust that is vital for therapeutic work to proceed. Group therapy with substance-abusing patients allows a modification of the characteristic reactive grandiosity to take place. A therapeutic breakthrough occurs when the chemically dependent patient takes the risk (trust) to share his or her ambivalence about drinking or drugs. By trusting the group with this information ("I still want to get wasted"; "I did get drunk last week."), self-sufficiency begins to evaporate. Acknowledgment of one's feelings or behavior is tantamount to an acceptance of help, information, or guidance from others and, thus, lessens pathological narcissistic defenses.

As with individual therapy, the phases of recovery described earlier are recognizable in the group setting. One of the advantages of a group approach is the power of example that the group can provide. The patient who is just recognizing his or her alcoholism, or who is in the compliance phase, feels the contrast between himself and the patient who has accepted his dependence.

In summary, by its intrinsic process and dynamics group therapy lends itself to the treatment of substance use disorders. Its acceptability by alcohol and drug dependent patients is also worth noting. The less intense transference to a therapist avoids premature exposure of emotions connected to competition, envy, dependency, or projection, which may interrupt a therapeutic alliance. Group therapy is also less costly, and its acceptability may be enhanced further by the patient's experience of peer support as gained through A.A. and N.A.

Common Themes in Group Psychotherapy

For nearly ten years, I have facilitated group psychotherapy sessions with professionals. Most of these groups have been for physicians, but some groups involved a mixture of attorneys, pharmacists, nurses, executives, and physicians. From this experience, I have noticed at least four themes salient to the recovery process. These themes are, of course, only fragments of group process but are highlighted both for their recurring nature and for their clinical relevance.

Occupational Concerns

From the onset of the discovery or exposure of a chemical dependency, professional patients fear that their careers will be ruined if the presence of this condition becomes known to others. Accepting treatment is often hindered and delayed because of a fear of exposure. The professional expects his or her reputation to decline or be permanently destroyed. Loss of job, income, or referrals is expected. In some instances, losses are severe. A license may be suspended, a staff appointment terminated, or the professional may be fired. If case finding is reasonably early, losses are usually minimal. In my experience, professionals who succeed in overcoming denial and who follow a successful program of recovery either do not experience major occupational consequences or, if they do, they recapture their former standing with time.

An advantage of group psychotherapy is that the experience of the more advanced members helps allay these occupational fears. The newcomer to the group sees others who may be six to 12 or more months into recovery. It is apparent that these men and women are thriving or, if not thriving, are overcoming the obstacles in their path. Such obstacles may include gaining hospital privileges, dealing with a malpractice suit, going through a divorce or child custody battle, reporting to State Boards, or facing hostility or distrust from colleagues.

A second occupational concern is the belief that "I can never have a bad day." The physician, nurse, or other professional is very self-conscious upon return to work. They expect to be scrutinized. They often live in fear that others will think they are drinking or taking drugs again. At times, this scrutiny is real and insensitive. Even so, the professional's self-consciousness is the major contributor to this form of stress. With time, both the professional and his colleagues appreciate that fatigue, irritability, forgetfulness, or variations in mood do not imply relapse and do not require confrontation. Often, upon return to the work environment, the professional appreciates the need to apply assertiveness skills. Group therapy is an excellent modality to acquire, practice, and gain confidence in being appropriately assertive.

For example, a physician found his clinical colleagues were closely monitoring his chart work. Week after week, small details were brought to his attention—details of no real consequence. The group suggested he confront his medical partners. The physician asked to meet with several of his partners to explain his problems with their scrutiny. He described how this made him feel, and then reviewed with them the safeguards built into his aftercare treatment and monitoring program. In other words, if he were relapsing, mechanisms were in place (for example, frequent unannounced urine drug screens) to detect the emergence of a problem. He felt better about "clearing the air" and both he and his partners developed a more open pattern of communication.

A third occupational concern is the embarrassment at having to report and explain a history of substance abuse and treatment. On applications or in interviews, the topic may come up. The best policy, clearly, is to be forthright and honest about one's history of chemical dependence, or psychiatric disorders, or any other medical matter. It is not necessary, however, to lead with your chin. I have seen many physicians, when invited to apply to a staff or interview for a position, prior to the interview and usually over the telephone, promptly report that they are in recovery, etc. My recommendation is that they participate in the interview process first, so that the prospective employer or partner can get a sense of them as a person and a professional. If rapport has been established, then their personal and medical history can be explained. Of course, if asked about such matters prior to or at anytime during an interview, forthright, honest answers should be given. The recovering professional's identity encompasses more than the identity of being an "alcoholic" or an "addict."

Family Concerns

Guilt and regret over past behaviors as they affected children, spouse, or parents is an omnipresent theme across the early years of recovery and, perhaps, beyond. Group therapy allows one to share these feelings. The capacity of the group to be empathic with concerns over the past softens the harshness of self-criticism. Further, the group experience enables one to gain a perspective on acts of omission or commission. Others, too, feel remorse over lost time with children, infidelity, abuse, and self-centeredness. A useful caveat is the reminder that the past should serve as a guidepost, not a whipping post.

Painful feelings from the past may pre-date the experience of the addiction. Some patients discover chronic feelings of resentment toward a parent. The feelings may derive from having been placed prematurely in a caretaker role while a child or adolescent. Others feel they did everything right, were the "family hero," but were taken for granted while attention focused on a troubled sibling. Some have memories of physical or sexual abuse at the hands of parents or others.

The here and now of day-by-day sobriety offers many patients painful emotional discord. Some are involved in divorce proceedings or child custody procedures. Most face rebuilding relationships. Trust has to be regained and this is a slow process. Disappointment in the spouse or other family members commonly occurs as the recovering chemically dependent patient feels misunderstood by them. For example, a young physician had been threatened with a lawsuit by the relative of a patient. Shaken, he confided his anxiety to his wife. Her reaction was to express fear that he would now promptly relapse. The physician had hoped that his wife would share his burden but was confronted instead with doubts.

Competition for time is an issue. Family members may resent the recovering person's absence for A.A. meetings or therapy sessions. Conflict over necessary recovery efforts may result. Group therapy often serves as a holding environment, wherein the recovering professional can sustain commitment to the change process, learn patience with others and himself or herself, and obtain practical guidance and advice on day-to-day issues.

Individual Concerns

The ability to ask for help requires continuing attention. Professional patients, especially physicians, delay reporting symptoms or personal concerns. A counterdependent attitude is common. For example, an older physician developed symptoms of angina. He delayed consulting a cardiologist and never did follow through with an angiogram. Another physician reported in group psychotherapy that he had been profoundly depressed for weeks, yet he postponed calling the psychiatrist who had successfully treated his depression in the past. In both instances, the therapy group urged and reinforced prompt attention to health-care matters.

A second expression of counterdependence is seen in relationship to a spouse. A reluctance to communicate one's feelings and report needs is readily apparent. Males, especially, wish to be understood and empathically responded to without the burden of direct communication. As a result frustration with the spouse is commonly reported.

In addition to counterdependent themes, professionals present with a heightened self-consciousness of stigma. The expectation that others will remain aware, or will all too quickly recall their troubled years haunts them, independent of a successful return to professional activities. When a referral goes to a colleague or a client sends some business to a different attorney, the thought occurs that one is doubted because of the past history of chemical dependence. This sense of stigma presents itself even when rational explanations for the referral patterns are apparent. Fears that one will be the first to be let go, or that one has to be "extra-competent" are burdens often borne over the initial years of recovery. A supportive group therapy experience is effective in toning down such anxieties.

Priorities

A fourth theme commonly addressed in group psychotherapy is that of "priorities," which means necessity to order one's life in a way that supports recovery, reduces stress, and serves to prevent relapse. Again, time demands are a major consideration. Tension between professional, family, and personal needs is inevitable. It remains necessary to emphasize adherence to a recovery plan: regular, consistent A.A. or N.A. attendance, including 12-step groups specific for each profession (if available); adherence to therapy appointments; use of medication as prescribed and not making changes without the permission of one's physician; utilization of A.A. or N.A. sponsor.

The priority concern is best settled by "scheduling" leisure time and by curbing tendencies to take on more and more work. For example, one young physician, as part of his aftercare treatment plan, agreed to resign from the staff of at least one hospital in the community and was mandated to take off a weekday afternoon for golf. This plan was supported by his county medical society impaired physicians committee, despite his initial protests, and proved to be beneficial. The need to save time for children and family activities, as well as exclusive time with the spouse cannot be overemphasized. This point applies equally to male and female professionals. It may seem trite to emphasize the importance of "scheduling" time for the family, but, in fact, when time pressure builds up, the family is usually cut out before professional activities. The recovering professional is learning to take care of himself or herself, learning to set limits, and time allotment and prioritizing are proving grounds for these tasks. As the physician cuts back on professional demands, stress reduction automatically occurs. The reinforcement provided by a closer relationship with one's children and spouse and/or the development of new interests or hobbies sustains this constructive change in behavior.

Again, in either the group or individual therapy setting, the therapist has the opportunity to monitor and process each of these themes.

MEDICATION

Three circumstances warrant consideration of the use of medication in patients with a substance use disorder: (1) associated organic brain syndromes; (2) comorbid psychiatric disorders ("dual diagnosis"); and (3) adjunctive treatment for the substance use disorder itself.

Organic Brain Syndromes

Organic brain syndromes originate in both rising and declining blood levels of abused substances. The following organic brain syndromes may be encountered in a substance-abusing patient: intoxication, idiosyncratic intoxication, withdrawal, withdrawal delirium, delirium, delusional disorder, hallucinosis, amnestic disorder, mood disorder, posthallucinogen perception disorder, and dementia. Table 13.3 lists the drugs associated with each organic brain syndrome.

Intoxication is undoubtedly the most commonly occurring organic brain syndrome but is only occasionally observed in the clinical setting. The most commonly treated organic brain syndrome is withdrawal. Appendix C outlines treatment approaches for the withdrawal syndromes.

Comorbid Psychiatric Disorders ("Dual Diagnosis")

Over the past decade, the considerable overlap between substance use and psychiatric disorders has been documented. Documentation is found in epidemiologic (Helzer & Pryzbeck, 1988) and clinical studies (Hesselbrock, Meyer, & Keener, 1985; Mirin, Weiss, & Michael, 1988; Penick, Powell, Liskow, Jackson, & Nickel, 1988; Weller & Halikas, 1985). Reviews of the prevalence, diagnosis, and treatment of "dual disorders" are available (Dackis & Gold, 1992; Mirin & Weiss, 1991; O'Connell, 1990).

The extent of psychiatric comorbidity in professionals with a substance use disorder has not been determined. Of the professions discussed in this book, only attorneys were found to exceed the expected incidence of major depression. Ten percent of attorneys, using nationwide epidemiologic data, met criteria for major depression compared to an expected

TABLE 13.3
Substance-Induced Disorders

A. Occurring During Intoxication By Substance

Delirium	Psychosis (hallucinations or delusions—not part of delirium)	Mood disorders (manic, depressive or mixed symptoms)	Anxiety disorders	Sleep disorders	Sexual dysfunction
alcohol	alcohol	alcohol	alcohol	alcohol	alcohol
amphetamines	amphetamines	amphetamines	amphetamines	amphetamines	amphetamines
cannabis	cannabis	cocaine	caffeine	caffeine	cocaine
cocaine	cocaine	hallucinogens	cannabis	cocaine	opioids
hallucinogens	hallucinogens	inhalants	cocaine	opioids	sedatives/hypnotics/anxiolytics
inhalants	inhalants	opioids	hallucinogens	sedatives/hypnotics/anxiolytics	
opioids	opioids	phencyclidine	inhalants		
phencyclidine	phencyclidine	sedatives/hypnotics/anxiolytics	phencyclidine		
sedative/hypnotics/anxiolytics	sedatives/hypnotics/anxiolytics				

B. Occurring During Withdrawal

Delirium	Psychosis	Mood disorders	Anxiety disorders	Sleep disorders
alcohol	alcohol	alcohol	alcohol	alcohol
sedatives/hypnotics/anxiolytics	sedatives/hypnotics/anxiolytics	amphetamines	cocaine	amphetamines
		cocaine	sedatives/hypnotics/anxiolytics	cocaine
		sedatives/hypnotics/anxiolytics		opioids
				sedatives/hypnotics/anxiolytics

C. Post-Acute Syndromes

Amnestic disorder	Dementia	Hallucinogen persisting perception disorder (flashbacks)
alcohol	alcohol	hallucinogens
sedatives/hypnotics/anxiolytics	inhalants	
	sedatives/hypnotics/anxiolytics	

(Modified from DSM-IV)

rate of 3 to 5% (Eaton et al., 1990), but the study did not address overlap of depression with alcohol or drug dependence.

A study of physicians admitted to a private psychiatric hospital (Nace, Davis, & Hunter, 1995) found a high rate of "dual diagnosis." Of the physicians admitted for substance abuse treatment, 57% had an additional Axis I psychiatric disorder (see APA, 1987 for description of diagnostic Axes). Of the physicians admitted for psychiatric treatment, 22% had a substance use disorder. Of particular interest is the focused nature of the comorbidity in this physician sample. For example, affective disorders were the predominant nonsubstance use diagnosis, with 93% of physicians admitted to a psychiatric unit having an affective disorder as the primary diagnosis. Of the physicians admitted to the substance abuse unit—if an additional Axis I disorder were present—it was an affective disorder in 96% of cases. In the majority of these physicians, the affective disorder was a unipolar depression. Thus, when comorbidity was present, it almost always involved depression.

Personality disorder also was commonly diagnosed in the physician sample. Sixty percent of the physicians—56% of the abuse group and 65% of the psychiatric group—carried an Axis II diagnosis. Of the 55 physicians diagnosed with a personality disorder, the following types of personality disorder were found: obsessive-compulsive (N = 21); personality disorder, not otherwise specified (N = 14); narcissistic (N = 11); passive-aggressive (N = 7); borderline (N = 1); and antisocial (N = 1). Thus, in this sample of physicians, there were fewer of the more malignant personality disorder diagnoses, such as antisocial and borderline. These data (Nace, Davis, & Hunter, 1995), because they were obtained in an inpatient sample, would be expected to incur a higher incidence of dual disorder than might be expected in professionals treated in outpatient settings.

The term *dual disorder* most typically refers to the patient who is both currently chemically dependent and also meets criteria, for example, for an anxiety or affective disorder. The designation dual disorder can apply also to the patient with a history of chemical dependence and an additional psychiatric disorder when only one of the conditions is clinically manifested. For example, a recovered alcoholic may develop a bipolar disorder or major depression after months or years of sobriety. If the affective disorder developed subsequent to the history of alcohol dependence, the alcohol dependence is "primary" and the affective disorder "secondary." Obviously, both require continuing attention.

It should be apparent that a chemically dependent patient with a coexisting psychiatric disorder should receive treatment for the latter. The judicious use of medications, including antidepressants, lithium, carbamazepine, valproic acid, buspirone, neuroleptics, benzodiaze-pines, or others, may be indicated. Individual and/or group psychother-apy is usually indicated and can complement the use of Alcoholics Anonymous or Narcotics Anonymous.

A discussion of specific treatments for psychiatric disorders is beyond the scope of this text. Conceptual guidelines for managing dual disorders are outlined below:

Primary versus secondary. Primary and secondary refer to the temporal sequences in which disorders develop and do not imply a hierarchy of clinical importance or etiologic development.

Does it matter which is primary and which secondary? Good clinical practice dictates that an effort be made to determine the primary/sec-ondary sequence. This exercise will help to distinguish whether two diagnoses apply or whether certain psychiatric symptoms are epiphe-nomena of the substance use disorder (Schuckit, 1983). For example, panic attack symptoms or depression may be described during or fol-lowing withdrawal from a drug, yet clear up as a drug-free state is acquired. A common example is panic symptoms associated with can-nabis abuse. It would be a mistake to assume the presence of a dual disorder unless a clear history of panic attacks were present before the use of marijuana or panic attacks continued well beyond termination of marijuana use.

A bipolar patient may drink heavily during manic episodes and subse-quently develop alcohol dependence. In this case, the bipolar disorder is primary—it developed first—and the alcoholism is secondary. An etiologic link is apparent as the alcoholism evolved from the heavy reli-ance on alcohol as a "tranquilizer" during manic episodes. Knowledge of this sequence will assist in clinical management if the patient develops a depressive episode. Given the history of bipolar disorder, any subse-quent symptoms of depression must be evaluated as a probable manifes-tation of bipolar disorder rather than assumed to be a temporary aftermath of alcohol use.

Determining the primary/secondary sequence may assist the clinician in recognizing potentially destructive interactions. For example, when some chemically dependent patients relapse, a secondary depression may evolve and, at times, has the potential for suicidal behavior, which occurred in a 39-year-old executive. Major depression was the primary disorder and responded to antidepressant medication. However, peri-odic bouts of alcohol abuse triggered not only depressive symptoms, but acute suicidal potential, as well.

Similarly, the alcohol or drug dependent patient is often at greater vulnerability for relapse when symptoms of a co-occurring psychiatric disorder emerge. An awareness of dual disorder and the interactions between such disorders over time provides the clinician and the patient with added tools to prevent relapse—relapse into alcohol or drug abuse, as well as relapse of psychiatric symptoms.

History and observation over time. In addition to a careful medical history, additional histories require attention:

1. A history of the use of each substance: age at onset, progression of use, route of administration, quantities used, how substance was attained, effects—including adverse and beneficial, reasons for starting and stopping substance, preferred substance and why.
2. A history of psychiatric symptoms: onset, precipitatory events, duration, progression, impact on relationships, impact of relationships, relationship of symptoms to occupation, degree of impairment, help-seeking behaviors.
3. A history of response to treatment: when was treatment first sought and why; what type of treatment and with what provider; medications used; type, duration, and intensity of psychotherapy; attendance at 12-step groups; reasons why treatment was discontinued; opinion on treatment received; what treatments helped, in what way, and which did not.

Despite our best efforts to obtain the patient's history, observation over time is necessary to unravel the fact of or the interactions between dual disorders. Basically, the clinician is making an effort to avoid undertreatment and overtreatment. Often, a patient is treated for one disorder only, and the second disorder is missed. For example, a 45-year-old physician sought psychiatric help for depression. Occupational stress was a major factor, and both benzodiazepines and an antidepressant were prescribed. Psychotherapy was not recommended, and medication check-ups were conducted every six months. Unknown to the psychiatrist was the physician-patient's addiction to synthetic narcotics. Eventually, a crisis led to recognition of the opioid dependence. Substance abuse treatment was begun and, over the course of several months, it was apparent that an additional disorder (i.e., affective disorder) was not present. In this case, initial treatment was limited to a possible affective disorder, while an addiction state remained disguised. When the addiction was treated, it became apparent that specific treatment for depression was not indicated.

A second case illustrates the reverse situation: A 63-year-old physician had been sober for five years following a successful rehabilitation program and extensive involvement in A.A. Only those close to him—wife, son, and a few A.A. friends—were aware of troublesome symptoms, in spite of his abstinence from alcohol or other drugs. Irritability, anger, withdrawal, poor concentration, and disturbed sleep patterns all remained unresponsive to his efforts to strengthen his "recovery program." An unexpected serious medical illness brought attention to his depression. Antidepressants soon resulted in improvement, but his refusal to continue with psychiatric care led to a rapid reemergence of depression. Only after his wife impressed upon both the treating psychiatrist and her physician-husband the difficulty she had in living with him did he agree to continuing treatment. Later treatment efforts struck an effective balance between outpatient psychiatric care and use of A.A.

Dual disorders are easily overdiagnosed if diagnoses are made too soon—for example, during withdrawal states or in the early days or weeks of recovery. Similarly, dual disorders may be missed if treatment personnel are not alert, or if patients and families do not provide the necessary information. Looking back (history-taking) and "following forward" (observation) provides the perspective necessary to make optimal treatment decisions.

Family history as a guide. Familial alcoholism is well-documented and has been extensively reviewed (Miller & Gold, 1991). The familial transmission of nonalcoholic drug abuse has not been documented as well, but seems to occur at a lower rate than that of alcoholism (Meller, Rinehart, Cadoret, & Troughton, 1988).

Family history can be a guide in ascertaining the presence of a dual disorder. The sons and daughters of alcoholic parents are at higher risk for alcoholism. Therefore, a positive family history of alcoholism in a patient presenting with psychiatric symptoms raises the index of suspicion for comorbidity. Data from McLean Hospital in Belmont, Mass. support the reverse consideration (Mirin, Weiss, Sollogub, & Michael, 1984): Drug abusers with a concurrent affective disorder had significantly more first-degree relatives with an affective disorder than did drug abusers without an affective disorder. These findings indicate that the presence of a comorbid psychiatric disorder should be considered in substance abusing patients with a family history positive for psychiatric disorders.

The use of medication. If a chemically dependent patient has a comorbid psychiatric disorder which is potentially responsive to medication, the benefits of the medication should be discusssed with the patient. The depressed, manic, or psychotic patient should be advised to use an appropriate psychopharmacologic regimen. Antidepressants, lithium, neuroleptics, anticonvulsants, beta-blockers, and others are not addicting, and patients should be reassured on that point. Occasionally, a chemically dependent patient is advised to the contrary by a sponsor or member of an A.A. or N.A. group. The treating physician needs to educate the patient as to the validity and safety of using medication and to reassure the patient that properly presented medications do not compromise the utilization of 12-step programs.

The situation may become complicated with anxiety disorders or other disorders with a significant anxiety component. Often, anxiety disorders respond to nonaddicting medications, such as tricyclic or monoamine-oxidase inhibitor (MAOI) antidepressants or buspirone. However, some patients require the anxiolytic relief of benzodiazepines. For example, a recovering alcoholic businessman had panic disorder and could not tolerate the side effects of tricyclics or MAOIs. After a trial of clonazepam (a benzodiazepine with relatively low abuse potential) proved ineffective, alprazolam (Xanax) was prescribed. Control of panic and anxiety followed without a pattern of alprazolam abuse. Another indication for the use of benzodiazepines in a "dual disordered" patient is illustrated by an executive with a history of both bipolar and polysubstance dependence. A disturbed sleep pattern in this patient heralded the onset of a hypomania, or manic state. His sleep disturbance was quickly corrected by either chlordiazepoxide or temazepam and affect stability was preserved.

The use of benzodiazepines in patients with a history of chemical dependence carries a risk of incurring a new dependence or triggering a relapse into the previous dependence. Nevertheless this risk is justified in selected cases, contingent on sufficiently severe or nonrespondent symptoms. Although clinicians are familiar with this risk, the incidence of renewed addictive behavior is not known. A review of benzodiazepine abuse among alcoholics stated: ". . . benzodiazepine use among alcoholics is greater than in the general population but comparable to the prevalence in psychiatric patients. The liability for abuse may also be greater for alcoholics, but the substantial methodologic deficiencies of anxiety studies preclude such a conclusion" (Ciraulo, Sands, & Shader, 1988).

Prevention or interruption of an abuse pattern can be accomplished by utilizing Dupont's Benzodiazepine Checklist for Long-Term Use (1992):

1. Problem being treated: Does the problem justify continued treatment with a benzodiazepine? Has the patient significantly benefited from benzodiazepine treatment?
2. Benzodiazepine Use: Does the patient's use of the benzodiazepine remain with the prescribed limits and duration of treatment? Has the patient avoided the use of other prescribed or nonprescribed agents?
3. Toxic Behavior: Has the patient been free of any signs of intoxication or impairment from the use of benzodiazepine medication, either alone or in combination with other agents?
4. Family Monitor: Does the patient's family monitor confirm that

there have been no problems with benzodiazepine use and that the patient has benefited from the use of the medication?

A summary statement on the treatment of dual disorders by Frances and Allen (1986) is both realistic and optimistic: "Patients who present with substance abuse and psychopathology have a poorer prognosis than those who have a single substance disorder without accompanying psychiatric disorders; however, they respond to treatment better when the multiple problems are addressed in a treatment tailored to their needs" (p. 436).

Adjunctive Medications

By adjunctive medications, I refer to medications that address the addictive state specifically, rather than comorbid psychiatric symptoms. These agents are useful when included in a comprehensive treatment program and are not a complete treatment in themselves. Methadone maintenance is not included in this section, as it is used very infrequently by professional patients (see the review of methadone maintenance by Lowinson, Marion, Joseph, & Dole, 1992).

Disulfiram (Antabuse)

Antabuse is rapidly absorbed from the gastrointestinal tract, is fat soluble, and, after 12 hours, is in full effect. It is metabolized by conjugation with glucuronic acid, oxidation to sulfate, or decomposition to carbon disulfide and diethylamine. The excretion is slow, with about one fifth remaining in the body after one week. Most of the drug is metabolized in the liver and excreted in the urine (Ritchie, 1975).

Disulfiram is a deterrent drug. The deterrent is the ethanol-disulfiram reaction. After alcohol is ingested, the ethyl alcohol molecule is metabolized to acetaldehyde by the enzyme alcohol dehydrogenase. The normal conversion of acetaldehyde to acetic acid is blocked by the effect of disulfiram on acetaldehyde dehydrogenase. There occurs, therefore, a rapid increase in serum acetaldehyde at levels 5 to 10 times normal. Acetaldehyde is toxic and produces the following effects, which are referred to as the Alcohol–Antabuse Reaction or ethanol-disulfiram reaction:

- flushing of the skin, particularly the face and upper chest
- throbbing headache
- nausea (and possibly vomiting)
- sweating

- hyperventilation and respiratory distress
- chest pain
- anxiety
- palpitations
- hypotension

If the reaction is severe, shock and cardiac arrhythmias can occur. The intensity of the reaction is proportional to the amount of alcohol ingested and the dose of disulfiram. The reaction usually lasts 30 to 60 minutes. Most reactions are mild, because the patient quickly stops drinking as symptoms emerge. The symptoms develop about 10 to 20 minutes after ingestion of alcohol. A mild reaction may occur with a blood alcohol level of 5 mg to 10 mg per 100 ml. A full reaction can be expected with a blood alcohol concentration of 50 mg to 100 mg per 100 ml, and consciousness may be lost if the blood alcohol concentration exceeds 125 mg per 100 ml.

A severe reaction may require treatment of shock, involving use of ephedrine for the hypotension and administration of oxygen. Intravenous antihistamines may abate some of the symptoms. Ascorbic acid (Vitamin C) given intravenously in a gram dose has a beneficial effect, presumably on the basis of ascorbic acid's antioxidant effect. This effect is believed to decrease the production of acetaldehyde by allowing alcohol to be excreted unchanged (Ayerst Laboratories, 1979). A patient reporting a disulfiram-ethanol reaction should be advised to see a physician or, in severe cases, to go to an emergency room.

Side effects of disulfiram include mild drowsiness, which usually subsides in 7 to 10 days. Since disulfiram is taken only once a day, a bedtime dosage schedule could be used to minimize this effect. A garlic or metallic-like taste may be noted. A lower dose may alleviate this effect. Other side effects include erectile dysfunction, fatigue, headaches, acneform skin eruptions, tremor, restlessness, and allergic dermatitis. Peripheral neuritis and a toxic psychosis with delirium and paranoid or affective features are possible, but uncommon. Rare side effects include hepatic dysfunction and optic neuritis.

Skin manifestations may be relieved by antihistamines, and most side effects respond to a lower dosage.

Antabuse is produced in 250 mg and 500 mg scored tablets. Some physicians routinely prescribe 250 mg daily. Others begin with 500 mg for 5 days, then decrease the dosage to 250 mg daily. Disulfiram should not be given until the blood alcohol level is zero. This requires at least a 12-hour interval after the last drink.

Alcohol abuse or alcohol dependence is an indication to consider the use of disulfiram, but neither is sufficient in itself to prescribe disulfiram.

To a proper diagnosis must be added an appropriate attitude on the part of the patient. Disulfiram is appropriate for an alcoholic patient who can view his or her use of Antabuse as "one additional weapon on my side against a return to alcoholism." If the patient feels positive about Antabuse, its prescription may be appropriate. If the patient is willing to take Antabuse only because his or her doctor is recommending it, to please the patient's spouse, or to "get people off my back about drinking," the prognosis is unfavorable. Resentment usually develops, and the patient may sabotage treatment. I explain to patients that they should not take Antabuse for someone else's benefit. If they feel better about themselves because they are taking Antabuse, then the drug will truly be an adjunct to treatment.

Apart from these attitudinal factors, contraindications are largely relative. The physician must weigh the risk of harm resulting from a possible ethanol-disulfiram reaction against the health consequences of drinking. Allergic reaction to disulfiram, severe heart disease, and psychosis are contraindications. If a patient is taking metronidazol (Flagyl), paraldehyde, or any alcohol-containing preparation, disulfiram should not be prescribed. The antituberculosis drug, isoniazid, may lead to a toxic reaction if given with disulfiram. The suicidal patient should not be prescribed disulfiram, nor should the patient whose judgment is easily compromised either by organic changes or by an impulsive personality disorder. If the clinician feels that a patient is likely to test Antabuse or forget that he or she is on Antabuse, it is best avoided.

Naltrexone (Revia)

Naltrexone is an opioid antagonist, which acts by binding to opioid receptors on the cell membrane. In the early 1970s, it was demonstrated that 50 mg of naltrexone would block the subjective effects of morphine for up to 24 hours (Martin, Jasinski, & Mansky, 1973). When the antagonist is present in sufficient quantities (50 mg dose once per day), all or nearly all opioid receptors are occupied, leaving no "room" on the cell membrane for subsequently ingested opiate molecules. As a result, the ingestion of an opioid results in a neutral subjective experience and can be considered a waste of time and money.

Naltrexone should not be administered until 7 to 14 days after the last use of an opiate, as it will displace from the receptor site any remaining opiate molecules and thereby precipitate a withdrawal syndrome. Naltrexone can be taken in a dose of 50 mg daily or, alternatively, 100 mg on Monday, 100 mg on Wednesday, and 150 mg on Friday. Side effects are usually not troublesome and may include some initial "sluggishness," nausea, and headache. Some patients report increased appetite while others lose weight (Greenstein, Arndt, McClellan, O'Brien, & Evans, 1984). Although endogenous opiates are blocked also by naltrexone, there is no evidence that depression results from long-term use of naltrexone and dysphoria is reported infrequently (Malcolm, O'Neil, Von, & Dickerson, 1987).

Naltrexone has been most successful in facilitating abstinence from opiates when used as part of a comprehensive treatment program. Middle-class patients and professionals have shown the most benefit. For example, 47 of 60 health professionals were considered much or moderately improved at an eight-month follow-up (Ling & Wesson, 1984), and business executives were opiate-free in 64% of cases, 12 to 18 months after completing a rehabiliation program and using naltrexone as part of their aftercare plan (Washton et al., 1984).

More recently, naltrexone has been marketed as Revia for the purpose of facilitating recovery from alcohol dependence. Studies have demonstrated that alcoholics taking Revia have less craving, fewer drinking days, and, if initiated, drinking is less likely to proceed to a full blown relapse. Again, it is necessary for Revia to be considered an adjunct to a fully comprehensive approach to alcoholism treatment. Initial studies on the use of naltrexone for the treatment of alcoholism are encouraging (Volpicelli, Alterman, Hayashida, and O'Brien, 1992; O'Malley, Jaffe, Chang, Schottenfeld, Meyer, and Rounsaville, 1992).

Buprenorphine (Buprenex)

Buprenorphine is a mixed agonist-antagonist; that is, it has opioid antagonist activity at kappa opiate receptors but agonist activity (partial) at the mu receptors. It is administered sublingually or parenterally, but not orally. At low doses, it acts like methadone and at high doses, like naltrexone. Sublingual doses have been employed in the range of 2 to 16 mg. Although experimental at this time, buprenorphine may prove useful in treating opiate dependence based on its: (a) euphoric blocking properties; (b) long duration of action; (c) limited withdrawal symptoms; and (d) morphine-like subjective effects (Greenstein, Fudala, & O'Brien, 1992).

Antidepressants

Several antidepressants have been tried in the treatment of cocaine abuse. The rationale is to correct the relative dopamine deficient state that follows chronic cocaine use and relieve the symptoms of anhedonia, depression, and craving, which occur during withdrawal from cocaine (Gawin & Kleber, 1986).

Desipramine (Norpramin, Pertofrane) has been most extensively studied and, at doses of 200 mg to 240 mg per day, assisted 65% of cocaine addicts to abstain compared to 20% on placebo (Gawin, Kleber, Byck, Rounsaville, Kosten, et al., 1989). Most studies have been short-term—about two months—and relapse rates are high when desipramine is stopped. Bupropion (Wellbutrin), an antidepressant with some degree of dopaminergic activity, has been found to assist in retaining cocaine addicts in treatment, and to lower both cocaine use and craving (Margolin, Kosten, Petrakis, Avants, & Kosten, 1991).

Serotonin reuptake inhibitors, such as fluoxetine (Prozac) and sertraline (Zoloft), are being studied also. Results in open trials are initially promising, but as with all pharmacologic approaches, the outcomes from double-blind controlled studies will be definitive (Kosten, 1993).

Dopaminergic Agents

Dopaminergic agents can be expected to increase the available dopamine in the neuronal synapse and have an onset of action within one day of starting—in contrast to antidepressants, which require two or more weeks before they will be effective.

Bromocriptine (Parlodel) and amantadine (Symmetrel) have been studied, and both agents demonstrate a favorable effect in decreasing craving. Amantadine has an advantage over bromocriptine because of its fewer side effects. The dosage of amantadine is typically 220 to 360 mg daily and of bromocriptine is 0.125 to 0.6 mg three times daily (Kosten, 1992).

There is no quick pharmacological cure for any chemical dependence. The above brief review of commonly used medications is presented in the interest of increasing the clinician's flexibility in treating substance abusing patients. Many patients chronically relapse. Perhaps, vigorous pharmacologic trials will strengthen a foothold on clean and sober living for some. The use of medications is effective only if carried out in the context of a therapeutic alliance and within a comprehensive treatment approach, which emphasizes use of A.A. or N.A., marital and family therapy, individual therapy, and group therapy, as indicated.

MONITORING

Monitoring of the impaired professional is a process that, if done properly, blends support, accountability, and documentation. Often, the process is conceived as "monitoring *of* the impaired professional"; more accurately, the process should be conceived as "monitoring *for* the impaired professional." The monitoring process can be viewed as intrusive, disciplinary, or punitive. Alternatively, monitoring may be viewed as complementary to treatment, psychologically supportive, and as a documentation of recovery. For example, an anesthesiologist was in recovery from cocaine addiction. When he returned to his clinical duties, following a course of inpatient treatment, he was aware that if something went wrong in the operating room or if some medications were unaccounted for, he would be a likely suspect. For this reason, he welcomed the hospital's monitoring procedures, which included urine and blood alcohol and drug screens. In addition to complying with the monitoring committee's periodic requests for a urine sample, this physician requested a drug/alcohol screen if something untoward happened during the course of an operation or during the recovery period. He also sought documentation of his being "clean and sober" when he was inadvertently involved in an automobile accident.

Technically, monitoring involves: (a) random or unannounced urine or blood screens for drugs and alcohol; (b) periodic contact between the chemically dependent individual and a designated monitor; (c) written reports from physicians, counselors, or employers on the status of the patient's recovery efforts; and (d) verification of attendance at A.A./N.A. meetings or verification of attendance at therapy sessions.

Urine/Blood Drug Screens

The technology for identifying substances in body fluids has advanced sufficiently that a credible monitoring program should make use of these techniques. Any initial positive screening test must be confirmed by the highly specific techniques of gas chromatography/mass spectrometry (GC/ms). The latter procedure is the most reliable technique currently available and provides a definitive "molecular fingerprint" (Hawks, 1986). Table 13.4 lists the drugs that qualified laboratories should be able to routinely test for (Vereby, 1992).

Urine testing is the most common screening method. If the urine cannot be obtained under proper observation, a blood specimen is preferable. Ingenious methods have been used by some individuals to avoid a positive urine test. For example, a female patient returned to the hospital from a pass with a condom filled with "clean" urine in her vagina. Her plan was to prick the condom with her fingernail when asked to provide a specimen.

The site of urine collection should be free of any contaminants (for example, soap, toilet bowl cleaner, etc.) that could be added to a specimen and foul the analytical procedure. The physical presence of an observer is essential when the specimen is voided. A policy for random

TABLE 13.4
Groups of Abused Drugs: Tests Performed or
Not Routinely Tested By Laboratories*

I [a]	II [b]	III [c]
amphetamines	barbiturates	LSD
cannabinoids	benzodiazepines	Fentanyl
cocaine	methadone	psilocybin
opioids	propoxydene	MDMA
phencyclidine	methaqualone	MDA
	ethanol	designer drugs

[a]Necessary to test for certification by the National Laboratory Certification Program administered by the National Institute on Drug Abuse.
[b]Tests performed by laboratories.
[c]Not routinely tested by laboratories.
*Reprinted with permission from Vereby, 1992. Diagnostic laboratory. In J. H. Lowinson, P. Ruiz, & R. B. Millman (Eds.), *Substance* abuse (p.428). Baltimore, MD: Williams & Wilkins.

drug screening used by the Texas Medical Association's Committee on Physicians Health and Rehabilitation is outlined below.

I. Procedures
    A. When a specimen is requested, it should be obtained within four hours of request. If the circumstances absolutely will not allow (e.g., client is in surgery), then the time frame should begin as soon as the client becomes free.
    B. There must be a documented photo-check of identification.
    C. Note all prescription and non-prescription medications the client may be taking.
    D. The specimen collection must be direct and watched.
    E. Specimen temperature should be checked within four minutes and recorded.
    F. A disclaimer should be signed explaining that any specimen found to be adulterated will be considered "dirty."
    G. The urine specimen must be at least two ounces.
    H. The chain of custody form should be followed perfectly when collecting *and* transferring the specimen.
II. The specimen must go to a reliable laboratory.
    A. Insist that the lab specify the individual drugs tested and not just drug categories.
    B. Insist that the initial screen must be an immunoassay type followed by a confirmatory GC/Mass Spec.

C. Insist that pH, creatine, and specific gravity be re-
   corded.
D. Laboratories approved by the National Institute of
   Drug Abuse are preferred.

Contact

The establishment of a supportive relationship between a designated monitor and the chemically dependent client is important. Who should monitor the professional client? A person of like profession is recommended—an attorney would monitor another attorney, for example. A recovered person with long sobriety often makes an excellent monitor. The monitor should not be a supervisor of the client nor a fellow employee, if possible. At times, staff from a treatment center will be monitors. The monitor should not be the client's therapist. Ideally, the monitoring would be done by a member of a state, county, or local institution peer assistance program.

The role of the monitor is not simply to arrange to collect a urine sample but, in addition, to convey to the client an ongoing interest in the client's welfare, recovery, and overall functioning. Weekly, biweekly, or monthly contact is recommended; the frequency of contact should be greater during the first six months of recovery and vary according to the client's response to a recovery program. Preferably, the contact will be face to face, but, in some circumstances, telephone contact will be necessary. The monitor should be knowledgeable about chemical dependence. A monitoring contract is essential.

Reports

As part of the monitoring process, reports from a treating psychiatrist or other physician or therapist may be requested. The proper release of information forms and agreements as to the information to be divulged must be established. I believe it is best to require the professional in recovery to assume the responsibility for notifying those submitting reports as to when the reports are due. Crosby and Bissell (1989) describe a monitoring technique whereby the professional in recovery forwards a monthly report to the monitor or monitoring agency which expresses his or her status from a subjective point of view.

Monitoring should be part of the recovery program for professionals because improved outcomes are the result; progress is documented; "slips" can be detected early or prevented, thus serving both the interests of public health, personal health, and career preservation; and the institution or "system" to which the professional returns gains confidence that problems, if they recur, will be detected early and that exposure will be lessened.

Monitoring involves a supportive yet objective co-professional who provides regular personal contact; urine or blood samples to test for drugs and alcohol, with specimens obtained randomly or unannounced and subject to chain of custody procedures and quality laboratory standards; reports from treating personnel and/or employers as to attendance, compliance, or changes in follow-up care; extended participation with 2 years post-initial treatment as the minimum and additional months or years should be decided on an individual basis.

CHAPTER 14

Twelve-Step Programs

Professionals often resist, indeed fear, involvement in Alcoholics Anonymous (A.A.) or other 12-step programs. The image of A.A. may be unappealing to them. They expect to be linked with the down and out, the dregs of humanity. Attendance at A.A. may symbolize the depth of their "fall," and they may prefer to believe that they aren't that bad, that they can manage this problem on their own or with the help of professional therapists.

In addition to such narcissistic issues, professionals may report additional hurdles to A.A. participation: The room is too smoky, the program consists of clichés, they can't identify with those who are marginally employed or unemployed. They may have considerable fear that a client, customer, patient, or colleague will see them there.

Of equal impact is the message of A.A.: Step One (see Table 14.1) asks for an admission of powerlessness; Step Two, a belief in "a Power greater than ourselves"; and Step Three, a decision to turn one's will and life over to the care of God. The professional, who has so highly valued self-sufficiency and self-efficacy, will cringe at the initial exposure to these steps. Yet as reviewed in this chapter (also see Kurtz, 1979, 1981), the deceptively simple steps of A.A. provide a fulcrum for critical changes, changes that are especially difficult, I believe, for professionals. These changes include the acceptance of one's limitations, a willingness to ask for help, and relief from acute shame.

In my opinion, any professional with a substance use disorder should, at the least, be encouraged to attend A.A. and, if necessary, urged, nudged, or cajoled into active involvement in A.A. Physicians, in particular, should increase their efforts in this direction because only 7% of A.A. members report that a physician attracted them to A.A. (Lawton, 1990).

Professionals are more likely to feel at home in A.A., in contrast to Narcotics Anonymous (N.A.), because A.A. offers more diverse groups socioeconomically, geographically, and by age. N.A. groups may not have as many members with long histories of abstinence and may be

185

TABLE 14.1
The Twelve Steps of Alcoholics Anonymous*

1. We admitted we were powerless and that our lives had become unmanageable.
2. Came to believe that a Power greater than ourselves could restore us to sanity.
3. Made a decision to turn our will and our lives over to the care of God as we understood Him.
4. Made a searching and fearless moral inventory of ourselves.
5. Admitted to God, to ourselves, and to another human being the exact nature of our wrongs.
6. Were entirely ready to have God remove all these defects of character.
7. Humbly asked Him to remove our shortcomings.
8. Made a list of all persons we had harmed, and became willing to make amends to them all.
9. Made direct amends to such people wherever possible, except when to do so would injure them or others.
10. Continue to take personal inventory and when we were wrong promptly admitted it.
11. Sought through prayer and meditation to improve our conscious contact with God as we understood Him, praying only for knowledge of His Will for us and the power to carry that out.
12. Having had a spiritual awakening as the results of these steps, we tried to carry this message to alcoholics, and to practice these principles in all our affairs.

*The Twelve Steps are reprinted with permission of Alcoholics Anonymous World Services, Inc. Permission to reprint this material does not mean that A.A. has reviewed or approved the contents of this publication, nor that A.A. agrees with the views expressed herein. A.A. is a program of recovery for alcoholism. Use of the Twelve Steps in connection with programs and activities that are patterned after A.A. but address other problems does not imply otherwise.

composed of more young people and "street" people than many A.A. groups. There are exceptions and some areas have very well-established, stable N.A. groups that appeal to a broad range of participants.

Nearly one third of A.A. members are women, and nearly one half of A.A. members have been addicted to other drugs. The average length of sobriety for those currently in A.A. is four years, and members attend, on the average, three meetings per week (Newman, 1992).

WHAT IS A.A.?

The "A.A. preamble," usually read at the start of a meeting, provides a concise description of A.A.:

Alcoholics Anonymous is a fellowship of men and women who share their experience, strength, and hope with each other that they may solve their common problem and help others to recover from alcoholism.

The only requirement for membership is a desire to stop drinking. There are no dues or fees to A.A. membership; we are self-supporting through our own contributions. A.A. is not allied with any sect, denomination, politics, organization, or institution; does not wish to engage in any controversy, neither endorses nor proposes any causes. Our primary purpose is to stay sober and help other alcoholics to achieve sobriety.

See also Table 14.2

AFFILIATION WITH A.A.

The 1989 A.A. General Services Office survey reports that 40% of newcomers were referred to A.A. by counselors and rehabilitation facilities, an increase of 4% from 1986. Thirty-four percent were attracted to A.A. by an A.A. member, 27% reported being self-motivated, 19% were influenced by a family member, and 7% were referred by a physician.

It would seem that A.A. could receive greater emphasis from physicians. Historically, things got off to a slow start with doctors. The first edition of *Alcoholics Anonymous*, known as the "Big Book," was published in 1939. A.A. members were enthusiastic about reaching out to the medical community and sent 20,000 announcements of the Big Book. Only two orders were received (Thomsen, 1975). Since then, of course, physicians have become much more aware of A.A.; one study from Great Britain reports that 65% of general practitioners believed that A.A. had something to offer beyond what could be obtained through medical efforts (Henry & Robinson, 1978). However, as noted, only 7% of A.A. members in 1989 reported being referred by a physician, a decline from the 10% reported in the 1986 survey.

Once someone gets to A.A., what are the chances he or she will stay? Figures from A.A. General Services Office surveys indicate that only 55% of those who come to A.A. remain more than 3 months. A review of A.A. affiliation (Ogborne & Glaser, 1981) found that about 20% of problem drinkers referred to A.A. attended regularly. In a four-year follow-up, of those who reported attending A.A. regularly, 39% had attended a meeting during the month prior to follow-up. In a more recent review of the literature (Emrick, 1987), dropout rates from A.A. varied from 68% before 10 meetings were attended to 88% by one year

TABLE 14.2
The Twelve Traditions of Alcoholics Anonymous*

1. Our common welfare should come first; personal recovery depends upon A.A. unity.
2. For our group purpose there is but one ultimate authority—a loving God as He may express Himself in our group conscience. Our leaders are but trusted servants; they do not govern.
3. The only requirement for A.A. membership is a desire to stop drinking.
4. Each group should be autonomous except in matters affecting other groups or A.A. as a whole.
5. Each group has but one primary purpose—to carry its message to the alcoholic who still suffers.
6. An A.A. group ought never endorse, finance, or lend the A.A. name to any related facility or outside enterprise, lest problems of money, property, and prestige divert us from our primary purpose.
7. Every A.A. group ought to be fully self-suppporting, declining outside contributions.
8. Alcoholics Anonymous should remain forever nonprofessional, but our service centers may employ special workers.
9. A.A., as such, ought never be organized; but we may create service boards or committees directly responsible to those they serve.
10. Alcoholics Anonymous has no opinion on outside issues; hence the AA name ought never be drawn into public controversy.
11. Our public relations policy is based on attraction rather than promotion; we need always maintain personal anonymity at the level of press, radio, and films.
12. Anonymity is the spiritual foundation of all our Traditions, ever reminding us to place principles before personalities.

*The Twelve Traditions are reprinted with permission of Alcoholics Anonymous World Services, Inc. Permission to reprint this material does not mean that A.A. has reviewed or approved the contents of this publication, nor that A.A. agrees with the views expressed herein. A.A. is a program of recovery for alcoholism. Use of the Twelve Traditions in connection with programs and activities that are patterned after A.A. but address other problems does not imply otherwise.

after discharge. There are no data on affiliation with A.A. by specific professional groups.

The "dropout" problem raises the question of who is likely to make a stable affiliation with A.A. Early research on this question (Bean, 1975; Boscarino, 1980; Ogborne & Glaser, 1981) suggests that those who join A.A. are middle-class, guilt-ridden, sociable, cognitively rigid, and socially stable. They also are more likely to be chronic alcoholics or loss-of-control drinkers and to have more alcohol-related problems. A comprehensive recent review (Emrick, 1987) of the affiliation process fails to support earlier findings. Emrick compared variables used to distinguish between stable and unstable affiliations and found that 64% bear no relationship, 29% show a positive relationship favoring A.A. affiliation, and only 7% bear a negative relationship to A.A. affiliation. This leads to the conclusion that most alcoholics have the possibility of making an affiliation with A.A. Only those whose goal is not to abstain from alcohol would be seen as exceptions.

Demographic variables such as education, employment, socio-economic status of the alcoholic or of the parents, social stability, religion, and measures of social competence are unrelated to the affiliative process. Age favors, though not consistently, older alcoholics' making a positive relationship to affiliation. Alcoholism variables bear little relationship to making a positive affiliation. For example, loss of control, quantity drunk daily, age at first drink, degree of physiologic dependence, and drinking style bear no consistent relationship to affiliation.

Currently, research indicates an unpredictability as to who will affiliate with A.A., which again emphasizes the importance of recommending A.A. to all who might benefit from affiliation.

WHY IS A.A. EFFECTIVE?

The reasons for A.A.'s effectiveness may be as varied as the individuals involved. At the most basic level, the program works because one follows the Twelve Steps. It may be that these deceptively simple steps provide a concrete, tangible course of action; they may trigger cognitive processes previously unformed, unfocused, or abandoned, and they may encapsulate powerful dynamics capable of having an impact on craving, conditioning, and character. The A.A. program revolves around the Twelve Steps, and most members would offer the commonsense explanation that working the steps keeps them sober. This sentiment is reflected in the Big Book's chapter on how it works: "Rarely have we seen a person fail who has thoroughly followed our path" (Alcoholics Anonymous, 1955).

AN EMPATHIC UNDERSTANDING OF THE ALCOHOLIC

In a series of classic papers, Bean (1975) emphasizes an empathic understanding of the alcoholic as a mechanism for A.A.'s effectiveness. A.A. has "accomplished a shift from a society-centered view of alcoholism to an abuser-centered one" (p. 6). For the bereft or discouraged alcoholic, this shift is a startling, powerful encounter. A.A. provides the alcoholic with a protected environment. After years of feeling debased and worthless, the alcoholic is offered an environment free from the conventional view of drunken behavior. The alcoholic discovers that his or her experience is of value and even interesting to others. Further, the alcoholic's experiences may be useful to someone else, and others thank him or her for sharing it. As Bean explains, "This idea, that a person's experience is of value, is gratifying to anyone and is especially heady stuff to the chronically self-deprecating alcoholic" (p. 10). This dynamic may have less impact on professionals since their own experience, views, and opinions typically have been valued.

However, A.A. provides a shift in what is expected of the alcoholic. First, the alcoholic is not asked to admit to being an alcoholic. A.A. simply asks that one have a desire to stop drinking. There is no effort to point out the error of one's ways or the evils of drink. In fact, the attraction of alcohol and the pleasure of alcohol are openly acknowledged, but linked with the statement that "We couldn't handle it." The alcoholic who comes to A.A. is not asked to change, only to listen, identify, and keep coming back.

The style of interpersonal contact is nonthreatening. Last names are not given, attendance is not taken, the setting is casual, and humor and friendliness abound. Nevertheless, the meeting is serious. Each member conveys that there is a lot to lose, regardless of how much has actually been lost, but also that there is much to gain—sobriety. Sobriety is the focus and remains so, unvaryingly. Not drinking is the coin of the realm. Relapses or "slips" do not represent a failure on the part of the alcoholic or of A.A. Rather, slips are further demonstration of the power of alcohol and, therefore, the necessity of A.A. as a counterforce.

Bean emphasizes the regressive effect of alcohol on the alcoholic's personality and functioning. The regression results from the toxic disinhibiting effect of alcohol on the brain, the stress of losing control, and the impact of opprobrium, failure, and stigma. A.A. is seen by Bean to facilitate surrendering immature defenses for mature defenses. Denial is relinquished partly as a result of the crisis that usually brings the alcoholic to A.A. in the first place, but also because the alcoholic is not expected to appreciate fully the consequences of his or her behavior. This would be overwhelming. The only expectation is to stop drinking one day at a time. Repression, therefore, replaces denial, according to Bean. Reaction formation and undoing are manifested in the change from love of drinking to love of sobriety.

The central point in Bean's explication of psychodynamic change through A.A. is that the drinking alcoholic is accepted as he or she presents. One is permitted to express oneself as he is rather than as others may wish him to be. The alcoholic in A.A. may continue unchanged in character and so is granted the opportunity to put his energy into abstinence. Ceasing to drink and following the A.A. way promote maturity, that is, a shift from primitive defenses to higher-order defenses.

As the alcoholic advances in recovery, self-esteem is protected by abstinence but threatened by remorse over the past. According to Bean (1975), A.A. techniques to handle this aspect of recovery are:

1. The decision not to drink—repent and reform to build upon the wreckage of the past.
2. Place blame on the illness, not on the alcoholic.
3. Avoid censure.
4. Reward good behavior—this is done by dispensing 30-day, 60-day, 90-day, or one-year "chips" as milestones in sobriety are achieved.
5. Allow expression of low self-esteem in nondestructive ways rather than by drinking.

A.A. does not ask the alcoholic to get a job, be a better family member, or become more responsible. Sobriety is the goal from which other desirable efforts may emerge. Bean finds the efficacy of A.A. to be based on the ability to identify the alcoholic's dilemma, despair, defenses, and needs.

ACCEPTING LIMITATIONS

The writings of Kurtz (1979, 1981) provide not only a definitive history of A.A. but also critical insights into A.A.'s effectiveness. The core dynamic of A.A. therapy, according to Kurtz (1981) is "the shared honesty of mutual vulnerability openly acknowledged . . ." (p. 30).

An essential insight of A.A. for the alcoholic is its recognition and acceptance that one is "not-God." With this term, Kurtz is referring to the necessity for the alcoholic to accept personal limitation. The First Step of A.A. communicates to the alcoholic: "We admitted that we were powerless over alcohol—that our lives had become unmanageable." The acceptance of personal limitation—a condition of existence for all—is a life-or-death matter for the alcoholic. A.A., in teaching that the first drink gets the alcoholic drunk, implies that the alcoholic does not have a drinking limit, the alcoholic is limited.

To experience limitation is tantamount to experiencing shame. As painful as the shame is, it is an affect pivotal to recovery. Acceptance of shame distinguishes the alcoholic who, in Tiebout's (1973) terms, complies rather than surrenders. Compliance is motivated by guilt, is superficial, and ultimately is useless to extended recovery. Surrender involves recognition of powerlessness (and the affect associated with feeling limited or of having fallen short). Through surrender, the alcoholic becomes open to the healing forces within A.A. Kurtz (1981) considers that Steps Two, Six, Seven, and Ten influence the experience of shame in the alcoholic. The A.A. program treats shame by enabling the alcoholic to accept his or her need for others, by promoting the acceptance of others as they are ("live and let live"), and by valuing and reinforcing traits of honesty, sharing, and caring.

THE SPIRITUAL DIMENSION

For an understanding of the A.A. process, the dimension of spirituality must be introduced and considered in the equation of A.A.'s effectiveness.

It was suggested that working the Twelve Steps is what makes A.A. effective. This simple explanation may disguise the impact of spirituality on the recovery process. Spirituality rarely is part of the lexicon of the mental health professional, but it is a dimension of the A.A. program understood by those who work and live the Twelve Steps. The spirituality of the A.A. program is distinct from religious dogma and may be understood as a series of overlapping themes (Kurtz, 1989) as reviewed in Chapter 11 of this book. The first theme is release, which refers to the "chains being broken"—freedom from the compulsion to drink. The experience of release is a powerful and welcome event for the alcoholic and seems to occur naturally or to be given rather than achieved.

A second theme of spirituality is gratitude. Gratitude may flow from the feeling of release and includes an awareness of what we have—for example, the gift of life. According to Kurtz (1989), the words "think" and "thank" share a common derivation. Thinking leads to remembrance (for example, as the A.A. speaker tells his or her story), and from remembrance an attitude of thankfulness (gratitude) may be experienced—gratitude, for example, that one is now sober.

The third theme is humility. Humility conveys the attitude that it is acceptable to be limited, to be simply human. The alcoholic's awareness of powerlessness over alcohol engenders humility.

Finally, a fourth theme or component of spirituality is tolerance. A tolerance of differences and limitations, of oneself and others, fosters the serenity often experienced by A.A. members.

These themes capture the healing process in mystical traditions as described by Deikman (1982) and reviewed in Chapter 11. According to Deikman, the process of attaining higher psychological development involves renunciation, humility, and sincerity. Renunciation refers to an attitude, a giving up of the attachment to the things of the world. The alcoholic's giving up alcohol would demonstrate renunciation. Humility, according to Deikman, is "the possibility that someone else can teach you something you do not already know, especially about yourself" (p. 81), and sincerity simply refers to honesty of intention. It is apparent that the professional client working the Twelve Steps (Table 14.1) is getting involved in the processes of renunciation, humility, and sincerity.

In addition to the spiritual themes mentioned above, an additional healing dynamic may be significant: forgiveness. The seeking of forgiveness is implied, not directly expressed, in the Twelve Steps. For example, Steps Six and Seven (see Table 14.1) ask God to remove defects of character and remove shortcomings. The behavior of A.A. members toward newcomers (welcoming, accepting, friendly, caring) communicates forgiveness. Forgiveness is neither asked for nor offered at A.A. The word itself may or may not be heard at A.A. meetings, but its meaning pervades the transactions of the meetings. For example, Bean (1975) writes:

> Alcoholics know how deeply and painfully ashamed and guilty other alcoholics are about their drinking, how they lie and minimize it, and how this reinforces their sense of worthlessness. The discovery that others have committed what they thought was their own uniquely unforgiveable crime brings longed-for solace. (p. 10)

Forgiveness may be a precondition for other dynamic forces to become operative. For example, forgiveness precedes hope. Hope is inevitably very tenuous for a newcomer to A.A. and requires a future orientation, an orientation minimized by A.A.'s emphasis on "one day at a time." Forgiveness is experienced in a moment and may be the foundation for a growing sense of hope. Abandoning narcissistic defenses, strengthening the capacity for self-governance, and accepting "powerlessness" over alcohol all may be contingent on feeling forgiven or feeling capable of being forgiven. To be forgiven and to feel forgiven imply being accepted, a common description of the A.A. experience. The experience of shame as a pivotal affect and the treatment of shame in A.A. may become possible only if preceded by a sense of being forgiven.

The concepts of spirituality, including forgiveness, are put forth only as a further effort to explain the impact and mechanisms of the A.A. program. Perhaps that which is effective in the A.A. program varies considerably from member to member. Many A.A. members have limited awareness of (and equally little interest in) the dynamic forces accounting for A.A.'s effectiveness. But possibly, for some, the program may be a secular expression of the Christian concept of grace—an unmerited gift from God.

TABLE 14.3

Modification of Differences between A.A. and Psychiatry

Subject	A.A.	Psychiatry	Modification
Cause of drinking	One drinks because one is an alcoholic. Therapy can lead to intellectualization and denial.	One needs to understand the dynamics that influence behavior in order for change to be lasting.	Initially, the emphasis is put on cessation of drinking; later an understanding of one's emotional pain or vulnerabilities.
Recovery	Simple—just follow program.	Lengthy therapeutic quest.	Explore with the alcoholic resistances to A.A., and/or why he or she can't avoid people, places, things that facilitate drinking.
A.A.	A divine gift. It saved my life.	It's rigid.	It's both. Early in treatment the alcoholic needs a concise, rigid formula to contain drinking impulses and to counter despair.
Controlled drinking	A myth that kills.	Sometimes it seems possible.	Controlled drinking is a very unlikely outcome for the large majority of alcoholics. Mildly dependent, early-stage alcoholics sometimes reverse loss of control.
Medication	It's bad.	Good—corrects biochemical defects	Medication may be essential.
Psycho-pathology	Alcoholics are normal once they stop drinking.	All alcoholics have specific conflicts that predate their alcoholism.	Psychotherapy often predates the alcoholism but many times is the result of drinking.
Treatment	The Twelve Steps	Medical and psychological	The two are not contradictory but can be used effectively by most alcoholics, with one receiving more emphasis at certain times.
Basis of treatment	Personal experience of others	Scientifically based and empirically validated procedures	Divergent sources of understanding enable the experience of many to make an impact on a complex disease.

THE MENTAL HEALTH PROFESSIONS AND A.A.

Chappel (1992) has described the compatibility of psychiatric treatment with patients who attend A.A. or N.A., and has emphasized that clinicians should attend several A.A. meetings themselves in order to familiarize themselves with A.A., and, thereby, better explain the program to patients. When clinicians demonstrate an active interest in which meetings a patient attends, how often, and with what results, the patient remains motivated to sustain A.A. involvement. Such active interest in the A.A. experience is likely to improve the 50% dropout rate that A.A. reports for participants within three months of their starting the program (Newman, 1992).

Many larger communities have A.A. meetings that are specific for a professional group—"Doctors Recovery Group," "Lawyers Concerned for Lawyers," "Nurses' A.A." Such groups can be very helpful in encouraging a patient who is a professional to affiliate and identify with 12-step programs. Professionals should attend these meetings, but not limit themselves to such specialized groups. "Regular" A.A., in addition to a professional group, will broaden the A.A. experience and counter any belief that "My addiction is different."

The clinician would be remiss to overlook, ignore, or disparage the value of A.A. for any patient with a substance use disorder. Familiarity with A.A. can be obtained by attending open A.A. meetings, developing friendly relationships with A.A. members, and insisting that one's patients meet with A.A. members for an initial, informed introduction to A.A. Such efforts can facilitate an alliance with the A.A. community and foster the development of mutual respect.

There are conceptual differences between A.A. and the treatments offered by the mental health field. Such differences may be discerned by professional patients and it is important to integrate what may seem to be divergent concepts. Table 14.3 on the preceding page outlines potential differences, and, for the sake of comparison, presents these differences in extreme form. A modification of the differences is suggested.

APPENDIX A

Guidelines for Taking a Substance Abuse History

1. Conceptualize drug or alcohol use as progressing through four stages (Dupont, 1984):
   a. Experimental: This is the first use of a substance and is limited to the initial experiences.
   b. Occasional: This refers to the situation where the individual is a passive user of a substance. That is, he or she does not actively seek the substance, but if it is offered or made available, will use the substance. Frequency of substance use during this stage is usually one to three times a month.
   c. Regular: At this stage, the user is actively pursuing the substance and usually spending money on it. Frequency of usage has increased to several times a week on the average.
   d. Substance abuse or dependence
2. Determine the age when experimentation with each substance occurred, then ascertain the following information: the *pattern* of drug use as reflected by: *route of administration, frequency of use, duration of use,* and *circumstances of use.* For example, "At age 13, John first smoked a joint of marijuana. It was provided by his older brother, who was a sophomore in high school at that time. Little effect was noted by John, but after the summer of ninth grade (age 15), he progressed to occasional use of marijuana. That is, he now accepted marijuana if it were offered to him and used it during his sophomore year in high school several times a month. By the time of his junior year, he was smoking marijuana on a daily basis, including lunch breaks at school and throughout the day on weekends."
3. Proceed with a similar history of all other substances ever used (including alcohol). This enables one to determine the variety of drugs used, the pattern of use, and the progression of use.
4. Determine the consequences of each substance used. For example, "Alcohol led to a DWI at the age of 18, and to a car accident one year later. Experimentation with LSD during the sophomore year of college resulted in a 'bad trip' characterized by anxiety and a brief period of depression. Marijuana had consistently produced a feeling of calm and 'no hassle' effects until six months ago, when anxiety would occasionally occur."

197

5. Inquire as to whether or not the individual has a favorite substance or any special preference. Try to understand why any one or two substances are preferred, what are the advantages of these substances for that individual. Similarly, determine what drugs are avoided by the user.

6. Inquire about periods of abstinence. How long has the person gone since he/she initiated the experimental stage without the use of any substances? Some patients who are alcoholic describe periods of abstinence for six to 12 months, but, if questioned, one learns they were smoking marijuana during that period or were on tranquilizers. Ascertain whether they have had completely substance-free periods and how they felt and functioned.

7. Carefully determine why evaluation or treatment is being sought at this time. Many times it is obvious by virtue of an external crisis, such as the threat of a jail sentence or a medical emergency. In other cases, it is more subtle, but it is useful to try to determine the process that led to a treatment decision. This helps determine motivating factors, but also becomes a paradigm for beginning to relate one's motivations, affect, and vulnerabilities in an open and honest manner.

Adult Recovery Services Chemical Dependency*

	MONDAY	TUESDAY	WEDNESDAY	THURSDAY	FRIDAY
6:30–7:00	Wake/Dress	Wake/Dress	Wake/Dress	Wake/Dress	Wake/Dress
7:30–8:00	Meditation	Meditation Community	Meditation	Meditation Community	Meditation
8:00–8:30	Breakfast	Breakfast	Breakfast	Breakfast	Breakfast
9:00–9:50	Poly-Addiction Series	Poly-Addiction Series	Poly-Addiction Series	Poly-Addiction Series	Poly-Addiction Series
10:00–10:50	Doctor's Process Group	Healthy Sexuality Relationship Group	Anger/Feeling Group	Personal Time	Doctor's Process Group
11:00–12:00	Weekly Progress Group	Dr.'s Addiction Group	Addiction Group Therapy	Dr.'s Addiction Group	Addiction Group Therapy
12:00–12:30	Lunch	Lunch	Lunch	Lunch	Lunch
12:30–1:30	Free Time	Free Time	Free Time	Free Time	Free Time
1:30–2:20	Process and Step Group (1:30)	Process and Step Group	Process and Step Group	ROPES (1:30–3:30)	ROPES (1:30–3:30)
2:45–3:45	Recreational Therapy	Bowling (Outing ends at 4:30 pm)	Recreational Therapy		
4:00–5:00	Family Education Group	Personal Time	Psychodrama (ends at 5:15)	Grief Resolution Boundaries Group	Community Group or Lecture
5:00–6:00	Dinner	Dinner	Dinner	Dinner	Dinner
6:00–6:30	Film or Big Book Led by Mayor	BOOKSTORE Every other Tues. (Recovery Books and Gifts for Sale —cash/check)	Film or Big Book Led by Mayor	FREE TIME	Film or Big Book Led by Mayor
6:30–7:00				Family and (Relationship) (Therapy) (ends at 9:15)	

7:00–8:00	12 STEP MEETING (Outside Hospital) OR In Hospital Focus Group	FREE TIME	FREE TIME		12 STEP MEETING (Outside Hospital) OR In Hospital Focus Group
8:00–9:30		12 STEP MEETING (IN)	12 STEP MEETING (IN)		
9:30–9:45	HIGHS/ LOWS	HIGHS/ LOWS	HIGHS/ LOWS	HIGHS/ LOWS	HIGHS/ LOWS
9:45–11:00	FREE TIME	FREE TIME	FREE TIME	FREE TIME	FREE TIME
11:00	LIGHTS OUT	LIGHTS OUT	LIGHTS OUT	LIGHTS OUT	LIGHTS OUT—12:00

0312L

*Reproduced with the permission of Charter Medical Corporation. Such programs are highly structured and are utilized by both inpatient and day hospital patients.

ADULT RECOVERY SERVICES
ALL ADDICTIONS
WEEKEND SCHEDULE

SATURDAY

7:30–8:00	Wake/Dress
8:00–8:30	Meditation
8:30–8:50	Breakfast
9:00–10:30	Process and Step Group
10:30–11:15	Break
11:15–12:00	Recreational Therapy
12:00–12:30	Lunch
12:30–1:30	IN-HOUSE AA/NA MEETING
1:30–4:00	VISITING HOURS

SUNDAY

7:30–8:00	Wake/Dress
8:00–8:30	Meditation
8:30–8:50	Breakfast
9:00–9:30	Chapel 1st Floor (optional)
9:30–10:30	Spirituality Film Series
11:00–12:00	Nursing Education
12:00–12:30	Lunch
12:30–4:00	VISITING HOURS
4:00–5:00	Recreational Therapy
5:00–5:30	Dinner

4:00–5:00	Personal Time
5:00–5:30	Dinner
6:00–7:00	Big Book Study
7:00–9:30	12 STEP MEETING (Outside Hospital) In-house Focus Group
9:30–9:45	HIGHS/LOWS
9:45–12:00	FREE TIME
12:00	LIGHTS OUT

6:00–7:00	Big Book Study Led by Unit Mayor
7:00–9:30	12 STEP MEETING (Outside Hospital) In-house Focus Group
9:30–9:45	HIGHS/LOWS
9:45–11:00	FREE TIME
11:00	LIGHTS OUT

0312L
*Reproduced with the permission of Charter Medical Corporation.

CHARTER HEALTH SYSTEMS— EVENING OUTPATIENT PROGRAM OUTPATIENT SCHEDULE

	SUNDAY	MONDAY	TUESDAY	WEDNESDAY	THURSDAY
2:00–4:00	Individual Therapy				
4:00–5:00	Group Therapy				
5:00–6:00		Individual Therapy (Schedule with staff) -OR-	Recovery Bookstore	Individual Therapy (Schedule with staff) -OR-	
5:00–6:00	Dinner (Cafeteria)	Dinner (Cafeteria)	Dinner (Cafeteria)	Dinner (Cafeteria)	
6:00–7:00	Spirituality Group	Group Therapy	Work on Homework	Step Study	
6:30–7:30			Aftercare Group (Cafeteria)	Lecture (Classroom)	Lecture (Classroom)
8:00–9:00			In-house AA Meeting (Cafeteria)	Group Therapy 7:30–8:30	Family Therapy (Classroom)

FRIDAY AND SATURDAY: (optional)

FRIDAY
4:00–5:00   Grief Group   6:00–7:00   Big Book Study
             (Classroom)   (Patient Lounge)

SATURDAY
9:00–10:00   Step Lecture
             (Classroom)

*Note—use of the weight room is also available to outpatients, ROPES is also available on Thursday and Friday afternoons. Please ask your Case Manager for details.

ALL PATIENTS WILL HAVE INDIVIDUAL SESSIONS TO REVIEW AND SET TREATMENT PLAN GOALS WHICH WILL BE INCORPORATED INTO THEIR TREATMENT. ADDITIONALLY PATIENTS WILL BE WORKING IN GROUPS AND ATTENDING LECTURES ON ASSIGNMENTS RELATED TO THEIR RECOVERY ISSUES, WORKING THROUGH THE 12 STEPS AND WORKING AN AFTERCARE PLAN. PATIENTS WILL BE EXPECTED TO ATTEND 12 STEP RECOVERY MEETINGS.

Reproduced with the permission of Charter Medical Corporation

APPENDIX C

Withdrawal Signs, Symptoms, Techniques

WITHDRAWAL SIGNS AND SYMPTOMS

These are the symptoms and signs seen during the postintoxication period of different substances:

1. *Alcohol, other sedative-hypnotics (including marijuana):* agitation, anxiety, sweating, headache, tremor, seizures, hallucinosis, irritability, sleep disturbance, intense dreaming
2. *Opioids:* abdominal cramps, diarrhea, nausea, vomiting, salivation, tearing, rhinorrhea, dilated pupils, bone pain, joint pain, lower back pain, headache, muscle twitching, gooseflesh, chills, sweating, sneezing, sniffling, "crawly" sensations
3. *Psychostimulants:* agitation, confusion, hypervigilance (paranoid thinking), short-term memory deficit, intense drug craving, jitteriness, irritability, fatigue, perseveration, skin hypersensitivity
4. *Psychedelics, inhalants:* hallucinosis, agitation, confusion, paranoid thinking, disorientation, delirium, irritability, short-term memory deficit, flashbacks, bizarre delusions
5. *Nicotine:* irritability, confusion, intense craving for a cigarette, anxiety, lethargy, drowsiness, difficulty concentrating, decreased attention span, short-term memory deficit, suspiciousness, hyperexcitability, mood swings, yawning, tremor, insomnia, hunger pangs

GUIDELINES FOR WITHDRAWAL OF PATIENTS FROM ALCOHOL

1. BENZODIAZEPINES:
   A. A Fixed Schedule:
       Loading dose: Librium (chlordiazepoxide) 50 mg once, daily
               Day 01: Librium (chlordiazepoxide) 25 mg QID
               Day 02: Librium (chlordiazepoxide) 25 mg TID
               Day 03: Librium (chlordiazepoxide) 25 mg BID
               Day 04: Librium (chlordiazepoxide) 25 mg HS
     If mild sedation develops, use lower doses. If agitated, double

the above doses. Oxazepam (Serax) is shorter-acting with no active metabolites to accumulate. Chlordiazepoxide is longer-acting and more likely to accumulate in the presence of liver disease.

In addition to the schedule above, a prn order for either benzodiazepine should be left (e.g., Serax, 30 mg p.o. or Librium 25 mg p.o. q 2 hours prn agitation or severe tremor for 72 hours).

B. Symptom-Triggered Benzodiazepines (Saitz, Mayo-Smith, Roberts, Redmond, Bernard, Calkins, 1994).

Chlordiazepoxide is given orally every hour in doses ranging from 25 to 100 mgs. The administration and dose of chlordiazepoxide is triggered by the presence of and severity of symptoms such as tremors, agitation, hallucinations, or illusions, headache, nausea, autonomic hyperactivity, disorientation, and anxiety.

2. THIAMINE: 100 mg p.o. or i.m. × 3 days (usually p.o. is satisfactory, unless there is vomiting or current gastritis).

3. MULTIVITAMIN PREPARATION: 1 p.o. daily. Folic acid and other B vitamins especially important. Avoid excess amounts of Vitamin A as liver function may be compromised.

4. DILANTIN (phenytoin): only if there is a past history of withdrawal seizures or other types of seizures: Photophobia may herald impending seizure. Give loading dose of 300 mg p.o. TID with food (1st 24 hours); 200 mg p.o. TID (2nd 24 hours); 100 mg p.o. TID.

Withdrawal seizures usually occur 24 to 48 hours after the last drink, are grand mal, nonfocal, brief, and usually consist of one or two seizure episodes. Discontinue Dilantin after 10 days—taper off over one to two weeks. If there is a seizure and the patient has not had a neurologic work-up, begin one.

5. Magnesium Sulfate 0.50% solution, 2 cc i.m. q 8 hours × 3 injections may be used if Serum MG is low. This is usually not necessary except in cases of poor nutrition and in cases of pronounced tremors not responding well to benzodiazepines.

6. Compazine Suppository, 25 mg q 4 hours prn vomiting.

7. Kaopectate 30 cc p.o. prn diarrhea.

8. Aspirin, 650 mg p.o. q 4 hours or Motrin, 600 mg p.o. q 4 hours prn headaches.

9. Temazepam, 30 mg p.o. hs prn × 3 days.

10. If hallucinations develop, haloperidol, 5 mg q 4 hours prn may be used.

If Delirium Tremens (D.T.s) develop—disorientation, fluctuating levels of consciousness, hallucinations, agitation, sweating, increasing temperature—consider transfer to a medical service.

D.T.'s usually develop in a patient who also has an infection, fracture, severe liver disease, G-I bleeding, or other medical complications.

Basic treatment* is:

1. Search for complicating medical/surgical illness.
2. Check for hypoglycemia.
3. Frequent vital signs: look for shock; look for increased temperature.
4. Correct any fluid/electrolyte imbalance—use I.V. fluids.
5. Parenteral vitamins.
6. Careful benzodiazepine sedation (do not oversedate); for example, lorazepam (Ativan) 0.5 mg I-V every 30 minutes until sedated.
7. Haloperidol, 5 mg p.o., i.m., or iv q 1–2 hours prn.
8. Cooling blanket for hyperthermia.
9. Quiet, well-lighted room; consistent attendants or family members.
10. If restraints are necessary, have constant nursing supervision to detect any sudden deterioration. Do not restrain in supine position because of danger of vomiting.

TECHNIQUES FOR WITHDRAWAL FROM CNS DEPRESSANTS

1. Ten Percent Rule: Estimate from history daily dosage and give same dose × 2 days; then decrease by 10% every day. This method can be used for any drug including benzodiazepines (BZDs). In the case of BZDs, a slower rate of withdrawal (15 to 21 days or more) is usually necessary.
2. Benzodiazepine withdrawal (Alexander & Perry, 1991; Dupont & Saylor, 1991)

Outpatient Schedule

A. Determine daily intake in diazepam (Valium) equivalents.
   For example, 1 mg Ativan (lorazepam) = 5 mg Valium
   25 mg Librium (chlordiazepoxide) = 5 mg Valium
B. Divide daily dose by 5: $\frac{30 \text{ mg Valium}}{5}$ = 6 mg (This is the amount decreased each week)

---

*See: Adams, 1987; Liskow & Goodwin, 1987; Castenada & Cushman, 1989.

C. Weekly decrease:
> Week one   - 24 mg Valium/day in four divided doses
> Week two   - 18 mg Valium/day in four divided doses
> Week three - 12 mg Valium/day in four divided doses
> Week four   - 6 mg Valium/day in four divided doses

Inpatient Schedule

1. Determine daily intake in diazepam (Valium) equivalents (For example, 100 mg Valium/day).
2. Take 40 percent (100 mg × .40 mg = 40 mg) and begin taper at that dose.
3. Decrease by 10%/day or every other day as tolerated.

Diazepam Tolerance Test

1. Nothing by mouth (NPO) except water or fruit juice for two hours
2. Give 20 mg of diazepam every two hours until one of the following develops: slurred speech, ataxia, nystagmus, drowsiness.
3. Begin taper at that dosage.

3. *Xanax* (alprazolam) detoxification is not substantially different from other benzodiazepine detoxification, although the patient may become more confused. If the patient has used Xanax, detoxification with *Klonopin* is preferred. 2 mg Klonopin = about 1 mg Xanax. Start with a loading dose (2–4 mg then 1–3 mg TID and reduce gradually over 14 days).
4. *Phenobarbital* detoxification for CNS Depressant withdrawal: start titration with 100 mg q half hour until patient gets drowsy. The total amount used becomes the total dose for the next 24 hours, in QID divided doses (usually 400–600 mg/day). Reduce over 10 days. Give p.o. or i.m.

WITHDRAWAL FROM OPIATES

Severity of symptoms is determined by:

1. Which narcotic used:
   a. Narcotics of short duration (heroin) produce more severe symptoms, but a briefer time course (5–10 days).
   b. Long lasting narcotics (methadone) yield milder symptoms over a longer period of time (14–21 days).
2. Total daily amount used: the higher the dose, the more pronounced the symptoms.
3. Duration of use: after 2–3 months of use, severity is no longer related to duration.

4. Physical health: sick, weaker patients are less able to tolerate the stress of withdrawal.
5. Psychological factors: personality, state of mind, treatment setting play a major role. If patient *expects* to get an abundance of medications, symptoms will be more severe.

Two classes of symptoms:

1. "Purposive"—goal-oriented, complaints, pleas, demands, manipulation, symptom mimicking.
2. "Nonpurposive"—independent of environment and will of patient: gooseflesh, mydriasis, rhinorrhea, lacrimation.

Clonidine Detoxification from Opiates

Clonidine (Catapres) is an alpha-adrenergic agonist successfully used for opiate detoxification.

The procedure for detoxification from opiates with clonidine is as follows:

1. Blood pressure determinations must be made prior to each dose and 20 minutes after each dose of clonidine. If the pressure is 85/55 or lower, subsequent dosage is best handled by monitoring blood pressure and having the patient lie down. Tolazoline is a clonidine antagonist and should be available for hypotensive crises, which are rare.
2. Dosage of clonidine:
   Day 01:   0.1 mg TID
   Day 02:   0.1 mg TID (0.4 mg maximum)
   Day 03:   0.5–0.6 mg maximum in three divided doses
   Day 04:   0.6–1.0 mg with a maximum of 1.2 mg
   Days 05–10: hold at established dose for control of symptoms
   Days 11–13: cut dosage in half each day. For example 0.11 mg is reduced to 0.6 mg to 0.3 mg to 0.1 mg

Antiwithdrawal effects of clonidine begin within 30 minutes and peak at 2–3 hours. Sedation is a commonly experienced side effect for the first few days, but usually remits. Dry mouth or facial pain are less common. Insomnia may occur during a clonidine detoxification and temazepam may be useful. Muscle aches, nervousness, and irritability are not typically relieved by clonidine detoxification. The addition of a benzodiazepine for a brief period of time may be useful. Advantages of clonidine in detoxification are that it is a nonnarcotic, noncontrolled substance and thus can be used in a wide range of clinical settings including outpatient detoxification. Also, the detoxification time is usually more brief than when methadone is used.

Methadone Detoxification from Opiates

Methadone Detoxification

1 mg methadone = 1–2 mg heroin
3–4 mg morphine
20 mg meperidine (Demerol)
½ mg hydromorphone (Dilaudid)
30 mg codeine

A Starting Regimen

Give 10–20 mg methadone after withdrawal symptoms begin (e.g., sweating, gooseflesh, dilated pupils, lacrimation, rhinorrhea, elevated vital signs).

Symptoms should be suppressed within 90 minutes.

If necessary, give 5–10 mg after two hours.

It may be necessary to repeat 10–20 mg 12 hours later.

If there is documented evidence of a narcotic habit greater than 40 mg methadone:

Suggested Withdrawal Pattern

Day	1	2	3	4	5	6	7	8	9	10	11	12
	40	40	35	30	25	20	15	10	8	6	4	2

Day	13	14
	0	0

It is usually not necessary to give more than 40 mg (2 doses of 20 mg) per day. The total dose necessary to stabilize the patient during the first 24 hours should be repeated the 2nd day.

Symptoms such as diarrhea, insomnia, anxiety/depression may be treated symptomatically.

Useful Medications for Symptom Control During Opiate Withdrawal

Provide medications the patient is allowed some control over:

Kaopectate 30 cc after a loose stool, prn

Pro-Banthine, 15 mg or Bentyl 20 mg q4h prn abdominal cramps

Tylenol, 650 mg q4h prn for headache

Feldene, 20 mg daily or Naprosyn, 375 mg q8h for back, joint, and bone pain

Mylanta, 30 ml q2h prn for indigestion

Compazine, 25 mg suppository q6h prn for vomiting

Librium, 25 mg q4h prn for anxiety
Atarax, 25 mg q4h prn nausea
Benadryl, 50 mg or temazepam 30 mg hs prn sleep

MARIJUANA
(delta-9 tetrahydrocannabinol, THC, hashish)

Usually no medication is necessary. Use benzodiazepines for agitation; neuroleptics (e.g., haloperidol) for paranoid thinking.

HALLUCINATIONS
PCP, LSD, MDMA, mescaline
and
INHALANTS
(glue, paint, polish, sprays, liquid paper, gasoline, etc.)

Benzodiazepines or neuroleptics for agitation and paranoid thinking.

PSYCHOSTIMULANTS
(Cocaine, amphetamine, PPA, MDMA, Ecstasy, MDEA, Eve)

Benzodiazepines for agitation
Haloperidol for paranoid thinking
Desipramine (125–250 mg/day) for anhedonia, depression, and reduction of craving

NICOTINE

Tobacco withdrawal symptoms:

*Anxiety   *Inadequate sleep
*Irritability   *Impatience
*Restlessness   *Craving tobacco
*Hunger   *GI upset
*Headaches   *Drowsiness
                *Difficulty Concentrating
Withdrawal may be treated with nicotine or clonidine skin patches

APPENDIX D

Impaired Health Professional's Treatment Contract

PHYSICIANS ASSISTANCE PROGRAM COMMITTEE OF THE TEXAS OSTEOPATHIC MEDICAL ASSOCIATION

IMPAIRED HEALTH PROFESSIONAL'S TREATMENT CONTRACT

Name: _____ Date: _____

1. The Physicians Assistance Program Committee of the Texas Osteopathic Medical Association agrees to assume an advocacy role with the D.E.A., D.P.S., state licensing boards, hospital boards, and other appropriate agencies provided _____, D.O., abides by the terms in the body of this contract.

2. I agree to the terms of this treatment contract for a period of _____ months from the date executed and witnessed on last page.

3. I am responsible for all expenses connected with my treatment including the evaluation and testing phases and drug screens.

4. My primary care physician (not a relative) in my locality is:
   (Name) _____
   (Address) _____
   (Telephone) _____

5. I agree to abstain completely from any mood-changing drug except as prescribed by my above designated primary care physician and/or treating psychiatrist, and when possible, with the consultation of the Physicians Assistance Program Committee.

6. I agree that the above named Primary Care physician is authorized by me to make reports to the Physicians Assistance Program Committee, upon request, as to any treatment rendered to me. Further, I authorize the Physicians Assistance Program Committee of the T.O.M.A. to make a copy of this contract agreement available to my Primary Care Physician as his authority to make such reports and further grant him immunity for the furnishing of such reports, of which I will not know the contents.

7. I agree to submit to the giving of supervised-observed urine/blood samples for drug screens, including alcohol, at the discretion of the Physicians Assistance Program Committee, my psychotherapist or psychiatrist, my primary care physician, or a representative of the hospital administration, where I am on staff, and that a report of this screen be made available to the committee.

8. I agree to continue with the outpatient treatment program as recommended by _____ under date of _____ and/or the Physicians Assistance Program Committee.

9. I authorize the above mentioned facility to furnish reports of my treatment and prognosis to the Physicians Assistance Program Committee of the T.O.M.A. I further authorize the Physicians Assistance Program Committee to make a copy of this contract agreement available to the above named facility for the furnishing of such reports, of which I will not know the contents.

10. In the event of relapse, I agree to immediately notify the Physicians Assistance Program Committee, and abide by their recommendations.

11. I agree to attend the specified _____ Alcoholics Anonymous or Narcotics Anonymous meetings in _____ days, and agree to attend on a maintenance basis thereafter a minimum of _____ meetings per week.

    I also agree to choose a person as a "sponsor" in the self-help group program. He or she will likewise attest to my attendance at the group meetings.

12. I agree to attend the weekly physicians' support meetings in either _____ or _____ Counties for the period of this contract, with a minimum of _____ meetings a month.

13. I agree to keep a list of all meetings attended on a form provided by the Physicians Assistance Program Committee and to submit same to the Committee at the T.O.M.A. address by the 10th of each month for the preceding month.

14. I agree to meet with the Physicians Assistance Program Committee on a quarterly basis or more frequently as the committee directs to report on my progress of recovery.

15. I agree that I will not treat in any manner, including the writing of prescriptions or furnishing of medication to members of my family, to include wife or husband, children, parents, brothers, sisters, in-laws and their families.

16. I agree that I will restrict the use of my Drug Enforcement Administration (D.E.A.) and Texas Controlled Substance (T.C.S.) Registrations to writing orders for the hospitalized patients of hospitals of which I am on staff.

17. I agree that if I leave the State of Texas to practice, that I will participate in the Impaired Physicians Program of the State where I relocate and further that I will notify the Physicians Assistance Program of the Texas Osteopathic Medical Association of such relocation with the name and address of the Chairman of the Program within fifteen (15) days of such move.

18. I authorize the program mentioned above to furnish reports of my aftercare program to the Physicians Assistance Program Committee of the T.O.M.A. as to my participation in their program. I further authorize the Physicians Assistance Program Committee to make a copy of this contract agreement available to the above named State Program as their authority to make such reports and further grant them immunity for the furnishing of such reports, of which I will not know the contents.

19. I understand that no member of the Physicians Assistance Program Commit-

tee of the T.O.M.A. can appear on my behalf in any court of law or in any legal matter except as mentioned in paragraph one of this contract.

20. I understand that if I do not adhere to the conditions of this contract, the Physicians Assistance Program Committee may elect to remove itself from any advocacy role and may so notify those agencies before which it has acted in my behalf, including the Texas State Board of Medical Examiners.

21. I agree to notify the Physicians Assistance Program Committee within ten (10) days of any change in my home, office, or practice address or telephone number.

My current home address is _____

Phone number _____

My current office address is _____

Phone number _____

My current practice address is _____

Phone number _____

                                         _____
                                         Affiant
                                         Date _____

_____
Witness

_____
Witness

References

Adams, P. (1987, Jan.). Delirium: An optimal treatment approach. *Hospital Therapy.*

Agahjanian, G. K. (1994). Serotonin and the action of LSD in the brain. *Psychiatric Annals, 24*(3): 137–141.

Alagna, S. W., & Morokoff, P. J. (1986). Beginning medical school: Determinants of male and female emotional reactions. *Journal of Applied Social Psychology, 16*(4): 348–360.

Alcoholics Anonymous. (1955). *Alcoholics Anonymous* (2nd ed.). New York: A.A. World Services.

Alterman, A., Tarter, R., Baughman, T., Borber, B., & Fabian, S. (1985). Differentiation of alcoholics high and low in childhood hyperactivity. *Drug and Alcohol Dependence, 15*(1–2): 111–121.

American Heritage illustrated encyclopedia dictionary. (1987). Boston: Houghton Mifflin.

American Medical Association Council on Mental Health. (1973). The sick physician: Impairment disorders including alcoholism and drug dependence. *JAMA, 223:* 684–687.

American Medical Association Council on Scientific Affairs. (1987). Results and implications of the American Medical Association–American Psychiatric Association Physician Mortality Project. *JAMA, 257:* 2949–2953.

American Medical Association Council on Scientific Affairs. (1988). Physician mortality and suicide: Results and implications of the American Medical Association–American Psychiatric Association Pilot Study. *Connecticut Medicine, 50*(1): 37–43.

American Psychiatric Association. (1984). *Psychiatric glossary.* Washington, DC: Author.

American Psychiatric Association. (1987). *Diagnostic and statistical manual of mental disorders* (3rd ed., rev.). Washington, DC: Author.

American Psychiatric Association. (1990). *Benzodiazepine dependence, toxicity and abuse: A task force report of the APA.* Washington, DC: Author.

American Psychiatric Association. (1994). *Diagnostic and statistical manual of mental disorders* (4th ed.). Washington, DC: Author.

Asby Wills, T., & Shiffman, S. (1985). Coping and substance use: A conceptual framework. In S. Shiffman & T. Asby Wills (Eds.), *Coping and substance abuse* (pp. 3–23). New York: Academic Press.

Asch, D. A., & Parke, R. M. (1988). The Libby Zion case: One step forward, or two steps backward? *NEJM, 318*: 771–775.

Ashem, B., & Donner, L. (1968). Covert sensitization with alcoholics: A controlled replication. *Behavioral Research Therapy, 6*: 7–12.

Ayerst Laboratories. (1979). Product profile: Antabuse (disulfiram) in alcoholism. New York: Author.

Baekland, F., Lundwall, L., & Shanahan, T. J. (1973). Correlates of patient attrition in the outpatient treatment of alcoholism. *Journal of Nervous and Mental Disease, 157*: 99–107.

Bailey, G. W. (1989). Current perspectives on substance abuse in youth. *Journal of the American Academy of Child and Adolescent Psychiatry, 28*(2): 151–162.

Baldwin Jr., D. C., Hughes, P. H., Conard, S. E., Storr, C. L., & Sheehan, D. V. (1991). Substance use among senior medical students. *JAMA, 265*(16): 2074–2078.

Bandura, A. (1986). *Social foundations of thought and action: A social cognitive theory.* Englewood Cliffs, NJ: Prentice-Hall.

Barry, H. (1988). Psychoanalytic theory of alcoholism. In C. D. Chaudron & D. A. Wilkinson (Eds.), *Theories on alcoholism* (pp. 103–141). Toronto, Canada: Addiction Research Foundation.

Bean, M. H. (1975). Alcoholics Anonymous: A.A. *Psychiatric Annals 1975, 5*(2): 3–64.

Bean, M. H. (1981).Denial and the psychological complications of alcoholism. In M. H. Bean & N. E. Zinberg (Eds.), *Dynamic approaches to the understanding and treatment of alcoholism* (pp. 55–96). New York: The Free Press.

Beck, A. T. (1993). Addictive set of beliefs. Presented at the Fourth Annual Symposium of the American Academy of Psychiatrists in Alcoholism Addictions. Palm Beach, FL, December 4.

Beck, A. T., & Freeman, A. (1990). *Cognitive therapy of personality disorders.* New York: Guilford Press.

Beck, A. T., Ward, C. H., Mendelson, M., Mock, J., & Erbaugh, J. (1961). An inventory for measuring depression. *Archives of General Psychiatry, 4*: 561–571.

Begleiter, H., Porjesz, B., Bihari, B., & Kisson, B. (1984). Event-related brain potentials in boys at risk for alcoholism. *Science, 225*: 1493–1496.

Behrens, U. J., Worner, T. M., Braly, L. F., Shaffner, F., & Lierer, S. S. (1988). Transferrin: A marker for chronic alcohol consumption in different ethnic populations. *Alcoholism, Clinical and Experimental Research, 12*(3): 427–432.

Benjamin, G. A. H., Darling, E. J., & Sales, B. (1990). The prevalence of depression, alcohol abuse, and cocaine abuse among United States lawyers. *International Journal of Law Psychiatry, 13*(3): 233–246.

Bergler, E. (1944). Contributions to the psychogenesis of alcohol addiction. *Quarterly Journal of Studies on Alcohol, 5*: 434–449.

Bissell, L., & Haberman, P. W. (1984). *Alcoholism in the professions.* New York: Oxford University Press.

Bissell, L., & Skorina, J. K. (1987). One hundred alcoholic women in medicine: An interview study. *JAMA, 257*: 2939–2344.

Bissell, L., Haberman, P. W., & Williams, R. L. (1989). Pharmacists' recovery from alcohol and other drug addictions: An intensive study. *American Pharmacy, 29*(6): 19–30.

Bjorksten, O., Sutherland, S., Miller, C., & Stewart, T. (1983). Identification of medical student problems and comparison with those of other students. *Journal of Medical Education, 58*: 759–767.

Blackwell, B. (1986). Prevention of impairment among residents in training. *JAMA, 255*(9): 1177–1178.

Blane, H. J. (1968). *The personality of the alcoholic: Guises of dependency.* New York: Harper & Row.

Blum, K. (1984). *Handbook of abusable drugs.* New York: Gardner Press.

Blum, K., & Trachtenberg, M. C. (1988). Alcoholism: Scientific basis of a neuropsychogenetic disease. *International Journal of the Addictions, 23*(8): 781–796.

Blum, K., Noble, E. P., Sheridan, P. J., Montgomery, A., Ritchie, T., Jagadeeswaran, P., Nogami, H., Briggs, A. H., & Cohn, J. B. (1990). Allelic association of human dopamine D-receptor gene in alcoholism. *JAMA, 263*(15): 2055–2060.

Blume, S. B. (1986). Women and alcohol: A review. *JAMA, 256*(11): 1467–1470.

Boisaubin, E., Laux, L., Lester, J., Rankin, B., Roessler, R., Thornby, J., & Merrill, J. (1983). Predicting those physicians who will find practice vexatious. *Clinical Research, 32*(2): 294A (Abstract).

Bolos, A. M., Dean, M., Lucas-Derse, S., Ramsburg, M., Brown, G. L., & Goldman, D. (1990). Population and pedigree studies reveal a lack of association between the dopamine D-receptor gene and alcoholism. *JAMA, 264*(24): 3156–3157.

Boscariro, J. (1980). Factors related to "stable" and "unstable" affiliation with Alcoholics Anonymous. *International Journal of Addictions, 15*(6): 839–848.

Boyle, B. P., & Coombs, R. H. (1971). Personality profiles related to emotional stress in the initial year of medical training. *Journal of Medical Education, 46*: 882–888.

Brewster, J. M. (1986). Prevalence of alcohol and other drug problems among physicians. *JAMA, 255*(14): 1913–1920.

Bromet, E. J., Parkinson, D. K., Curtis, E. C., & Schulberg, H. C. (1990). Epidemiology of depression and alcohol abuse/dependence in a managerial and professional work place. *Journal of Occupational Medicine, 32*: 10.

Brook, J. S., Whiteman, M., Gordon, A. S., & Cohen, P. (1989). Changes in drug involvement: A longitudinal study of childhood and adolescent determinants. *Psychological Reports, 65*(3, pt. 1): 707–726.

Brown, S., & Yalom, I. D. (1977). Interactional group therapy with alcoholics. *Journal of Studies on Alcohol, 38*(3): 426–456.

Canavan, D. I. (1983a). The subject of impairment. *Journal of the Medical Society of New Jersey, 80*(1): 47–48.

Canavan, D. I. (1983b). The Impaired Physicians Program: Identification. *Journal of the Medical Society of New Jersey, 83*: 292–293.

Carroll, J. R. (1992, Mar.). When your colleague is hooked. *Texas Bar Journal*, 268–270.

Cashaw, J. L., Geraghty, C. A., McLaughlin, B. R., & Davis, V. E. (1987). Effects of acute ethanol administration on brain levels of tetrahydropapaveroline in L-dopa treated rats. *Journal of Neuroscience Research, 18*: 497–503.

Casper, E., Dilts, S. L., Soter, J. J., Lepoff, R. B., & Shore, J. H. (1988). Establishment of the Colorado Physician Health Program with a legislative initiative. *JAMA, 260*(5): 671–673.

Castaneda, R., & Cushman, P. (1989). Alcohol withdrawal: A review of clinical management. *Journal of Clinical Psychiatry, 50*(8): 278–284.

Cautela, J. R. (1967). Covert sensitization. *Psychological Reports, 20*: 459–468.

Cermak, T. L. (1986). Diagnostic criteria for codependency. *Journal of Psychoactive Drugs, 18*(1): 15–20.

Chandler, L. J., Sumners, C., & Crews, F. T. (1991). Ethanol inhibits NMDA-stimulated excitoxicity. *Alcohol, 15*: 323.

Chappel, J. N. (1992). Effective use of Alcoholics Anonymous and Narcotics Anonymous in treating patients. *Psychiatric Annals, 22*(8): 409–418.

Chappel, J. N., Jordan, R. D., Treadway, B. J., & Miller, P. R. (1977). Substance abuse attitude changes in medical students. *American Journal of Psychiatry, 134*(4): 377–384.

Chiles, J. A., Benjamin, A. H., & Cahn, T. S. (1990). Who smokes? Why? Psychiatric aspect of continued cigarette usage among lawyers in Washington State. *Comprehensive Psychiatry, 31*(2): 176–184.

Chrousos, G. P., & Gold, P. W. (1992). The concepts of stress and stress system disorders. *JAMA, 267*: 1244–1252.

Ciraulo, D. A., Sands, B. F., & Shader, R. I. (1988). Critical review of liability for benzodiazepine abuse among alcoholics. *American Journal of Psychiatry, 145*(12): 1501–1506.

Cisin, I. H. (1978). Formal and informal social controls over drinking. In J. A. Ewing & B. A. Rouse (Eds.), *Drinking: Alcohol in American society—issues and current research* (pp. 145–158). Chicago: Nelson-Hall.

Clark, A., Kay, J., & Clark, D. (1988). Patterns of psychoactive drug prescriptions by house officers for nonpatients. *Journal of Medical Education, 63*: 44–50.

Clark, D. C., & Zeldow, P. B. (1988). Vicissitudes of depressed mood during four years of medical school. *JAMA, 260*(17): 2521–2528.

Clark, D. C., Dougherty, S. R., Zeldow, P. B., Eckenfels, E. J., & Silverman, C. (1986). Alcohol use patterns of first-year medical students: II. Psychosocial characteristics associated with drinking levels. *Alcoholism, 10*(1): 65–70.

Clark, D. C., Eckenfels, E. J., Dougherty, S. R., & Fawcett, J. (1987). Patterns of alcohol use and abuse by medical students: A longitudinal study of one class. *JAMA, 257*: 2921–2926.

Clark, D. C., Gibbons, R. D., Dougherty, S. R., & Silverman, C. M. (1987). Model for quantifying the drug involvement of medical students. *International Journal of the Addictions, 22*(3): 249–271.

Clark, D. C., Salazar-Grueso, E., Grabler, P., & Fawcett, J. (1984). Predictors of depression during first 6 months of internship. *American Journal of Psychiatry, 141*(9): 1095–1098.

Cloninger, C. R. (1987). Neurogenetic adaptive mechanisms in alcoholism. *Science, 236*: 410–416.

Cloninger, C. R., Bohman, M., & Sigvardsson, S. (1981). Inheritance of alcohol abuse. *Archives of General Psychiatry, 38*: 861–868.

Cloninger, C. R., Bohman, M., Sigvardsson, S., & von Knorring, A. (1985). Psychopathology in adopted-out children of alcoholics: The Stockholm Adoption Study. In M. Galanter (Ed.), *Recent developments in alcoholism* (vol. 3). New York: Plenum Press.

Cohen, P., Johnson, J., Lewis, S. A., & Brook, J. S. (1990). Single parenthood and employment: Double jeopardy? In J. Eckenrode & S. Gore (Eds.), *Stress between work and family* (pp. 117–132). New York: Plenum Press.

Cohen, S. (1984). Drugs in the workplace. *Journal of Clinical Psychiatry, 45*(12, sec. 2): 4–8.

Cohen, S. (1985). *The substance abuse problem. Vol. 2. New issues for the 1980s.* New York: The Haworth Press.

Colford Jr., J. M., & McPhee, S. J. (1989). The ravelled sleeve of care: Managing the stress of residency training. *JAMA, 261*(6): 889–893.

Conger, J. J. (1956). Alcoholism: Theory, problem and challenge. II. Reinforcement theory and the dynamics of alcoholism. *Quarterly Journal of Studies in Alcohol, 17*: 296–305.

Cox, W. (1988). Personality theory. In C. D. Chaudron & D. A. Wilkinson (Eds.), *Theories on alcoholism* (pp. 143–172). Toronto, Canada: Addiction Research Foundation.

Crosby, L., & Bissell, L. (1989). *To care enough: Intervention with chemically dependent colleagues.* Minneapolis, MN: Johnson Institute.

Crowley, T. J. (1986). Doctors' drug abuse reduced during contingency-contracting treatment. *Alcohol and Drug Research, 6*: 299–307.

Dackis, C. A., & Gold, M. S. (1985). Bromocriptine as a treatment for cocaine abuse. *Lancet, 2*: 1151–1152.

Dackis, C. A., & Gold, M. S. (1992). Psychiatric hospitals for treatment of dual diagnosis. In J. H. Lowinson, P. Ruiz, & R. B. Millman (Eds.), *Substance abuse: A comprehensive textbook* (2nd ed.) (pp. 467–485). Baltimore, MD: Williams & Wilkins.

Davis Jr., L. J., de la Fuente, J., Morse, R. M., Landa, E., & O'Brien, P. C. (1989). Self-Administered Alcoholism Screening Test (SAAST): Comparison of classificatory accuracy in two cultures. *Alcoholism, 13*(2): 224–228.

Davis, M. S. (1989). Detecting and preventing stress: The Cedars-Sinai House Officer Model. *The Resident Advocate, 4*(1): 1–8.

Davis, V. E., & Walsh, M. D. (1970). Alcohol, amines, and alkaloids: A possible basis for alcohol addiction. *Science, 167*: 1005–1007.

Deikman, A. J. (1982). *The observing self and mysticism in psychotherapy.* Boston: Beacon Press.

Derogatis, L. R., & Melisaratos, N. (1983). The brief symptom inventory: An introductory report. *Psychological Medicine, 13*: 595–605.

Devor, E. J., & Cloninger, C. R. (1989). Genetics of alcoholism. *Annual Review of Genetics, 23*: 19–36.

Dickstein, L. J., Stephenson, M. S., & Hinz, L. D. (1990). Psychiatric impairment in medical students. *Academic Medicine, 65*: 588–593.

Dodes, L. M. (1984). Abstinence from alcohol and long-term individual psychotherapy with alcoholics. *American Journal of Psychotherapy, 38*(2): 248–256.

Duffy, M. (1983). The demand for alcoholic drink in the United Kingdom. *Applied Economics, 15*: 125–140.

Dupont, R. L. (1984). *Getting tough on gateway drugs: A guide for the family.* Washington, DC: American Psychiatric Press.

Dupont, R. L. (1992). Choosing the right treatment for the patient with anxiety. *Modern Medicine, 60*: 64–76.

Dupont, R. L., & Sayler, K. E. (1991). Sedatives/hypnotics and benzodiazepines. In R. J. Frances & S. Miller (Eds.), *Clinical textbook of addictive disorders* (pp. 69–102). New York: Guilford Press.

Eaton, W. W., Anthony, J. C., Mandel, W., & Garrison, R. (1990). Occupations and the prevalence of major depression disorders. *Journal of Occupational Medicine, 32*(11): 1079–1087.

Eddy, N. B., Halback, H., Isbell, H., & Seevers, M. H. (1965). Drug dependence: Its significance and characteristics. *Bulletin of the World Health Organization, 32*: 721–733.

Elaine B., Claire M., June S., & Janet A. (1974). Helping the nurse who misuses drugs. *American Journal of Nursing, 74*(9): 1665–1671.

Emrick, C. (1987). Alcoholics Anonymous: Affiliation process and effectiveness as treatment. *Alcoholism, Clinical and Experimental Research, 11*(5): 416–423.

Ewing, J. A., & Rouse, B. A. (1978). *Drinking: Alcohol in American society—issues and current research.* Chicago: Nelson-Hall.

Fagerstrom, K. O. (1991). Towards better diagnoses and more individual treatment of tobacco dependence. *British Journal of Addiction, 86*(5): 543–547.

Fels, A. (1991, Nov. 10). Review of *Learning to play God: The coming of age of a young doctor* by Robert Marion. *The New York Times Book Review,* p. 20.

Fielding, J. E., Knight, K. K., Goetzel, R. Z., & Laouri, M. (1991). Prevalence and characteristics of employees reporting heavy or problem drinking. *Preventive Medicine, 20*: 316–327.

Fiore, M. C., Jorenby, D. E., Baker, T. B., & Kenford, S. L. (1992). Tobacco dependence and the nicotine patch: Clinical guidelines for effective use. *JAMA, 268*(19): 2687–2694.

Fisher, J. C., Mason, R. L., Keeley, K. A., & Fisher, I. V. (1975). Physicians and alcoholics: The effect of medical training on attitudes toward alcoholics. *Journal of Studies on Alcohol, 36*(7): 949–955.

Frances, R. J., & Allen, M. H. (1986). The interaction of substance use disorders with nonpsychotic psychiatric disorders. In R. Michels & J. O. Cavernar Jr. (Eds.), *Psychiatry* (vol. 1). New York: Basic Books.

Frances, R. J., & Miller, S. I. (Eds.). (1991). *Clinical textbook of addictive disorders.* New York: Guilford Press.

Frances, R., Alexopoulos, G., & Yandow, J. (1984). Lawyers' alcoholism. In B. Stimmel (Ed.), *Alcohol and drug abuse in the affluent* (pp. 59–66). New York: The Haworth Press.

Frank, B., Marel, R., Schmeidler, J., & Lipton, D. S. (1984). An overview of substance use among New York State's upper income householders. In B. Stimmel (Ed.), *Alcohol and drug abuse in the affluent* (pp. 11–26). New York: The Haworth Press.

Gabbard, G. O. (1985). The role of compulsiveness in the normal physician. *JAMA, 254*(20): 2926–2929.

Gabbard, G. O., & Menninger, R. W. (1989). The psychology of postponement in the medical marriage. *JAMA, 261*(16): 2378–2381.

Galanter, M. (1993). Network therapy for addiction: A model for office practice. *American Journal of Psychiatry, 150*(1): 28–36.

Garetz, F. K., Raths, O. N., & Morse, R. H. (1976). The disturbed and the disturbing psychiatric resident. *Archives of General Psychiatry, 134*: 446–450.

Garfinkel, P. E., & Waring, E. M. (1981). Personality, interests, and emotional disturbance in psychiatric residents. *American Journal of Psychiatry, 138*: 51–55.

Gavin, D. R., Ross, H. E., & Skinner, H. A. (1989). Diagnostic validity of the Drug Abuse Screening Test in the assessment of the DSM-III drug disorders. British Journal of Addiction, *84*:301–307.

Gawin, F. H. (1991). Cocaine addiction: Psychology and neurophysiology. *Science, 251*: 1580–1586.

Gawin, F. H., & Kleber, H. D. (1984). Cocaine abuse treatment: Open pilot trial with desipramine and lithium carbonate. *Archives of General Psychiatry, 41*: 903–909.

Gawin, F. H., & Kleber, H. D. (1986). Abstinence, symptomatology, and psychiatric diagnosis and cocaine abusers. *Archives of General Psychiatry, 43*: 107–113.

Gawin, F. H., Kleber, H. D., Byck, R., Rounsaville, B. J., Kosten, T. R., Jatlow, P. I., & Morgan, C. (1989). Desipramine facilitation of initial cocaine abstinence. *Archives of General Psychiatry, 46*(2): 117–121.

Gelernter, J., Goldman, D., & Risch, N. (1993). The A1 allele at the D2 dopamine receptor gene and alcoholism. *JAMA, 263*: 1673–1677.

Gill, K., & Amit, Z. (1989). Serotonin uptake blockers and voluntary alcohol consumptions: A review of recent studies. In M. Galanter (Ed.), *Recent developments in alcoholism* (vol. 7) (pp. 225–248). New York: Plenum Press.

Giannetti, V. J., Galinsky, A. M., & Kay, D. H. (1990). Education, assistance and prevention program for chemical dependency problems among pharmacy students. *American Journal of Pharmaceutical Education, 54*: 275–281.

Goby, M. J., Bradley, N. J., & Bespalec, D. A. (1979). Physicians treated for alcoholism: A follow-up study. *Alcoholism, 3*(2): 121–124.

Godfrey, C., & Maynard, A. (1988). An economic theory of alcohol consumption and abuse. In C. D. Chaudron & D. A. Wilkinson (Eds.), *Theories on alcoholism* (pp. 411–435). Toronto, Canada: Addiction Research Foundation.

Gold, M. S., Pottash, A. C., Sweeney, D. R., & Kleber, H. D. (1980). Opiate withdrawal using clonidine. *JAMA, 243*(4): 343–346.

Goldstein, A. (1978). Endorphins: Physiology and clinical implications. *Annals of the New York Academy of Science, 311*: 49–58.

Gomberg, E. S. (1988). Alcoholic women in treatment: The question of stigma and age. *Alcohol and Alcoholism, 23*(6): 507–514.

Goodwin, D. W. (1983). The role of genetics: Overview. In M. Galanter (Ed.), *Recent developments in alcoholism* (vol. 1) (pp. 3–8). New York: Plenum Press.

Goodwin, D. W., Schulsinger, F., Hermansen, L., Guza, S. B., & Winokur, G.

(1973). Alcohol problems in adoptees raised apart from alcoholic biological parents. *Archives of General Psychiatry, 28*: 238–243.

Gottheil, E., Druley, K. A., Pashko, S., & Winstein, S. P. (Eds.). (1987). *Stress in addiction.* New York: Brunner/Mazel.

Greenstein, R. A., Arndt, I. C., McClellan, A. T., O'Brien, C. P., & Evans, B. (1984). Naltrexone: A clinical perspective. *Journal of Clinical Perspective, 45*: 25–28.

Greenstein, R. A., Fudala, P. J., & O'Brien, C. P. (1992). Alternative pharmaco-therapies for opiate addiction. In J. H. Lowinson, P. Ruiz, & R. B. Millman (Eds.), *Substance abuse: A comprehensive textbook* (2nd ed.) (pp. 562–573). Baltimore, MD: Williams & Wilkins.

Griffin, M. L., Weiss, R. D., Mirin, S. M., & Lange, U. (1989). A comparison of male and female cocaine abusers. *Archives of General Psychiatry, 46*(2): 122–126.

Gulatieri, A. C., Consentino, J. P., & Becker, J. S. (1983). The California experi-ence with a divergent program for impaired physicians. *JAMA, 249*(2): 226–229.

Haack, M. R., & Harford, T. C. (1984). Drinking patterns among student nurses. *International Journal of the Addictions, 19*(5): 577–583.

Hawks, R. L. (1986). Analytical methodology. In R. L. Hawks & N. C. Chiang (Eds.), *Urine testing for drugs of abuse* (NIDA Research Monograph 73) (pp. 30–42). Washington, DC: U.S. Government Printing Office.

Heath, A. C., Jardine, R., & Martin, N. G. (1989). Interactive effects of genotype and social environment on alcohol consumption in female twins. *Journal of Studies on Alcohol, 50*(1): 38–48.

Heath, D. B. (1988). Emerging anthropological theory and models of alcohol use and alcoholism. In C. D. Chaudron & D. A. Wilkinson (Eds.), *Theories on alcoholism* (pp. 353–410). Toronto, Canada: Addiction Research Foundation.

Heinz, M., Fahey, S. N., & Leiden, L. I. (1984). Perceived stress in medical, law, and graduate students. *Journal of Medical Education, 59*: 169–179.

Helzer, J. E., & Pryzbeck, T. R. (1988). The co-occurrence of alcoholism with other psychiatric disorders in the general population and its impact on treatment. *Journal of Studies on Alcohol, 49*(3): 219–224.

Hendrie, H. C., Clair, D. K., Brittain, H. M., & Fadul, P. E. (1990). A study of anxiety/depressive symptoms of medical students, house staff, and their spouses/partners. *Journal of Nervous and Mental Disease, 178*(3): 204–206.

Henry, S., & Robinson, D. (1978). Understanding Alcoholics Anonymous. *Lan-cet, 2*: 372–375.

Herrington, R. E. (1979). The impaired physician: Recognition, diagnosis, and treatment. *Wisconsin Medical Journal, 78*: 21–23.

Herzog, D. B., Wyshak, G., & Stern, T. A. (1984). Patient-generated dysphoria in house officers. *Journal of Medical Education, 59*: 869–874.

Hesselbrock, M. N., Meyer, R. E., & Keener, J. (1985). Psychopathology in hospitalized alcoholics. *Archives of General Psychiatry, 42*: 1050–1055.

Hill, D. R., Krantz, D. S., Contrada, R. J., Hedges, S. M., & Ratliff-Crain, J. A. (1987). Stability and change in Type A components and cardiovascular reactivity in medical students during periods of academic stress. *Journal of Applied Social Psychology, 17*(8): 679–688.

Hochschild, A. (1989). *The second shift: Working parents and the revolution at home.* New York: Viking Press.

Hoffer, G. L., & Macleod, J. S. (1988). How attorneys in law firms in Maryland's major urban areas view the quality of their professional lives and issues facing the profession. A pilot study conducted by PayCor, Inc., for the Maryland Bar Association.

Holden, C. (1991). Probing the complex genetics of alcoholism. *Science, 251*: 163–164.

Holder, H. D., James, K., Mosher, J., Saltz, R., Spurr, S., & Wagenaar, A. C. (1993). Alcoholic beverage server liability and the reduction of alcohol-involved problems. *Journal of Studies on Alcohol, 54*(1): 23–36.

Hser, Y. I., Anglin, M. D., & McGlothlin, W. H. (1987). Sex differences in addict careers. 1. Initiation of use. *American Journal of Drug and Alcohol Abuse, 13*(1–2): 33–57.

Hsu, K., & Marshall, V. (1987). Prevalence of depression and distress in a large sample of Canadian residents, interns, and fellows. *American Journal of Psychiatry, 144*(12): 1561–1566.

Hughes, P. H., Brandenburg, N., Baldwin Jr., D. C., Storr, C. L., Williams, K. M., Anthony, J. C., & Sheehan, D. V. (1992). Prevalence of substance use among U.S. physicians. *JAMA, 267*: 2333–2339.

Hughes, P. H., Conard, S. E., Baldwin, D. C., Storr, C. L., & Sheehan, D. V. (1991). Resident physician substance use in the United States. *JAMA, 265*(16): 2069–2112.

Hull, J. G. (1981). A self-awareness model of the causes and effects of alcohol consumption. *Journal of Abnormal Psychology, 90*: 586–600.

Hurwitz, T. A., Beiser, M., Nichol, H., Patrick, L., & Kozak, J. (1987). Impaired interns and residents. *Canadian Journal of Psychiatry, 32*(3): 165–169.

Hutchinson, S. (1986). Chemically dependent nurses: The trajectory toward self-annihilation. *Nursing Research, 35*(4): 196–201.

Jacobson, G. R. (1989). A comprehensive approach to pretreatment evaluation: I. Detection, assessment, and diagnosis of alcoholism. In R. K. Hester & W. R. Miller (Eds.), *Handbook of alcoholism treatment approaches: Effective alternatives* (pp. 17–53). New York: Pergamon Press.

Janes, K., & Gruenewald, P. J. (1991). The role of formal law in alcohol control systems: A comparison among states. *American Journal of Drug and Alcohol Abuse, 17*(2): 199–214.

Johnson, R. P., & Connelly, J. C. (1981). Addicted physicians: A closer look. *JAMA, 245*(3): 253–257.

Johnson, V. E. (1973). *I'll quit tomorrow.* New York: Harper & Row.

Johnston, L., O'Malley, P., & Bachman, J. (1989). Drug use, drinking, and smoking: National survey results from high school, college, and young adult populations. *National Institute on Drug Abuse*, Pub. 89: 1638.

Kandel, D. B., & Logan, J. A. (1984). Patterns of drug use from adolescence to young adulthood: I. Periods of risk for initiation, continued use, and discontinuation. *American Journal of Public Health, 74*: 660–666.

Kaprio, J., Koskenvuo, L., Langinvainio, H., Romanov, K., Sarna, S., & Rose, R. J. (1987). Genetic influences on use and abuse of alcohol: A study of 5638 adult Finnish twin brothers. *Alcoholism, Clinical and Experimental Research*, 11(4): 349–356.

Karabensh, J. K. (1988, Jan.-Feb.-Mar.). One hundred years of pharmacy. *The Apothecary*, 100.

Kaufman, E., & Reoux, J. (1988). Guidelines for the successful psychotherapy of substance abusers. *American Journal of Drug and Alcohol Abuse*, 14(2): 199–209.

Kellner, R., Wiggins, R. J., & Pathak, D. (1986). Distress in medical and law students. *Comprehensive Psychiatry*, 27(3): 220–223.

Khantzian, E. J. (1981). Some treatment implications of the ego and self-disturbance in alcoholism. In M. H. Bean & N. E. Zinberg (Eds.), *Dynamic approaches to the understanding and treatment of alcoholism* (pp. 163–188). New York: The Free Press.

Khantzian, E. J. (1985a). The injured self, addiction, and our call to medicine: Understanding and managing addicted physicians. *JAMA*, 254(2): 249–252.

Khantzian, E. J. (1985b). The self-medication hypothesis of addictive disorders: Focus on heroin and cocaine dependence. *American Journal of Psychiatry*, 142(aa): 1259–1264.

Khantzian, E. J. (1988). The primary care therapist and patient needs in substance abuse treatment. *American Journal of Drug and Alcohol Abuse*, 14(2): 159–167.

Khantzian, E. J., Halliday, K. S., & McAuliffe, W. E. (1990). *Addiction and the vulnerable self: Modified dynamic group therapy for substance abusers*. New York: Guilford Press.

Khantzian, E. J., & Mack, J. E. (1989). Alcoholics Anonymous and contemporary psychodynamic theory. In M. Galanter (Ed.), *Recent developments in alcoholism* (vol. 7) (pp. 67–89). New York: Plenum Press.

Kleber, H. D., Riordan, C. E., & Rounsaville, B. (1985). Clonidine in outpatient detoxication from methadone. *Archives of General Psychiatry*, 42: 391–395.

Kleber, H. D., Topazian, M., Gaspari, J., Riordan, C. E., & Kosten, T. (1987). Clonidine and naltrexone in the outpatient treatment of heroin withdrawal. *American Journal of Drug and Alcohol Abuse*, 13(1–2): 1–17.

Knight, R. P. (1937). The psychodynamics of chronic alcoholism. *Journal of Nervous and Mental Disease*, 86: 538–548.

Kohut, H. (1971). *The analysis of the self*. New York: International Universities Press.

Kohut, H. (1977). *The restoration of the self*. New York: International Universities Press.

Koob, G. F., & Bloom, F. E. (1988). Cellular and molecular mechanisms of drug dependence. *Science*, 242: 715–723.

Kosten, T. R. (1992). Pharmacotherapies. In T. R. Kosten & H. D. Kleber (Eds.), *Clinician's guide to cocaine addiction: Theory, research, and treatment* (pp. 273–289). New York: Guilford Press.

Kosten, T. R. (1993, Feb.). Pharmacotherapies for cocaine abuse: Neurobiological abnormalities reversed with drug intervention. *The Psychiatric Times*, pp. 25–26.

Krakowski, A. J. (1982). Stress and the practice of medicine: II. Stressors, stresses, and strains. *Psychotherapy Psychosomatic, 38*: 11–23.

Krakowski, A. J. (1984). Stress in the practice of medicine: III. Physicians compared with lawyers. *Psychotherapy Psychosomatic, 42*: 143–151.

Kurtz, E. (1979). *Not God: A history of Alcoholics Anonymous.* Center City, MN: Hazelden.

Kurtz, E. (1981). *Shame and guilt: Characteristics of the dependency cycle. An historical perspective for professionals.* Center City, MN: Hazelden Foundation.

Kurtz, E. (1989, Jun. 9). Alcoholics Anonymous and spirituality. Workshop presented in Dallas, TX.

Kurtz, E., & Ketcham, K. (1992). *The spirituality of imperfection.* New York: Bantam.

Landau, C., Hall, S., Wartman, S., & Macko, M. B. (1988). Stress in social and family relationships during the medical residency. *Journal of Medical Education, 61.*

Lawton, M. J. (Ed.). (1990). *The Addiction Letter, 6,* p. 6.

Lazarus, R., & Folkman, S. (1984). *Stress, appraisal, and coping.* New York: Springer.

Lehman, W. E. K., & Simpson, D. D. (1990). Patterns of drug use in a large metropolitan workforce. *National Institute on Drug Abuse Research Monograph Series,* Monograph 100, vol. II, pp. 45–62.

Lester, D. (1988). Genetic theory: An assessment of the heritability of alcoholism. In C. D. Chaudron & D. A. Wilkinson (Eds.), *Theories on alcoholism* (pp. 1–28). Toronto, Canada: Addiction Research Foundation.

Levine, D. G., Preston, P. A., & Lipscomb, S. G. (1974). A historical approach to understanding drug abuse among nurses. *American Journal of Psychiatry, 131*(9): 1036–1037.

Lewis, J. M., Barnhardt, F. D., Howard, B. L., Carson, D. I., & Nace, E. P. (1993a, Feb.). Work satisfaction in the lives of physicians. *The Journal of Texas Medicine,* pp. 54–61.

Lewis, J. M., Barnhardt, F. D., Howard, B. L., Carson, D. I., & Nace, E. P. (1993b, Feb.). Work stress in the lives of physicians. *The Journal of Texas Medicine,* pp. 62–67.

Ling, W., & Wesson, D. R. (1984). Naltrexone treatment for addicted health care professionals: A collaborative private practice experience. *Journal of Clinical Psychiatry, 45*: 46–48.

Linn, L. S., Yager, J., Cope, D., & Leake, B. (1985). Health status, job satisfaction, job stress, and life satisfaction among academic and clinical faculty. *JAMA, 254*: 2775–2782.

Linnoila, M. I. (1989). Anxiety and alcoholism. *Journal of Clinical Psychiatry, 50*(11) (suppl.): 26–29.

Lipp, M. R., Benson, S. G., & Taintor, Z. (1971). Marijuana use by medical students. *American Journal of Psychiatry, 128*(2): 99–105.

Liskow, B. I., & Goodwin, D. W. (1987). Pharmacological treatment of alcohol intoxication withdrawal and dependence: A critical review. *Journal of Studies on Alcohol, 48*: 365–370.

Lloyd, C., & Gartrell, N. K. (1981). Sex differences in medical school mental health. *American Journal of Psychiatry, 138*: 1346–1351.

Lowinson, J. H., Marion, I. J., Joseph, H., & Dole, V. P. (1992). Methadone maintenance. In J. H. Lowinson, P. Ruiz, & R. B. Millman (Eds.), *Substance abuse: A comprehensive textbook* (2nd ed.) (pp. 550–561). Baltimore, MD: Williams & Wilkins.

Lowinson, J. H., Ruiz, P., & Millman, R. B. (1992). *Substance abuse: A comprehensive textbook* (2nd ed.). Baltimore, MD: Williams & Wilkins.

Luborsky, L., & Crits-Cristoph, P. (1989). A relationship pattern measure: The core conflictual relationship theme. *Psychiatry, 52*(3): 250–259.

Lutsky, I., Abram, S. E., Jacobson, G. R., Hopwood, M., & Kampine, J. P. (1991). Substance abuse by anesthesiology residents. *Academic Medicine, 66*(3): 164–166.

Machell, D. E. (1990). The lethality of the corporate image in the recovering corporate executive alcoholic. *Journal of Alcohol and Drug Education, 36*(1): 1–5.

Mack, J. E. (1981). Alcoholism, A.A. and the governance of the self. In M. A. Bean & N. E. Zinberg (Eds.), *Dynamic approaches to the understanding and treatment of alcoholism* (pp. 128–162). New York: The Free Press.

Maddux, J. F., Hoppe, S. K., & Costello, R. M. (1986). Psychoactive substance use among medical students. *American Journal of Psychiatry, 143*: 187–191.

Maddux, J. F., Timmerman, I. M., & Costello, R. M. (1987). Use of psychoactive substances by residents. *Journal of Medical Education, 62*: 852–854.

Malcolm, R., O'Neil, P. M., Von, J. M., & Dickerson, P. C. (1987). Naltrexone and dysphoria: A double blind placebo controlled trial. *Biological Psychiatry, 22*(6): 710–716.

Margolin, A., Kosten, T. R., Petrakis, I. L., Avants, S. K., & Kosten, T. A. (1991). Bupropion reduces cocaine abuse in methadone-maintained patients. *Archives of General Psychiatry, 48*(1): 87.

Marlatt, G. A. (1987). Alcohol, the magic elixir: Stress expectancy and the transformation of emotional states. In E. Gottheil, K. A. Druley, S. Pashko, & S. P. Weinstein (Eds.), *Stress and addiction* (pp. 302–322). New York: Brunner/Mazel.

Martin, B., Bloom, A., Howlett, A., & Welch, S. (1988). Cannabinoid action in the central nervous system. *Problems of Drug Dependence, 1988*, NIDA Research Monograph 90: 275–283.

Martin, W. R. (1987). Opioid antagonists. *Pharmacological Reviews, 19*: 463–521.

Martin, W. R., Jasinski, D., & Mansky, P. (1973). Naltrexone: An antagonist for the treatment of heroin dependence. *Archives of General Psychiatry, 28*: 784–791.

Marx, J. (1990). Marijuana receptor gene cloned. *Science, 249*: 624–625.

Mawardi, B. H. (1979). Satisfaction, dissatisfaction, and causes of stress in medical practice. *JAMA, 241*(14): 1483–1486.

Mazie, B. (1985). Job stress, psychological health, and social support of family practice residents. *Journal of Medical Education, 60*: 935–941.

McAuliffe, W. E., Rohman, M., Santangelo, S., Feldman, B., Magnuson, E., Sobol, A., & Weissman, J. (1986). Psychoactive drug use among practicing physicians and medical students. *New England Journal of Medicine, 315*(13): 805–809.

McAuliffe, W. E., Santangelo, S. L., Gingras, J., Rohman, M., Sobol, A., & Magnuson, E. (1987). Use and abuse of controlled substances by pharmacists and pharmacy students. *American Journal of Hospital Pharmacy, 44*: 311–317.

McAuliffe, W. E., Wechsler, H., Rohman, N., Soboloff, S. H., Fishman, P., Toth, D., & Friedman, R. (1984). Psychoactive drug use by young and future physicians. *Journal of Health and Social Behavior, 25*: 34–54.

McClelland, D. C., Davis, W. N., Kalin, R., & Wanner, E. (1972). *The drinking man*. New York: The Free Press.

McCord, W., & McCord, J. (1980). *Origins of alcoholism*. Stanford, CA: Stanford University Press.

McCue, J. D. (1982). The effects of stress on physicians and their medical practice. *New England Journal of Medicine, 306*: 458–463.

McLellan, A. T., Luborsky, L., Woody, G. E., & O'Brien, C. P. (1980). An improved diagnostic evaluation instrument for substance abuse patients: The Addiction Severity Index. *Journal of Nervous and Mental Disease, 168*: 26–33.

McShane, J. V. (1992, Mar.). Disability probation and monitoring programs. *Texas Bar Journal*, 273–275.

Mechanick, P., Mintz, J., Gallagher, J., Lapid, G., Rubin, R., & Good, J. (1973). Nonmedical drug use among medical students. *Archives of General Psychiatry, 29*: 48–50.

Meller, W. H., Rinehart, R., Cadoret, R. J., & Troughton, E. (1988). Specific familial transmission in substance abuse. *International Journal of the Addictions, 23*(10): 1029–1039.

Mellinger, G. D., Balter, M. B., & Uhlenhuth, E. N. (1984). Antianxiety agents: Duration of use and characteristics of users in the USA. *Current Medical Research Opinion, 85*: 21–35.

Menk, E. J., Baumgarten, R. K., Kingsley, C. P., Culling, R. D., & Middaugh, R. (1990). Success of reentry into anesthesiology training programs by residents with a history of substance abuse. *JAMA, 263*(22): 3060–3062.

Mercer, P. W., & Khavari, K. A. (1990). Are women drinking more like men? An empirical examination of the convergence hypothesis. *Alcoholism, Clinical and Experimental Research, 14*(3): 461–466.

Michels, P. J., & Johnson, N. P. (1990). Medical student stress, alcohol and other drug use in early medical education. *Substance Abuse, 11*(2): 78–83.

Miller, N. S. (Ed.). (1991). *Comprehensive handbook of drug and alcohol addiction*. New York: Marcel Dekker.

Miller, N. S., & Gold, M. S. (1991). Alcohol and other drug dependence and withdrawal characteristics. In M. S. Gold (Ed.), *Alcohol*. New York: Plenum Press.

Miller, W. R. (1989). Matching individuals with interventions. In R. K. Hester & W. R. Miller (Eds.), *Handbook of alcoholism treatment approaches* (pp. 261–271). New York: Pergamon Press.

Millon, T. (1969). *Modern psychopathology: A biosocial approach to maladaptive learning and functioning*. Philadelphia: W. B. Saunders.

Mirin, S. M., & Weiss, R. D. (1991). Substance abuse in mental illness. In R. J. Frances & S. I. Miller (Eds.), *Clinical textbook of addicted disorders* (pp. 271–298). New York: Guilford Press.

Mirin, S. M., Weiss, R. D., & Michael, J. (1988). Psychopathology in substance abusers: Diagnosis and treatment. *American Journal of Drug and Alcohol Abuse*, *14*(2): 139–157.

Mirin, S. M., Weiss, R. D., Sollogub, A., & Michael, J. (1984). Psychopathology in the families of drug abusers. In S. M. Mirin (Ed.), *Substance abuse and psychopathology* (pp. 80–106). Washington, DC: American Psychiatric Press.

Modlin, H., & Montes, A. (1964). Narcotic addiction in physicians. *American Journal of Psychiatry*, *121*: 358–365.

Morse, R. M., Martin, M. A., Swenson, W. M., & Niven, R. G. (1984). Prognosis of physicians treated for alcoholism and drug dependence. *JAMA*, *251*(6): 743–746.

Morse, R. M., Mitchell, M. M., & Martin, M. A. (1977). Physicians' attitudes toward alcoholism: A positive trend? In F. Seixas (Ed.), *Currents in alcoholism* (vol. 2) (pp. 207–224). New York: Grune & Stratton.

Murray, R. M., Clifford, C. A., & Gurling, H. M. D. (1983). Twin and adoption studies: New goal is the evidence for a genetic role. In M. Galanter (Ed.), *Recent developments in alcoholism* (vol. 1) (pp. 25–48). New York: Plenum Press.

Myers, R. D., & Melchior, C. L. (1977). Alcohol drinking: Abnormal intake caused by tetrahydropapaveroline in brain. *Science*, *196*: 554–556.

Myers, T., & Weiss, E. (1987). Substance use by interns and residents: An analysis of personal, social and professional differences. *British Journal of Addiction*, *82*(10): 1091–1099.

Nace, E. P. (1982). The role of craving in the treatment of alcoholism. *National Association of Private Psychiatric Hospitals Journal*, *13*(1): 27–31.

Nace, E. P. (1987). *The treatment of alcoholism*. New York: Brunner/Mazel.

Nace, E. P. (1990). Substance abuse and personality disorder. In D. F. O'Connell (Ed.), *Managing the dually diagnosed patient: Current issues in clinical approaches* (pp. 183–198). New York: The Haworth Press.

Nace, E. P., & Isbell, P. G. (1991). Alcohol. In R. J. Frances & S. I. Miller (Eds.), *Clinical textbook of addictive disorders* (pp. 43–68). New York: Guilford.

Nace, E. P., Davis, C., & Hunter, J. (1995, spring). A comparison of male and female physicians treated for substance use and psychiatric disorders. *American Journal of Addictions*, *14*(2):156–162.

Nace, E. P., O'Brien, C. P., Mintz, J., Ream, N., & Myers, A. L. (1977). Drinking problems among Vietnam veterans. In F. A. Seixas (Ed.), *Currents in alcoholism* (vol. 2). New York: Grune & Stratton.

Nadelson, C., Notman, M., & Preven, D. (1982). Medical student stress, adaptation and mental health. In S. Scheiber & B. Doyle (Eds.), *Impaired physicians*. New York: Plenum Press.

Naranjo, C. A., Sellers, E. M., & Lawrin, M. O. (1986). Modulation of ethanol intake by serotonin uptake inhibitors. *Journal of Clinical Psychiatry*, *47*(suppl. 4): 16–22.

Newman, A. (1992, Oct.). Psychiatrist hopes to mend ties with A.A. (interview with Dr. John Chappel). *Clinical Psychiatry News*, p. 10.

Nicholi Jr., A. M. (1983). The nontherapeutic use of psychoactive drugs. *New England Journal of Medicine*, 308(18): 925–933.

Niven, R. G., Hurt, R. D., Morse, R. M., & Swenson, W. M. (1984). Alcoholism in physicians. *Mayo Clinic Proceedings*, 59: 12–16.

Noble, B. P. (1993, Jan. 10). Pushing nurses to a breaking point. *The New York Times*, p. F25.

Norris, J., Pierson, F., & Waugama, W. (1988). Critical factors associated with substance abuse and chemical dependency in nurse anesthesia. *Journal of Alcohol and Drug Education*, 33(2): 6–13.

North, C. S., Clouse, R. E., Spitznagel, E. L., & Alpers, D. H. (1990). The relation of ulcerative colitis to psychiatric factors: A review of findings and methods. *American Journal of Psychiatry*, 147(8): 974–981.

Notman, M. T., Salt, P., & Nadelson, C. C. (1984). Stress and adaptation in medical students: Who is most vulnerable? *Comprehensive Psychiatry*, 25: 355–356.

O'Brien, C. P., Nace, E. P., Mintz, J., Myers, A. L., & Ream, N. (1980). Follow-up to Vietnam veterans: I. Relapse to drug use after Vietnam service. *Drug and Alcohol Dependence*, 5: 333–340.

O'Connell, D. F. (Ed.). (1990). *Managing the dually diagnosed patient: Current issues in clinical approaches*. New York: The Haworth Press.

Ogborne, A. C., & Glaser, F. B. (1981). Characteristics of affiliates of Alcoholics Anonymous. *Journal of Studies on Alcohol*, 42(7): 661–675.

O'Malley, S. S., Jaffe, A. J., Chang, G., Schottenfeld, R. S., Meyer, R. E., & Rounsaville, B. (1992) Naltrexone and coping skills therapy for alcohol dependence: A controlled study. *Archives of General Psychiatry*. 49:881–887.

Parker, D. A., & Farmer, G. C. (1988). The epidemiology of alcohol abuse among employed men and women. In M. Galanter (Ed.), *Recent developments in alcoholism* (vol. 6) (pp. 113–130). New York: Plenum Press.

Parker, D. A., Wolz, M. W., Parker, E. S., & Harford, T. C. (1980). Sex roles and alcohol consumption: A research note. *Journal of Health and Social Behavior*, 21: 43–48.

Parkerson Jr., G. R., Broadhead, W. E., & Tse, C. J. (1990). The health status and life satisfaction of first-year medical students. *Academic Medicine*, 65(9): 586–589.

Pasternak, G. W. (Ed.). (1988). *The opiate receptors*. Clifton, NJ: Humana Press.

Patient placement criteria for the treatment of psychoactive substance use disorders. American Society of Addiction Medicine, 1991.

Penick, E. C., Powell, B. J., Liskow,B. I., Jackson, J. O., & Nickel, E. J. (1988). The stability of coexisting psychiatric syndromes in alcoholic men after one year. *Journal of Studies on Alcohol*, 49(5): 395–405.

Pepitone-Arreola-Rockwall, F., Rockwell, D., & Core, N. (1981). Fifty-two medical students' suicide. *American Journal of Psychiatry*, 138: 198–201.

Pert, C. B., & Snyder, S. H. (1973). Opiate receptor: Demonstration in nervous tissue. *Science*, 179: 1011–1014.

Piazza, N. J., Vrbka, J. L., & Yeager, R. D. (1989). Telescoping of alcoholism in women alcoholics. *International Journal of Addictions*, *24*(1): 19–28.

Pohorecky, L. A. (1991). Stress and alcohol interaction: An update of human research. *Alcoholism, Clinical and Experimental Research*, *15*(3): 438–459.

Polich, J., & Bloom, F. E. (1988). Event-related brain potentials in individuals at high and low risk for developing alcoholism: Failure to replicate. *Alcoholism, Clinical and Experimental Research*, *12*(3): 368–373.

Pollock, V. E., Volavka, J., Goodwin, D. W., Medrick, S. A., Gabrielli, W. F., Knop, J., & Schulsinger, F. (1983). The EEG after alcohol in men at risk for alcoholism. *Archives of General Psychiatry*, *40*(8): 857–864.

Popham, R., Schmidt, W., & de Lint, J. (1978). Government control measures to prevent hazardous drinking. In J. A. Ewing, & B. A. Rouse (Eds.), *Drinking: Alcohol in American society—issues and current research*. Chicago: Nelson-Hall.

Racy, J. (1990). Professionalism: sane and insane. *Journal of Clinical Psychiatry*, *51*(4): 138–140.

Regier, D. A., Boyd, J. H., Burke Jr., J. D., Rae, D. S., Myers, J. K., Kramer, M., Robins, L. N., George, L. K., Karns, M., & Locke, B. Z. (1988). One-month prevalence of mental disorders in the United States: Based on five epidemiologic catchment area sites. *Archives of General Psychiatry*, *45*(1): 977–986.

Reuben, D. B. (1985). Depressive symptoms in medical house officers. *Archives of Internal Medicine*, *145*: 286–288.

Rich, C. L., & Pitts Jr., F. N. (1979). Suicide by male physicians during a five year period. *American Journal of Psychiatry*, *136*: 1089–1090.

Richman, J. A., & Flaherty, J. A. (1990). Alcohol-related problems of future physicians prior to medical training. *Journal of Studies on Alcohol*, *51*(4): 296–300.

Ritchie, J. M. (1975). *Pharmacological basis of therapeutics* (4th ed.). New York: Macmillan.

Roessler, R., Lester, J. W., Butler, W. T., Rankin, D. B., & Collins, F. (1978). Cognitive and non-cognitive variables in the prediction of pre-clinical performance. *Journal of Medical Education*, *53*: 678–689.

Roy, A., DeJong, J., Lamparski, D., Adinoff, B., George, T., Moore, V., Garnett, D., Kerich, M., & Linnoila, J. (1991). Mental disorders among alcoholics: Relationship to age of onset and cerebrospinal fluid neuropeptides. *Archives of General Psychiatry*, *48*(5): 423–427.

Russell, A. T., Pasnau, R., & Taintor, Z. C. (1975). Emotional problems of residents in psychiatry. *American Journal of Psychiatry*, *132*(3): 263–267.

Sachs, M. H., Frosch, W. A., Kesselman, M., & Parker, L. (1980). Psychiatric problems in third-year medical students. *American Journal of Psychiatry*, *137*(7): 822–825.

Sales, J. B. (1989, Mar.). The Lawyers' Assistance Program: A responsible and effective alternative for the substance-impaired lawyer. *Texas Bar Journal*, 273–274.

Sanhel, C. L. (1989, Mar.). The impact of impaired attorneys on the Texas grievance process. *Texas Bar Journal* 312–314.

Schilit, R., & Gomberg, E. L. (1987). Social support structures of women in treatment for alcoholism. *Health and Social Work, 12*(3): 187–195.

Schnall, P. L., Piper, C., Schwartz, J. E., Karasek, R. A., Schlussel, Y., Devereux, R. B., Ganau, A., Alderman, N., Warren, K., & Pickering, T. G. (1990). The relationship between "job strain," work place diastolic blood pressure, and left ventricular mass index: Results of a case-control study. *JAMA, 263*(14): 1929–1935.

Schuckit, M. A. (1983). Alcoholic patients with secondary depression. *American Journal of Psychiatry, 140*: 711–714.

Schuckit, M. A. (1985a). Genetics and the risk for alcoholism. *JAMA, 254*(28): 2614–2617.

Schuckit, M. A. (1985b). Ethanol-induced changes in body sway in men at high alcoholism risk. *Archives of General Psychiatry, 42*: 375–379.

Schuckit, M. A., & Russell, J. W. (1983). Clinical importance of age at first drink in a group of young men. *American Journal of Psychiatry, 140*(9): 1221–1222.

Schuckit, M. A., Goodwin, D. A., & Winokur, G. (1972). A study of alcoholism in half-siblings. *American Journal of Psychiatry, 128*: 1132–1136.

Schuckit, M. A., Irwin, M., & Mahler, H. I. M. (1990). Tridimensional Personality Questionnaire scores of sons of alcoholic and nonalcoholic fathers. *American Journal of Psychiatry, 147*(4): 481–487.

Schuster, C. (1993). Alcohol abuse and dependence. In J. Kahn (Ed.), *Mental health in the workplace: A practical psychiatric guide* (pp. 366–387). New York: Van Nostrand Reinhold.

Schwartz, A. J., Black, E. R., Goldstein, M. G., Jozefowicz, R. F., & Emmings, F. G. (1987). Levels of causes of stress among residents. *Journal of Medical Education, 62*: 744–753.

Schwartz, R. H., Lewis, D. C., Hoffman, N. G., & Kyriazi, N. (1990). Cocaine and marijuana use by medical students before and during medical school. *Archives of Internal Medicine, 150*: 883–886.

Seixas, F. A. (1983). The Missouri Alcoholism Severity Scale as a predictor of transfer from outpatient to inpatient treatment. *Substance and Alcohol Action/ Misuse, 4*: 423–443.

Selzer, M. L. (1971). The Michigan Alcoholism Screening Test (MAST): The quest for a new diagnostic instrument. *American Journal of Psychiatry, 127*: 1653–1658.

Senay, E. C. (1992). Diagnostic interview and mental status examination. In J. H. Lowinson, P. Ruiz, R. B. Millman, & J. G. Langrod (Eds.), *Substance abuse: A comprehensive textbook* (2nd ed.) (pp. 416–424). Baltimore, MD: Williams & Wilkins.

Seventh special report to the U.S. Congress on alcohol and health, National Institute of Alcohol Abuse and Alcoholism, U. S. Department of Health and Human Services, January 1990.

Sheffield, J. W. (1991a, Jan.-Mar.). Breaking through impairment. *The Apothecary*, 7–14.

Sheffield, J. W. (1991b, Jan.). Texas recovery program leads the way. *Missouri Pharmacist*, 21–22.

Sheffield, J. W., O'Neill, P., & Fisher, C. (1992). Women in recovery: From pain to progress. *Texas Pharmacy, 36*: 29–31.

Shore, E. R. (1985). Norms regarding drinking behavior in the business environment. *The Journal of Social Psychology, 125*(6): 735–741.

Shore, J. H. (1982). The impaired physician four years after probation. *JAMA, 248*(23): 3126–3139.

Single, E. W. (1988). The availability theory of alcohol-related problems. In C. D. Chaudron & D. A. Wilkinson (Eds.), *Theories on alcoholism* (pp. 325–351). Toronto, Canada: Addiction Research Foundation.

Skelly, F. J. (1992, Apr. 27). The perils of perfectionism. *American Medical News,* pp. 33–35.

Skinner, H. A. (1982). The Drug Abuse Screening Test. *Addictive Behavior, 7*: 363–370.

Smart, R. G. (1978). Do some alcoholics do better in some types of treatment than others? *Drug and Alcohol Dependence, 3*: 65–77.

Smith, C. (1989). Current issues: Physicians. In T. W. Hester (Ed.), *Professionals and their addictions* (pp. 159–166). Macon, GA: Charter Medical Corp.

Smith, E. M., Cloninger, C. R., & Bradford, S. (1983). Predictions of mortality in alcoholic women: A prospective follow-up study. *Alcoholism, 7*: 237–243.

Smith, J. W., Denny, W. F., & Witzke, D. B. (1986). Emotional impairment in internal medicine house staff. *JAMA, 255*: 1155–1158.

Speller, J. L. (1989). *Executives in crisis* (p. 87). San Francisco: Jossey-Bass.

Stevens, A. (1993, Aug.). *The Wall Street Journal,* p. 1.

Stibler, H., & Hultcrantz, R. (1987). Carbohydrate-deficient transferrin in serum in patients with liver diseases. *Alcoholism, 11*(5): 468–473.

Stout-Wiegand, N., & Trent, R. B. (1981). Physician drug use: Availability or occupational stress? *International Journal of Medicine, 16*(2): 317–330.

Strunk, C. L., Bailey, B. J., Scott, B. A., Cummings, C. W., Lucente, F. E., Beatty, C. W., Neel, H. B., Pillsbury III, H. C., Rice, D. H., Bryan, M. D., & Hokanson, J. A. (1991). Resident work hours and working environment in otolaryngology: Analysis for daily activity and resident perception. *JAMA, 226*: 1371–1374.

Sullivan, E. J. (1987). Comparison of chemically dependent and nondependent nurses on familial, personal, and professional characteristics. *Journal of Studies on Alcohol, 48*(6): 563–568.

Suzdak, P. D., Glowa, J. R., Crawley, J. N., Skolnick, P., & Paul, S. M. (1988). Is ethanol antagonist selective for ethanol? *Science, 239*: 648–650.

Tabakoff, B., & Hoffman, P. L. (1988). A neurobehavioral theory of alcoholism. In C. D. Chaudron & D. A. Wilkinson (Eds.), *Theories of alcoholism* (pp. 29–72). Toronto, Canada: Addiction Research Foundation.

Tabakoff, B., Hoffman, P. L., Lee, J. M., Saio, T., & Willard, B. (1988). Differences in platelet enzyme activity. *New England Journal of Medicine, 313*: 134–139.

Talbott, G. D., & Benson, E. B. (1980). Impaired physicians: The dilemma of identification. *Post Graduate Medicine, 68*(6): 58–64.

Talbott, G. D., Gallegos, K. V., Wilson, P. O., & Porter, T. L. (1987). Medical

Association of Georgia's Impaired Physicians Program: Review of the first 1,000 physicians. Analysis of specialty. *JAMA, 257*(21): 2927–2930.

Tarter, R. E., Alterman, A. I., & Edwards, K. L. (1988). Neurobehavioral theory of alcoholism etiology. In C. D. Chaudron & D. A. Wilkinson (Eds.), *Theories on alcoholism* (pp. 73–102). Toronto, Canada: Addiction Research Foundation.

Tarter, R., Hegedus, A., & Gavaler, J. (1985). Hyperactivity in sons of alcoholics. *Journal of Studies on Alcohol, 46*: 259–261.

Tarter, R., McBride, H., Buonpane, N., & Schneider, D. (1977). Differentiation of alcoholics: Childhood history of minimal brain dysfunction, family history and drinking patterns. *Archives of General Psychiatry, 34*: 761–768.

Tennant, F., & Berman, M. L. (1988). Stepwise detoxification from cocaine. *Postgraduate Medicine, 84*(2): 225–234.

Thomas, C. B. (1971). Suicide among us: Habits of nervous tension as potential predictors. *Johns Hopkins Medical Journal, 129*: 190–201.

Thomas, C. B. (1976). What becomes of medical students: The dark side. *Johns Hopkins Medical Journal, 138*(5): 185–195.

Thomas, L. (1979). *The medusa and the snail.* New York: Viking Press.

Thomas, R. B., Luber, S. A., & Smith, J. A. (1977). A study of alcohol and drug use in medical students. *Diseases of the Nervous System, 38*, 41–43.

Thompson, K. M., & Wilsnack, L. J. (1984). Drinking and drinking problems among female adolescents: Patterns and influences. In S. C. Wilsnack & L. K. Beckman (Eds.), *Alcohol problems in women: Antecedents, consequences, and interventions.* New York: Guilford Press.

Thomsen, R. (1975). *Bill W.* New York: Harper & Row.

Tiebout, H. N. (1973). *Direct treatment of a symptom.* Center City, MN: Hazeldon Foundation.

Topel, H. (1988). Beta-endorphin genetics in the etiology of alcoholism. *Alcohol, 5*(2): 159–165.

Treaster, J. B. (1992, Jul. 22). Executive's secret struggle with heroin's powerful grip. *The New York Times,* p. 1.

Trent, R. B. (1981). Physician drug use: Availability or occupational stress? *International Journal of the Addictions, 16*(2): 317–330.

Tucker, D. R., Gurnee, M. D., Baldwin, J. N., Sylvestri, M. F., & Roche, E. B. (1988). Psychoactive drug use and impairment markers in pharmacy students. *American Journal of Pharmacy Education, 52*: 42–47.

Ullmann, D., Phillips, R. L., Beeson, W. L., Dewey, H. G., Brin, B. N., Kuzma, J. W., Mathews, C. P., & Hirst, A. E. (1991). Cause-specific mortality among physicians with differing life-styles. *JAMA, 265*(18): 2352–2359.

Vaillant, G. E. (1971). Theoretical hierarchy of adaptive ego mechanisms. *Archives of General Psychiatry, 24*: 107–118.

Vaillant, G. E., & Milofsky, E. S. (1982). The etiology of alcoholism: A prospective viewpoint. *American Psychologist, 37*: 497–503.

Vaillant, G. E., Brighton, J. R., & McArthur, C. (1970). Physicians' use of mood altering drugs: A twenty year follow-up report. *New England Journal of Medicine, 282*: 365–370.

Vaillant, G. E., Sobowale, N. C., & McArthur, C. (1972). Some psychologic vulnerabilities of physicians. *New England Journal of Medicine, 287*: 372–374.

Valko, R. J., & Clayton, P. J. (1975). Depression in the internship. *Diseases of the Nervous System, 38*: 28–29.

Vanderberry, R. C. (1990). North Carolina Physicians Health and Effectiveness Program: The first full year. *North Carolina Medical Journal, 51*(7): 347–349.

Vereby, K. (1992). Diagnostic laboratory: Screening for drug abuse. In J. H. Lowinson, P. Ruiz, & R. B. Millman (Eds.), *Substance abuse: A comprehensive textbook* (pp. 425–436). Baltimore, MD: Williams & Wilkins.

Vitaliano, P. J., Maiuro, R. D., Russo, J., Mitchell, E. S., Carr, J. E., & Van Citters, R. L. (1988). A biopsychosocial model of medical student distress. *Journal of Behavioral Medicine, 11*(4): 311–324.

Vitaliano, P. P., Russo, J., Carr, J. E., & Heerwagen, J. H. (1984). Medical school pressures and their relationship to anxiety. *Journal of Nervous and Mental Disease, 172*(12): 730–736.

Volpicelli, J. R., Alterman, A. I., Hayashida, M., & O'Brien, C. P. (1992). Naltrexone in the treatment of alcohol dependence. *Archives of General Psychiatry, 49*:876–880.

Voss, H. L., & Clayton, R. R. (1987). Stages in involvement with drugs. *Pediatrician, 14*: 24–31.

Wallace, J. (1988). The relevance to clinical care of recent research in neurobiology. *Journal of Substance Abuse Treatment, 5*(4): 207–217.

Ward, C. F., Ward, G. C., & Saidman, L. J. (1983). Drug abuse in anesthesia training programs. *JAMA, 250*(7): 922–925.

Washton, A. M., Pottash, A. C., & Gold, M. S. (1984). Naltrexone in addicted business executives and physicians. *Journal of Clinical Psychiatry, 45*(9, sec. 2): 39–41.

Webster's new twentieth century dictionary of the English language (2nd ed., unabridged). (1980). William Collins Publishers.

Weller, R. A., & Halikas, J. A. (1985). Marijuana use in psychiatric illness: A follow-up study. *American Journal of Psychiatry, 142*(7): 848–850.

Welner, A., Martin, S., & Wochnick, E. (1979). Psychiatric disorders among professional women. *Archives of General Psychiatry, 36*: 169–173.

Westermeyer, J. (1988a). Substance abuse among medical trainees: Current problems and evolving resources. *American Journal of Drug and Alcohol Abuse, 14*(3): 393–404.

Westermeyer, J. (1988b). The pursuit of intoxication: Our 100-century old romance with psychoactive substances. *American Journal of Drug and Alcohol Abuse, 14*(2): 175–187.

Westermeyer, J. (1991). Historical and social context of psychoactive substance disorders. In R. J. Frances & S. I. Miller (Eds.), *Clinical textbook of addictive disorders* (pp. 23–40). New York: Guilford Press.

Whipple, S. L., Parker, E. S., & Noble, E. P. (1988). An atypical neurocognitive profile in alcoholic fathers and their sons. *Journal of Studies on Alcohol, 49*(3): 240–244.

Wieder, H., & Kaplan, E. H. (1969). Drug use in adolescents: Psychodynamic meaning and pharmacologic effect. In R. S. Eissler, A. Freud, H. Hartmann,

S. Lustman, & M. Kris (Eds.), *Psychoanalytic study of the child* (vol. 24) (pp. 399–431). New York: International Universities Press.

Wilford, B. B. (1981). *Drug abuse: A guide for the primary care physician* (p. 25). Chicago: American Medical Association.

Wilsnack, S. C. (1973, Apr.). Femininity by the bottle. *Psychology Today*, p. 39.

Wolf, K. (1991, Feb.). Assisting the substance abusing attorney. *Michigan Bar Journal*, 148–151.

Woody, G. E., McLellan, A. T., Luborsky, L., & O'Brien, C. P. (1986). Psychotherapy for substance abuse. *Psychiatric Clinics of North America, 9*: 547–562.

Wurmser, L. (1974). Personality disorders and drug dependency. In J. R. Lion (Ed.), *Personality disorders: Diagnosis and management* (pp. 113–142). Baltimore, MD: Williams & Wilkins.

Wyshak, G., Lamb, G. A., Lawrence, R. S., & Curran, W. J. (1980). A profile of the health-promoting behaviors of physicians and lawyers. *New England Journal of Medicine, 303*(2): 104–107.

Zeldow, P. B., & Clark, D. (1985). Masculinity, femininity, Type A behavior, and psychosoical adjustment in medical students. *Journal of Personality and Social Psychology, 48*(2): 481–492.

Zeldow, P. B., Daugherty, S. R., & McAdams, D. P. (1988). Intimacy, power, and psychological well-being in medical students. *Journal of Nervous and Mental Disease, 176*(3): 182–186.

Zimberg, S. (1982). Psychotherapy in the treatment of alcoholism. In E. M. Pattison & E. Kaufman (Eds.), *Encyclopedic handbook of alcoholism* (pp. 999–1010). New York: Gardner Press.

Zoccolillo, M., Murphy, G. E., & Wetzel, R. D. (1986). Depression among medical students. *Journal of Affective Disorders, 11*: 91–96.

Name Index

Subject Index